BLACK BANGOR

*Revisiting New England: The New Regionalism*

SERIES EDITORS

Siobhan Senier, University of New Hampshire
Darren Ranco, Dartmouth College
Adam Sweeting, Boston University
David H. Watters, University of New Hampshire

This series presents fresh discussions of the distinctiveness of New England culture. The editors seek manuscripts examining the history of New England regionalism; the way its culture came to represent American national culture as a whole; the interaction between that "official" New England culture and the people who lived in the region; and local, subregional, or even biographical subjects as microcosms that explicitly open up and consider larger issues. The series welcomes new theoretical and historical perspectives and is designed to cross disciplinary boundaries and appeal to a wide audience.

Richard Archer, *Fissures in the Rock: New England in the Seventeenth Century*

Judith Bookbinder, *Boston Modern: Figurative Expressionism as Alternative Modernism*

Donna M. Cassidy, *Marsden Hartley: Race, Region, and Nation*

Nancy L. Gallagher, *Breeding Better Vermonters: The Eugenics Project in Vermont*

Sidney V. James, *The Colonial Metamorphoses in Rhode Island: A Study of Institutions in Change*

Maureen Elgersman Lee, *Black Bangor: African Americans in a Maine Community, 1880–1950*

Christopher J. Lenney, *Sightseeing: Clues to the Landscape History of New England*

Donald W. Linebaugh, *The Man Who Found Thoreau: Roland W. Robbins and the Rise of Historical Archaeology in America*

Pauleena MacDougall, *The Penobscot Dance of Resistance: Tradition in the History of a People*

Diana Muir, *Reflections in Bullough's Pond: Economy and Ecosystem in New England*

James C. O'Connell, *Becoming Cape Cod: Creating a Seaside Resort*

Priscilla Paton, *Abandoned New England: Landscape in the Works of Homer, Frost, Hopper, Wyeth, and Bishop*

Jennifer C. Post, *Music in Rural New England Family and Community Life, 1870–1940*

David L. Richards, *Poland Spring: A Tale of the Gilded Age, 1860–1900*

Mark J. Sammons and Valerie Cunningham, *Black Portsmouth: Three Centuries of African-American Heritage*

Adam Sweeting, *Beneath the Second Sun: A Cultural History of Indian Summer*

*Maureen Elgersman Lee*

❧❦❧

# BLACK BANGOR

## African Americans in a Maine Community, 1880 – 1950

❧❦❧

University of New Hampshire Press

*Durham, New Hampshire*

PUBLISHED BY UNIVERSITY PRESS OF NEW ENGLAND

HANOVER AND LONDON

University of New Hampshire Press
Published by University Press of New England,
One Court Street, Lebanon, NH 03766
www.upne.com
© 2005 by University of New Hampshire Press
Printed in the United States of America

5   4   3   2   1

Library of Congress Cataloging-in-Publication Data
Lee, Maureen Elgersman.
Black Bangor : African Americans in a Maine community, 1880–1950 /
Maureen Elgersman Lee.
    p.   cm.—(Revisiting New England)
Includes bibliographical references and index.
ISBN-13: 978-1-58465-498-8 (cloth : alk. paper)
ISBN-10: 1-58465-498-8 (cloth : alk. paper)
ISBN-13: 978-1-58465-499-5 (pbk. : alk. paper)
ISBN-10: 1-58465-499-6 (pbk. : alk. paper)
1. African Americans—Maine—Bangor—History.   2. African Americans—Maine—Bangor—Social conditions—19th century.   3. African Americans—Maine—Bangor—Social conditions—20th century.   4. Ethnic neighborhoods—Maine—Bangor—History.   5. Community life—Maine—Bangor—History.   6. Bangor (Me.)—Social conditions—19th century.   7. Bangor (Me.)—Social conditions—20th century.   8. Bangor (Me.)—Race relations. I. Title. II. Series.
F29.B2L44 2005
305.896′07307413—dc22        2005015533

*For my father, Fred Elgersman, who died
during my journey to this book, and whose
own life stories I sorely miss.*

⌘

*And for my mother, Sophie Elgersman, who never
doubted my journey would be completed.*

# Contents

# Acknowledgments

This book's seminal work began in late 1998 and early 1999 in preparation for a Black History Month photograph exhibition at the University of Southern Maine (USM). The show, "Re-membering Maine's Past — African American Portraiture as Historical Text," marked my first major exhibition as the faculty scholar for the University's African American Collection, part of the Jean Byers Sampson Center for Diversity in Maine. It featured more than fifty predominately studio photographs of African American men, women, and children. Drawn exclusively from the Gerald E. Talbot Collection, most photos were taken across the state of Maine. Many of those were taken in Bangor. "Re-Membering Maine's Past" was installed in Portland and Lewiston, before coming to Bangor in the summer of 1999. A public, lunchtime talk at the local library revealed that Bangor had hosted a vibrant African American community from the turn of the century through the 1940s. Some members of this community still resided in the area and the excitement of their memories was absolutely infectious. Thus began a long journey to discover more about this incredible time in Maine's history. Eventually, I even dared to dream that the community's history could be reconstructed on paper.

Despite the vast amount of information uncovered in the past years and incorporated into this text, parts of this local history remain elusive. I do not have information on every person or even every family that was part of the Black community. Clearly, some people have garnered more attention than others. Nonetheless, in this book I have tried to capture both the zeitgeist — the spirit of the times — and the gestalt — the sense that this community was more than the sum of its parts — of Black Bangor.

This study has been some of the most challenging work I have done thus far. It has also been some of the most rewarding. Many people have assisted me in this work, and I want to thank them for their interest, encouragement, and support over the past few years. USM President Richard L. Pattenaude and past and current provosts, Mark Lapping and Joseph S. Wood, have my sincere thanks. I am equally grateful for the financial support of the College of Arts and Sciences Research and Creative Activity Fund, which helped defer the cost of several illustrations. I wish to recognize my colleagues in the History Department, and to thank Susie R. Bock, head of USM's Special Collections, and David Andreasen, Special Collections library assistant, for their technical support.

I also need to recognize University of Maine faculty members Richard Judd and Ann Schonberger for their support and feedback as I tried to piece together this history in drafts of various papers. My thanks also go out to Deborah Gray White of Rutgers University and to members of both the American Historical Association (AHA) and the Canadian Historical Association (CHA) for scholarly feedback and criticism. I would like to thank my editor, Phyllis Deutsch, for her extensive comments on previous drafts and for enthusiastically guiding me through the publication process. I would also like to thank my external reviewers for their close reading of the manuscript and sage advice for improvement.

From the very beginning, it was Roxanne Moore Saucier, a columnist at the *Bangor Daily News*, who got behind my work, getting the news of the show and the project to the public. This work could not have been completed without the help of Sarah Martin and Dana Lippitt at the Bangor Museum and Center for History (formerly the Bangor Historical Society). Bill Cook and the staff at the Bangor Public Library greatly assisted much of this research, and gave me access to a variety of valuable sources. William Barry at the Maine Historical Society, Earl G. Shettleworth, Jr., of the Maine Historic Preservation Commission, and the African American Historical and Genealogical Society–New England chapter (AAHGS–NE) all proved to be wonderful sources of information and encouragement.

I owe the greatest scholarly debt to Randolph Stakeman, for pioneering scholarship on African Americans in Maine and for providing me access to an incredible database of information on Bangor's African American households. I personally would like to thank Gerald Talbot, Sterling Dymond, Jr., Earl Johnson, Dorothy Simmons, Lloyd George, Herbert Heughan, and H. Althea Warner Mandel for welcoming and initiating interviews. Your histories created in me the passion to uncover the story of *Black Bangor* and bring it to light.

To family and friends, in Canada and the United States, your sustained interest and encouragement in seeing this project to completion has meant more than I can say. Last, but certainly not least, I need to thank my husband, Christopher Lee. Thank you for all the hot tea and back rubs you gave me while I worked on this project. Even more than that, I thank you for encouraging me and for modeling passion and engagement in everything that you do.

# Introduction

The city of Bangor is located in eastern Maine, 140 miles from Portland and 250 miles from Boston, Massachusetts. Situated 60 miles from the coast, the city borders the Penosbcot River and is divided by the smaller Kenduskeag Stream (illustration 1). Settled by the English in 1769 as Kenduskeag Plantation, Bangor was incorporated as a town in 1791 and as a city in 1834. By 1840, the city was home to more than eight thousand residents, a number that more than doubled by 1870. By the turn of the century, Bangor had a population in excess of twenty-one thousand people, and in 1950 more than thirty-one thousand were living in the city. While growing its population has been a struggle at times, Bangor has consistently remained one of Maine's largest and most important cities.[1]

Bangor also has had to reinvent itself over the years. During the mid- to late 1800s, Bangor was the self-proclaimed lumber capital of the world and the lumber port with the highest productivity. It was responsible for approximately one-third of the entire Maine cut, which, at its peak in the early twentieth century, reportedly produced 1.1 billion board feet of lumber. By the early decades of the twentieth century, Bangor had become more of a mercantile area that could be accessed by road, water, and rail. Emerging paper giants like the Great Northern Paper Company fueled the city's economies, and by marketing its proximity to the Maine woods and its convenience to coastal sites such as Bar Harbor, Bangor was able to attract an increasing number of tourists. Dow Air Force Base opened in 1942 and brought a new source of revenue and employment closer to the heart of the city. The base injected more money into the local economy until its deactivation in 1968.[2]

The physical history of Bangor is marked by two disasters: the flood of 1902 and the fire of 1911. In 1902, an ice jam caused the Penobscot River to flood. The force of the water destroyed the center span of the bridge connecting Bangor and Brewer, and flooded downtown Bangor in approximately four feet of water (illustration 2). The events of 1911, however, soon eclipsed

ILLUSTRATION 1. Bangor waterfront, c. early twentieth century. *Collections of the Bangor Museum and Center for History.*

those of 1902, when a small fire broke out in an Exchange Street business and quickly consumed a large part of the city. Flames devastated the city. The Post Office, Customs House, Bangor High School, Central Fire Station, and the Bangor Savings Bank all were destroyed. The library lost its entire collection; the University of Maine Law School was also a complete loss. When the flames were extinguished on 1 May 1911, more than 285 residences and more than 100 businesses lay in ruins (illustration 3).[3]

Bangor's commercial and material histories conceal another, equally engaging history—that of the city's African American population. *Black Bangor* serves to uncover that saga and fill a void in Maine's historical narrative. *Black Bangor* reconstructs the lives and community history of Blacks from the United States, Canada, and the Caribbean who lived in this eastern Maine city from 1880 to 1950. It explores how African Americans created a cohesive, vibrant community for themselves and their children by the early twentieth century and sustained it through mid-century. The Black population declined sharply in numbers after World War II, as outmigration and mortality took its toll. *Black Bangor* serves as a study of African American community formation and identity in one of the nation's whitest states. The community was a successful, although relatively short-lived experiment in how Blacks could parlay their ultraminority status as less than 1 percent of the city's population into a vibrant community. During this extraordinary period, Black men and women spanned the labor spectrum from professionals to service workers; lived in large, multi-room houses that they owned or in modest dwellings that they rented; they participated in the city's institutions while fashioning others to meet their own needs. The questions guiding *Black Bangor* are straightforward, yet highly complex. What did it mean to be Black in Bangor during these seventy years? What was the Black community's nativity profile? How and where did Blacks work, live, worship, learn, and play? How did African Americans' experiences in Bangor compare to those of Blacks in other New England cities such as Portsmouth, New Hampshire; New Haven, Connecticut; New Bedford, Massachusetts; and Newport, Rhode Island? In sum, this study is about both the challenges and possibilities of Black community, identity, and institutions in largely homogeneous cultures. It also may serve as a basis for studying other similar communities elsewhere in the United States and Canada.

ILLUSTRATION 2. The 1902 Flood, Broad Street view. *Collections of the Bangor Museum and Center for History.*

ILLUSTRATION 3. The fire of 1911 burning along Kenduskeag Stream. *Collections of the Bangor Museum and Center for History.*

Chapter 1 introduces in depth the individuals and the families whose migration built Bangor's African American community. Dubbed the gateway generation, these people moved to Bangor from across Maine, the eastern United States, Canada, and the Caribbean. As part of a labor migration from Maritime Canada or as spin-offs of the Great Migration out of the American South, Blacks established and expanded their families in Bangor. The migration tide crested in 1910, and when the population peaked in 1930, Black Bangor was more than twice its pre-1880 size.

Chapter 2 focuses on African Americans' labor experiences in the city. Although Black men and women were employed across the labor spectrum, distinct features are discernable. There were few Black professionals. Black men from Canada often worked in the lumber or pulp and paper industries; those from the United States often worked in the railroad industry. Black women found their primary employment in domestic service work, even if they had professional training.

Chapter 3 explores daily life in the African American community. Residency, home ownership, foodways, consumer culture, and racial representations all figure prominently in the discussion of the forces, both internal and external, that shaped Black Bangor's day-to-day activities. African Americans lived throughout the city, but in 1930, almost half of the Black population lived in a relatively small area known as the Parker Street neighborhood. By this same time, roughly half of the city's African Americans were homeowners, with property ranging in value from several hundred to several thousand dollars. While not necessarily conspicuous, Blacks were active consumers of such middle-class items as new cars and player pianos. Whether or not they had middle-class finances, many Blacks clearly had middle-class appetites.

Chapter 4 is, in many ways, the heart of this book. All discussions of migration, labor, and daily life ultimately inform this chapter. It explores how African Americans attended the city's institutions, but went to great lengths to create those of their own. Bangor's Blacks established a chapter of the Grand United Order of Odd Fellows (G.U.O.O.F.) and its ladies auxiliary, the Household of Ruth, by 1919. They hosted a chartered branch of the National Association for the Advancement of Colored People (NAACP), and a Mothers' Club all by the early 1920s. Additionally, they had a lodge of Black Masons, a Junior Mothers' Club, and a Black United Service Organization (U.S.O.). It was in and through these institutions that Blacks in Bangor thrived, and where the most persistent communal memories were created. Despite Black Bangor's remarkable institutional development and maturation, its small size appears to have been its downfall, limiting its ability to maintain most of these institutions over the long term. Eventually, mortality and outmigration left a vacuum in Black institutional life. Today, the vestiges of that life are found in the Black Masons and the subsequently reorganized local NAACP.

The Epilogue provides a brief glimpse into African American life in Bangor in the twenty-first century. While the Black population remains substantial — even larger than it was in 1930 — most of the institutions that defined Black life in the previous century are gone. Various family names such as Dymond, Johnson, and Talbot are still found in the city directory, but Black Bangor's golden age is clearly over.

I purposely begin each chapter with a brief historical sketch of two or three members of the community whose experiences are relevant to that particular chapter's theme. As much as possible, I want the reader to know who these people were, where they worked, how they lived, and, most importantly, how they thrived. I use the terms "African American" and "Black" interchangeably to refer to the subjects of this book, people of African descent drawn primarily from birthplaces in the United States, Canada, and the Caribbean.

Bangor's size creates some research problems. It is not large enough to be included among the larger cities in federal census schedules. For example, tables that profile Black labor at the city level consistently have omitted Bangor because its population has never reached the benchmark of 50,000 people. We are required, therefore, to take the available state-level statistics and generalize them to the local level. Evidence from the manuscript census, whether anecdotal or cumulative, does help fill the gaps in these cases.

The manuscript census has its own drawbacks. Some Black families were identified as White; others may have been missed, requiring me to rely on a variety of textual, visual, and oral sources to locate the Black population. The 1880 manuscript census for Bangor is not entirely legible, making some of my statements and conclusions possibly erroneous by either misinterpretation or omission. Fire destroyed the 1890 manuscript census, but the 1900 through 1920 manuscript censuses are readily available. Fortunately, the 1930 manuscript census was released in 2003 — in time to be incorporated integrally into this text. I place particular emphasis on the year 1930 for a number of reasons. It is the most recent year for which a U.S. manuscript census is available. As such, it is also the most recent year for which I can corroborate information from the federal census and locally generated information like that found in the city directory and the *Bangor Daily News*. Coincidentally, Bangor's Black population reached its peak of 228 people in 1930 as well.

*Black Bangor* is designed to fill a void in Maine's African American historiography, one that has been concerned primarily with slavery and abolition, select families and institutions, and the modern civil rights movement. Elizabeth Donnan's *Documents Illustrative of the Slave Trade* (1930) and Lorenzo J. Greene's *The Negro in Colonial New England* (1942) were two of the earliest studies to shine a light on Maine slavery. Since then, the topic of slavery in Maine has garnered significant in-state attention.[4] The first documented African (or possibly African American) in Maine is believed to have been "a negro boy named Mingo," sold in York in 1663 by Thomas Bolt.[5] Whether Mingo was the first Black resident of Maine is difficult to say. His sale in 1663 may have been his introduction to the colony or it simply may have marked his movement from one Maine owner to another.[6] Attempting to put together the history of Mingo and others like him is an "occupational hazard" for early African Americanists, who have the unenviable task that William D. Piersen characterizes as "hav[ing] to fry whatever fish they catch."[7]

While studies admit of only a few hundred Blacks enslaved in Maine, they denote that slavery was a significant, discernable status symbol. Notable eighteenth-century southern Maine families, including the Pepperells, Frosts, and McClellans, were slaveholders, their names repeatedly invoked when the discussion of Maine slavery arises. Both Sir William Pepperell (also Pepperell) and his son, Colonel William Pepperell, owned slaves. Local lore reports that the senior Pepperell was rowed down the Saco River by several of the Blacks he owned. This very public spectacle must have reinforced the position that Pepperell held as one of Kittery's wealthy merchants; it also may have impressed observers with some ideas about the attractiveness of owning slaves. A man of property, Major Charles Frost of Kittery was a slave owner who willed a few slaves—Cesar, Hector, Prince, and Pompey—to his sons. Gorham's William McClellan is seen as having been more benevolent. After his slave Prince was manumitted for his Revolutionary War service, McClellan provided him and his wife, Chloe, with several acres of land on which to reside. Prince died in 1829.[8]

Randolph Stakeman's research on African Americans in Maine has included a critical study of slavery in which he characterizes the institution as "a privilege of the small colonial upper class and more an aristocratic trapping than a mode of production." However, Stakeman argues that slavery is not "an aberration in Maine's history, but a prologue" that would serve as the foundation for race relations in the state for the coming centuries.[9]

Abolitionism also has garnered attention in Maine historiography. The 1834 formation of the Maine Antislavery Society marked its entry on the abolitionist stage, and from the 1830s through the 1860s, Maine gave audience to various abolitionists. Abolitionist, orator, and former fugitive slave Frederick Douglass spoke in Portland during the 1840s. Writer and activist Frances Ellen Watkins worked for the Maine Antislavery Society from 1854 to 1856, and was one of its most prominent agents. Harriet Beecher Stowe, author of *Uncle Tom's Cabin* (1852), lived for a time in Maine. Fugitives William and Ellen Craft took refuge in Portland on their way to Canada and ultimately to England. The Crafts' 1860 narrative, *Running a Thousand Miles for Freedom*, chronicles their escape from plantation slavery in Georgia after the Fugitive Slave Act of 1850 strengthened the power of slaveholders or their agents to retrieve runaways and made the lives of even free northern Blacks perilous.[10]

Even as it served as an abolitionist forum in its own right, Portland's Abyssinian Church was established in the late 1820s by Blacks who felt un-welcome in the city's other churches. The institution served not only as a house of worship, but as a school and a public meeting house. In November 1898, the 281 foot SS *Portland* sank off the coast of Cape Cod in what has become known as the "Great Portland Gale." The loss of nearly twenty Abyssinian supporters and members weighed heavily on the church and the community. The Abyssinian went into decline by the late 1890s, and in 1917 it closed.[11]

The historiography of African Americans in Maine tends to gloss over the late nineteenth century and the first half of the twentieth century. It has not yet explored whether Maine women participated in the Black Women's Club Movement, whether the Great Migration penetrated Maine's borders, or whether Maine cities such as Portland and Bangor were sites of Black institutional development and maturation. Stakeman's study of largely nineteenth-century Black nativity moves the discourse in this direction by identifying Virginia and New Brunswick as key sources of Black migration through the turn of the twentieth century. Perhaps more than any other published work, it serves as a foundation for studying Black Bangor.[12]

Established research on Blacks in twentieth-century Maine revolves around Ku Klux Klan (KKK) activity of the 1920s and civil rights activism of the 1960s and 1970s. Although Maine historiography consistently emphasizes the state's Franco-American, Catholic, and Jewish populations as the Klan's primary targets, historical documents record Klan threats against the Black population as well. Ku Klux Klan membership in Maine may have reached fifty thousand during this decade, but historians caution that such figures have been exaggerated.[13]

The dawn of the 1960s began an enduring struggle to improve African American employment, housing, and civil rights. In the early 1960s, the Central Maine chapter of the NAACP was organized in Lewiston. African Americans from Maine joined hundreds of thousands of Blacks nationwide, traveling to the March on Washington in August 1963. At home, they registered voters, welcomed freedom riders, and marched in the streets following the April 1968 assassination of Martin Luther King, Jr. In 1964, the Portland chapter of the NAACP reorganized and began an unprecedented stretch of continuous activity in the area. In 2004, it celebrated its fortieth anniversary.[14]

The successes of Maine's civil rights activities bore fruit. In 1972, longtime Portland resident Gerald E. Talbot became the first African American to be elected to the Maine state legislature. During his three consecutive terms in the legislature, he introduced a number of bills designed to eradicate practical and symbolic instances of racism and intolerance. Talbot's signature legislation outlawed the use of the term "nigger" to designate any place name or physical feature in the state of Maine. Talbot left the state legislature in 1978, but continued to work in official or advisory capacities for various state and national organizations including the Maine Human Rights Commission and the American Association of Retired People (AARP). The 1980s and 1990s saw more Blacks enter political offices. Two Maine cities even elected Black mayors: William Burney became mayor of Augusta in 1988 and John Jenkins was elected mayor of Lewiston in 1993. In 2004, Jill Duson became Portland's first African American mayor and the first African American woman in Maine to hold mayoral office.[15] At the beginning of the twenty-first century, African Americans in Maine can look back and see that, as a group, they have moved into spheres and spaces that few might have dreamed of a century earlier.

Maine's Black population rose from 1,319 in 1900 to 5,138 in 1990. The 2000 Census recorded that 6,760 of the state's more than 1.2 million people identified themselves as Black or African American alone, and an additional 2,793 people identified themselves as Black or African American in combination with another race. Together these two groups numbered more than 9,500 people and accounted for 0.7 percent of the state's 2000 population.[16] Despite Maine's enduring Black presence and its growing population, the historiography of African Americans in Maine remains largely episodic at best. Rather than resurrecting the histories of slavery, abolition, and civil rights, it is time to ask new questions: Other than being small in number, what discerns Maine's Black experience from those of other African Americans? Realized or unrealized, what ties bind Blacks in Maine to other parts of New England? What historical lessons can Maine's African American past teach us if we only pay attention? How did Blacks in Bangor create a thriving community, and what lessons can the story of this community teach?

In this study, I use the term "Black Bangor" not just as a convenient title for the book, but as an expression of a particular time, place, and way of life for African Americans in this eastern Maine city. It was not just the coming together of Blacks from different parts of the Americas. It was that they built a community despite differences in origin; that they supported themselves despite being relegated to some of the least prestigious and lowest paying jobs in the labor market; that they housed themselves comfortably as both renters and homeowners; that they were welcomed in most of the city's institutions but still desired to establish others for themselves. This is the story of *Black Bangor*. It builds between 1880 and 1910, it levels off between 1910 and 1945, and it declines by 1950. *Black Bangor* existed for a specific moment in time, under a specific set of circumstances that probably are not to be repeated again.

## Chapter 1

◦∞◦

# ONE FAMILY AT A TIME

## *Building Black Bangor*

When William A. Johnson arrived in Bangor in the late 1870s, the Black community of less than one hundred was much smaller than that of his birthplace, Norfolk, Virginia; it was also significantly smaller than the Boston community from which he had migrated most recently (illustration 4). Nonetheless, Johnson established a successful clothes-cleaning business in Bangor, which he later expanded to trade in second-hand merchandise. Johnson married Caribbean native Edith Mae Delaney (also Delany), and together they raised one of the largest and most prominent Black families in the city. None of Johnson's parents or siblings accompanied him to Maine; at the time of his death in 1913, he was survived by four brothers, all of whom lived in Norfolk.[1]

In the spring of 1901, William Leek and his wife, Evalena McCarty Leek, lived in Kingsclear, New Brunswick, with their six sons and three daughters. All the Leek children, aged one to fifteen years, were at least third-generation Canadians with deep roots in the Maritime province. But by 1910, William and Evalena's two eldest daughters, Gertrude and Margaret, had left Kingsclear and were living in Bangor. During the next decade, two of the Leeks' sons, Wallace and Goodridge (also Goodrich), moved to Bangor; by 1930 two more of their sons, Earl and Alton, had taken up residence there as well. Despite the departure of at least half of their family, William and Evalena Leek remained in Canada. Both died in New Brunswick in the 1930s, and they were buried in the province, near Fredericton.[2]

Charles Alvin Talbot was born in northern Maine in 1858. As a young man, Talbot moved to Bangor, married Canadian native Frances ("Fannie")

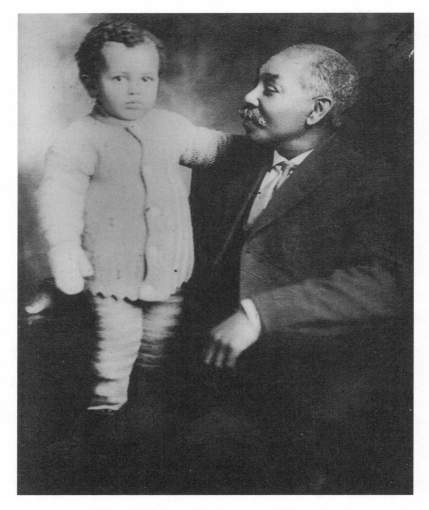

ILLUSTRATION 4. William A. Johnson and his youngest son, Earl, c. 1912–1913. *Courtesy Earl R. Johnson Collection.*

Saunders, and raised a family. Over time, Bangor would be home to several generations of the Talbot family, a long line of men and women who enjoyed the esteem of residents both Black and White. Charles A. Talbot saw Bangor's Black population more than double in size during his lifetime. The African American community that had numbered less than one hundred in 1880 increased to more than two hundred by 1910. At this historical moment,

African Americans' proportion of Bangor's population was the highest it had ever been. Black Bangor would go on to reach a peak population of 228 residents in 1930, but by 1910, the high tide of migration had crested and the majority of migrants had arrived.[3]

The fifty years between 1880 and 1930 serve as the backdrop of a larger, national shift in the African American population. Between 1880 and 1910, the tides of the Great Migration—the unprecedented northern migration of Southern-born Blacks—began to swell. The South lost an estimated more than four hundred thousand Blacks during this time. The largest south-to-north population shift among African Americans was yet to come, however, as more than 1.2 million Blacks would relocate between the years 1910 and 1930.[4] Very few of these 1.2 million people came to Bangor, for during those same twenty years, the city's African American population grew by a mere twenty-three people. Nonetheless, they, and others from Canada and the Caribbean, did come.

The Johnsons, the Leeks, the Talbots, and many others like them formed Black Bangor's gateway population—those Blacks, born primarily in the United States, Canada, and the Caribbean, whose migration to Bangor, particularly between 1880 and 1910, gave the city's African American population unprecedented increase. For the Canadians in particular, Bangor was the destination of a labor migration. Others' attraction to the city is less clear, but they may have been drawn by regional marketing, migratory momentum, or simple opportunity. Whatever their reasons for coming, these people and their offspring built and profoundly shaped Black Bangor—individual by individual, and family by family.

### Population Growth

The number of Blacks in Bangor was indeed small in 1870 (see table 1.1). The mere 84 African Americans in a city of more than 18,000 comprised less than one-half of 1 percent of its total population. At the turn of the next century, census takers identified 176 Blacks living in the city. By 1910, that number had grown to 205, and when Black Bangor's population peaked at 228 in 1930, it represented an increase of more than 170 percent over its 1870 figure. During the same time period of 1870 to 1930, the city of Bangor grew by 57 percent. This increase tempered the African American population growth, holding Black Bangor to less than 1 percent of the city's total population. By 1940, the number of African Americans in Bangor had begun a slow decline. An influx

TABLE I.I    Bangor's Black Population as Part of the City's Total Population, 1870–1950

| Year | Black population | Bangor population | Percent of total |
|------|------------------|-------------------|------------------|
| 1870 | 84 | 18,289 | 0.46 |
| 1880 | 87 | 16,856 | 0.52 |
| 1890 | 67 | 19,103 | 0.35 |
| 1900 | 176 | 21,850 | 0.81 |
| 1910 | 205 | 24,803 | 0.83 |
| 1920 | 208 | 25,978 | 0.80 |
| 1930 | 228 | 28,749 | 0.79 |
| 1940 | 222 | 29,822 | 0.74 |
| 1950 | 112 | 31,558 | 0.35 |

*Source:* U.S. Bureau of the Census, 1870–1950 Censuses of the United States (Population) (Washington, D.C.: GPO); U.S. Bureau of the Census, *Negro Population in the United States 1790-1915* (New York: Arno Press and the *New York Times*, 1968), 98. Percentage figures have been rounded up.

of Black military service personnel stationed at Bangor's Dow Air Force Base temporarily inflated the local population, but a post–World War II out-migration reduced Black Bangor to virtually half of its 1940 size. By 1950, Black Bangor was reduced to 112 people, a size more reminiscent of the nine-teenth century than the twentieth.[5]

In stark contrast to Bangor's Black community stood the African Ameri-can population of Lewiston, in central Maine. In 1890, the Census counted only 48 Blacks in the city. By 1930 that number was a mere 25 in a city of al-most 35,000 people; by 1940, there were a mere 8 in a growing, industrial city of more than 38,000.[6]

During the entire period of 1880 to 1950, Blacks remained less than 1 per-cent of the city's population. Nonetheless, the rise in Bangor's African Amer-ican population parallels Black Bangor's increase in proportion to the popu-lation. African Americans peaked at 0.83 percent of the city in 1910. Between 1910 and 1930, the Black population continued to grow, but was outpaced by the city's growth. The result was a slight decrease in Black Bangor's propor-tion. By 1950, Bangor's total population exceeded 30,000 people, and a de-clining Black population accounted for little more than one-third of 1 percent of the city.

Bangor's place in what historically has been one of the country's least racially diverse states begs the question of how many African Americans in the city actually were born in Maine. A review of the manuscript censuses for Bangor reveals that of Blacks born in Maine, Blacks born elsewhere in the

United States, and Blacks born outside of the country, Maine-born Blacks comprised the single largest group of Blacks for all years between 1900 and 1930. In 1900, Maine-born residents accounted for approximately 53 percent of the city's Black population, and approximately 52 percent in 1910. The proportion of Maine-born Blacks dropped to approximately 49 percent in 1920, but rebounded to approximately 55 percent in 1930.[7] These figures compare favorably to the statewide trends for the number of Blacks born in Maine and living in the state. In 1900, for example, 748 or almost 57 percent of African Americans in the United States who had been born in Maine still resided in the state. By 1900, that ratio had dropped 6 percent, and of the 1,321 African Americans in the United States who had been born in Maine, 802 or nearly 51 percent were still living in the state.[8]

Those who were at least full, second-generation Mainers, according to the 1900 census, included teamster Charles A. Talbot; barbers John M. Mason, Alvin A. Talbot, and Frank Oree; homemaker May Dunn; husband and wife, Andrew and Maggie Burtt. Those whom the 1900 census recorded as being at least third-generation Mainers include Clara Talbot Matheas and Andrew and Maggie Burtt's daughter, Clara.[9] Other Maine-born Blacks living in Bangor in 1900 included Annie Warner and her two sons, and Daniel and Jennie Mason and their three children, James, Mary, and Elizabeth.[10]

Maine's ability to retain its native-born Black population was markedly lower than that of Rhode Island, Massachusetts, and Connecticut, but higher than neighboring New Hampshire and Vermont. In 1900, for example, Rhode Island had the highest retention rate of all New England, with 81 percent of its instate-born Black population still living there. Massachusetts ranked second with 78.2 percent, and Connecticut ranked third with 76.4 percent. Maine followed with the fourth highest rate of nearly 57 percent, followed by the two lowest states, New Hampshire with 48.4 percent and Vermont with 37.5 percent of African Americans born in the state still residing there.[11]

African Americans born in Maine accounted for a good proportion of Black Bangor's population, but the number of Blacks in the city who were born in Maine and whose mother and father were both born in Maine was actually quite small. Of the more than ninety Maine-born Blacks living in Bangor in 1900, only 19 percent had both a Maine-born father and mother. In 1910, that number was approximately 21 percent, and in 1920 it was approximately 22 percent. In 1930, it was a meager 10 percent.[12] For all manuscript censuses from 1900 through 1930, less than one-quarter of Maine-born

Blacks living in Bangor were at least full, second-generation Mainers. Three-quarters of Maine-born Blacks in Bangor were born in families where one or both parents had been born outside of the state.[13] It is clear, therefore, that even after the migration to Bangor decreased, the migration watermark remained visible in Black family demographics.

## The Great Migration

The migration of African Americans to Bangor coincided with a larger northern, eastern, and midwestern movement of southern-born Blacks known as the Great Migration. Blacks had already been leaving the South during the Reconstruction years of the mid-1860s to the late 1870s. Slavery as a popular institution had been invalidated by the Thirteenth Amendment, and Blacks sought to escape the debt peonage of sharecropping, the oppressive nature of Black Codes, and the escalating brutality of groups like the Ku Klux Klan. During the 1870s, the South had an estimated net outmigration of 60,000 African Americans. During the next decade, that number rose an additional 10,000, and for the 1890s, Black net outmigration from the South was 168,000. The twentieth century saw record-setting numbers of southern-born Blacks who moved west or north. The new century's first decade reported 170,000 African Americans gone, and the next decade saw that figure more than double at 454,000. The years 1920 to 1930 witnessed an unprecedented net outmigration of 749,000 Blacks. From the beginning of U.S. involvement in World War I to the first full year of the Great Depression, more than one million African Americans left the South, with an estimated 400,000 leaving between 1916 and 1918 alone.[14]

The migration scholarship of Carole Marks, Joe William Trotter, Jr., Darlene Clark Hine, Nell Irvin Painter, and others articulates that nineteenth- and twentieth-century Black population movement was a combination of push and pull factors—conditions that made it easy for Blacks to leave one place and those that attracted them to another. The idea of urban living, better schools, and gainful industrial employment made relocation attractive, as did the chance to leave behind southern living, sharecropping, and overt racism. Scholars also have mapped out the migration streams of African Americans from various parts of the south and southeast. Blacks born in Mississippi, Arkansas, Alabama, Louisiana, and Texas tended to migrate to Chicago, while Blacks from Florida, Georgia, South Carolina, and Virginia headed to other prominent cities such as New York and Detroit. From their initial or primary destinations, some African American migrants also fanned out into outlying cities, often in indirect and even circular fashion.[15]

The preponderance of southern-born Blacks' migration to cities such as Chicago, Detroit, Cleveland, New York, Philadelphia, and Pittsburgh during the twentieth century's opening decades, coupled with the nominal number of southern-born African Americans in Bangor, reveals that the eastern Maine city was not a primary or significant destination.[16] But although native-born Blacks did not come to Bangor in large numbers, they did come. Bangor's water and rail transportation were principal industries that would have made it easy for Blacks to move to Bangor from Boston. From 1909 to 1935, the steamship *City of Belfast* had an established route between Bangor and Boston, and the Eastern Steamship Company routinely carried passengers between the two cities until 1936. The Bangor and Aroostook Railroad's 1891 completion helped eclipse river transportation, expanded ground transportation networks, and made Bangor more of a mercantile center. In the early twentieth century, America's growing fondness for the automobile was not lost on Bangor. Ad campaigns widely promoted local sightseeing opportunities, and scenic drives to nearby Bar Harbor were widely marketed, quickly attracting wealthy tourists who often brought their African American servants with them as they traveled. Steamers, passenger trains, and personal automobiles all linked Bangor with other cities and increased opportunities for Black migration.[17]

As steamship passenger traffic declined and railroad passenger traffic increased, so did opportunities for Black porters to come to Bangor. The Pullman Company operated Maine lines that stopped in Portland and Bangor. The 1907 completion of Bangor's Union Station helped mark the amalgamation of different local rail lines and served as a symbol of Black migration and employment in Bangor. Maryland native William Derricks was a Pullman porter, and many other Blacks worked as railroad porters, cooks, and repairmen; still others worked as janitors and boot blacks at the station. The expansion of railroad service, the extensive use of Black porters nationally, the opportunities for contact between Bangor and Boston, and Bangor's increased marketing as a desirable place to work and vacation were probably all factors in interstate migration to the city. Bangor did not have the highly industrialized economy of other, larger American cities, and, likewise, the interstate migration of Blacks to Bangor apparently was not "orchestrated in the board rooms of northern industrial enterprise."[18]

Bangor stands in strong contrast to New Haven and Waterbury, Connecticut, as the wartime demand for labor prompted the New York, New Hampshire, and Hartford Railroad Company to bring in one hundred Black workers from Norfolk, Virginia. The 20 July 1916 edition of the *New York Age* reported the following concerning attempts to solve "New Haven's Labor Problem":

> On July 15, one hundred southern Negroes reach [*sic*] New Haven from Norfolk. They were divided into two groups, one going to Berlin Junction; the other coming to Waterbury. Both groups are now on construction work. They are in good physical condition, seem to be contented with their prospects and were ready for work the next morning after their arrive [*sic*] despite their long, tiring trip.
>
> The duration of their employment rests solely with them. They can remain permanently. The only stipulation is that they must remain sixty days during which time the New Haven Company will shelter and supply them with food. After that time, if they remain, they are to shelter themselves. If not, they will be returned home by the company.[19]

Bangor-based railroad companies do not appear to have solicited Black migrants in the manner of New Haven, Connecticut, and most Blacks in the city who worked for either the Maine Central Railroad, the Bangor and Aroostook Railroad, or at Union Station worked on the trains or in the stations rather than in constructing or maintaining track. Very few Blacks in Bangor worked in a manufacturing setting; most remained tied to the railroad or to individual private and mercantile labor.[20]

### The Gateway Populations: The Americans

Horton and Horton's study of Black life in antebellum Boston reveals that the birthplaces of Blacks who migrated to the Massachusetts city before the Civil War were strikingly similar to the birthplaces of those who migrated to Bangor during the postbellum period. Whether born in the northern or southern states, most Black Americans in Bangor had been born along the east coast, anywhere from Massachusetts to Florida. There were a few Blacks from the more interior states of Kentucky, Tennessee, and Ohio, and fewer still from states west of the Mississippi River. Of the New England, mid-Atlantic, and south-Atlantic regions of the country, most Black American migrants to Bangor were born in New England.[21]

From 1880 to 1950, Massachusetts was the New England state with the highest African American population, and each decennial census between 1900 and 1930 recorded that a few more families and individuals of Massachusetts birth had trickled into Bangor. A significant source of African American migrants, Massachusetts served as the geographical entrance to northern New England; the port city of Boston probably served as a conduit for African Americans to migrate to Bangor either by boat or by train.[22]

Housewife Gertrude Buck and deck hand George Walker were a few of the Massachusetts-born Blacks in the city in 1900. This group was so small however, that the movement of three families—the Stewarts, the Davises, and the Shears—was sufficient to create a noticeable flourish in the presence of African Americans from this state. Lenora Stewart was a native of Massachusetts, while her husband, William, had been born in the West Indies. All of the Stewart children—William, twelve; Emma, nine; and Sophia, six—had been born in Massachusetts, revealing that the family would have moved to Bangor sometime between 1904 and early 1910.[23] The number of Massachusetts-born Blacks in Bangor had no notable increase until the Davis family arrived. Dean Davis was born in Maine, but his wife, Marianne, and the couple's two young boys, Dean, four, and George, three, had all been born in Massachusetts. Based on the age and birthplace of their children, the Davis family probably moved to Bangor sometime between 1927 and 1930.[24] Other Blacks of Massachusetts birth in Bangor included Eunice Shears and chauffeur Carlton Cromwell.[25]

Black Bangor's other New England populations derived primarily from Connecticut and Rhode Island. Railroad steward James H. Warner and boat iceman Louis Farham were both from Connecticut and living in Bangor at the turn of the century (illustration 5).[26] Connecticut native Elizabeth Jackson came to Bangor sometime between 1908 and 1912, and, soon after, married a recently widowed Warner. Elizabeth Jackson Warner spent her next forty years in Bangor, raising her two daughters, Beryl and Helen Althea. Elizabeth Jackson Warner's younger sisters, Helen and Rose Jackson, also moved to Bangor. Both in their thirties in 1920, the women lived with their sister and made their livings as housemaids to private families.[27] Mabel Derricks (also Derrick) was born in Connecticut and lived in the Bangor with her husband, Pullman porter William H. Derricks.[28] Bangor's Connecticut-born Black population remained small.

Blacks of Rhode Island birth were even fewer in number than those born in Connecticut. Rhode Island native Edward Palmer worked as a railroad porter. Married to Canadian native Mona Sunth Palmer, he lived in Bangor

ILLUSTRATION 5. Connecticut native and railroad steward James
H. Warner. *Courtesy Dr. H. Althea Warner Mandel Collection.*

with their two children, his wife's parents, and his wife's six younger siblings.
The Palmers' daughter, Vera, had been born in Rhode Island and their son,
Eric—a mere two months old at the time of the 1910 census—was born in
Maine. The extended Sunth and Palmer families do not appear to have
stayed long in Bangor; they are absent from both the 1920 and 1930 manu-
script censuses, and are not listed in the Bangor city directory.[29]

Despite their states' proximity to Maine, Blacks born in New Hampshire
and Vermont were conspicuously absent from Black Bangor's nativity profile
(see table 1.2). Geographic location was not an absolute predictor of migration; a better indicator is overall Black population. African Americans born
in New England and residing in Bangor consistently were traced to birth-

places in the states with the largest Black populations—Massachusetts, Connecticut, and Rhode Island—as opposed to states with the smallest number of Blacks—New Hampshire and Vermont.

Various Blacks living in Bangor were born in the mid-Atlantic region of the United States that comprises New York, New Jersey, and Pennsylvania. In 1900, John Smith, of New York, was working in the city as a steamship barman. At the same time, Edgar (also Edward) S. Buck, of either New York or New Jersey, worked as a waiter. Widow Delia Murray had been born in New York in 1824, and at seventy-five years of age, she lived in Bangor with her daughter, Adell Murray Johnson, a local caterer.[30]

One of the most prominent African Americans to take up his residency in Bangor during this era was Bangor's "little minister," Milton Roscoe Geary. Born in Boiling Springs, Pennsylvania, in 1885, and raised in Marlboro, Massachusetts, Milton Geary probably moved to Bangor sometime around 1910. He came to the city by train, and, by his own account, arrived with a meager twelve dollars in his pocket and an instant affinity for the city. As he reported to the *Bangor Daily News* in 1963, "I felt the minute I stepped into Bangor—here is where I want to stay." Geary worked through "the lean years of bean soup and rented rooms" and reached his goal of becoming a lawyer. He received his bachelor's degree from the University of Maine Law School in 1913, and when he died in June of 1964, Milton Geary was known as the state's only African American lawyer and the only attorney ordained as a minister.[31]

The Geary household comprised Milton, his Canadian-born wife, Fahy Heughan Geary, and his father, William H. Geary. Born in the early 1840s,

TABLE 1.2   African American Population of New England States, 1900–1930

|  | 1900 | 1910 | 1920 | 1930 |
|---|---|---|---|---|
| Maine | 1,319 | 1,363 | 1,310 | 1,096 |
| New Hampshire | 662 | 564 | 621 | 790 |
| Vermont | 826 | 1,621 | 572 | 568 |
| Massachusetts | 31,974 | 38,055 | 45,466 | 52,365 |
| Rhode Island | 9,092 | 9,529 | 10,036 | 9,913 |
| Connecticut | 15,226 | 15,174 | 24,046 | 29,354 |

*Source:* U.S. Bureau of the Census, *Negro Population in the United States, 1790–1915* (New York: Arno Press and the *New York Times*, 1968), 43; Donald B. Dobb, ed., *Historical Statistics of the United States: Two Centuries of the Census, 1790–1990* (Westport, Conn.: Greenwood Press, 1993), 15–92, passim.

William Geary was at least a second-generation Virginian and, according to his son, he had also been a fugitive from slavery. [32]

> [Milton's] father, William H. Geary, as a slave in Virginia became a good friend of abolitionist John Brown by forewarning Brown of several plots against his life. This is something his son remember[ed] with a great deal of pride. It was after his escape from Virginia that the elder Geary settled in Pennsylvania where Milton Geary was born.[33]

Black Bangor's south-Atlantic population also included some highly visible individuals. William H. Derricks, for example, was born in Maryland in the early 1860s, and by 1920, he was counted among Bangor's railroad porters.[34] Virginian William A. Johnson arrived in Bangor in the late 1870s after spending an undetermined amount of time living and working in Boston. According to the *Daily News*, Johnson arrived in Bangor on the steamship *Governor*. He established what would prove to be a prosperous enterprise in cleaning and pressing clothes, before expanding the business to sell second-hand merchandise and rent costumes. Virginians Lee and Iva Leplayne lived in the Johnson household in the 1920s. Listed as a boarder and a servant, respectively, thirty-two-year-old Lee Leplayne was a farm truck driver and twenty-five-year-old Iva was a domestic. It is unclear if the Leplaynes were husband and wife or, perhaps, siblings; it is equally unclear if they were relatives of William Johnson, who, by 1913, had passed away. The Leplaynes are absent from the 1930 census and may have left the city before the end of the decade.[35]

Charles Smallwood was at least a second-generation Virginian who worked in Bangor first as a barber and then as a steamship saloon man. His wife, Josephine, was a native of Maine, but had Kentucky parentage.[36] Louise Irene Mahoney had been born in Virginia — possibly in Richmond — around 1885. In 1920, she was thirty-five years old, living in Bangor, and married to James Robert Mahoney, of Washington, D.C. Louise Mahoney operated her own beauty salon, while her husband joined William Derricks among the ranks of the city's Black porters. Other Virginia-born Blacks living in Bangor in the early twentieth century included Horace Dunn, a fish market clerk; William Brown, who worked odd jobs; and Benjamin Wilson, a roomer with no given occupation.[37]

Relatively few Blacks in Bangor were born in the Carolinas, Georgia, or Florida. Counted among this small group, however, were day laborer Benjamin Wilson of North Carolina; cook Hattie Brown of South Carolina; garage laborer Lucius Wickers of Georgia; and gardener George Bart of Florida.[38]

Bangor was also home to a small group of residents born in more interior states. Kentucky native Samuel Guess, for example, lived in Bangor. Residents Arthur Washington and George Jones were both at least second-generation Ohioans. Washington worked as an electric lineman and Jones worked as a hotel cook.[39] Those African Americans living in Bangor but born even further west of the Ohio Valley region were even fewer in number. One such person was stonemason Edgar L. Joseph of Minnesota.[40]

The small number of Black Bangor's population born in interior states magnifies the east coast nativity of Black Americans born outside of Maine. Blacks born in states up and down the eastern seaboard helped comprise Black Bangor, but no single state was overrepresented in the city's African American population. This pattern seems to play out at the state level as well. In 1910, for example, Maine was home to 1,126 U.S.-born African Americans. Of those, 802 (71.2 percent) were born in Maine, 310 (27.5 percent) were born in other states, and 14 (1.2 percent) were "other native births." Those Blacks born outside of Maine, but living in the state, were born primarily in Massachusetts, Virginia, North Carolina, Maryland, Pennsylvania, South Carolina, and New York.[41]

### The Canadians

Canadians comprised Black Bangor's largest immigrant group. In 1900 and 1910, they were approximately 94 percent of the city's Black non-native population. The number of Canadian-born Blacks remained static in the next two decades, and Black Canadians were 96 percent of the foreign-born Black population in both 1920 and 1930. Black Canadians averaged 95 percent of Bangor's non-native Black population during the first thirty years of the twentieth century.[42] The Canadian presence was felt at the community level as well. In 1900, Canadians accounted for approximately 35 percent of the city's Black residents. By 1910, that rose to approximately 37 percent, but dropped back to approximately 35 percent by 1920. In 1930, the proportion of Black Canadians as part of Black Bangor's total population had continued to decline to approximately 31 percent. Over the four decennial censuses of 1900 through 1930, Black Canadians accounted for an average of 34 percent of Black Bangor's residents.[43]

Most Black Canadians came from Fredericton, Kingsclear, and Woodstock, New Brunswick. They were typically third-, fourth-, and even fifth-generation Canadians who, when they crossed the border into the United

States, left behind a regional history that reached back more than two hundred years and well into Canada's colonial past. Blacks in present-day New Brunswick began arriving as early as the seventeenth century when enslaved Africans were brought to French Acadia; they increased in number after the British gained control of the region in 1713. African slavery was not the foundation of the Maritime region's economy, but it was a popular institution. The city of Halifax, which was constructed in 1749 using slave labor, stands as one of Canadian slavery's most enduring symbols.[44] After the American Revolution, the migration of British Loyalists to the Canadian colonies increased the number of free and enslaved Blacks. Conflicts in governance soon divided the region, and in 1784 New Brunswick was created as a separate colony from Nova Scotia. The War of 1812 brought more Blacks, both free and enslaved, to New Brunswick, and by the time of its first census, Blacks were living in every county in the colony, including the centers of Fredericton, Kingsclear, and Woodstock.[45] Britain's Imperial Act of 1833 ended slavery in its Canadian and West Indian colonies effective 1 August 1834. It is believed that the number of Blacks still enslaved in Canada when the legislation took effect was negligible.[46]

Despite its own experiment with slavery, Canada consistently has been constructed as a haven for Blacks escaping slavery. African Americans left the United States for the Canadian colonies in the late 1790s and early 1800s. The numbers rose dramatically after the 1850 Fugitive Slave Law strengthened southern slave owners' power to retrieve their property, mandated the public to assist, and increased penalties for harboring runaways. Historians believe that most Blacks were destined for Canada West (Ontario) and Canada East (Quebec), but some fugitive routes did extend through Maine into the Maritimes. Because United States legislation also made life perilous for free Blacks, the year 1850 set off a migration of free Blacks to Canada in unprecedented numbers.[47] According to historian of Black Canada, Robin Winks, the arrival of the fugitives from American slavery not only inflated the Black population, it also created tensions within the existing, largely Loyalist-derived Black population—tensions that would divide Blacks well into the twentieth century. "Old-line Loyalist [Blacks] of Kingsclear, near Fredericton," Winks wrote, "looked down upon the fugitive-line [Blacks] who lived nearer the city" and even refused inter-group marriage.[48]

Randolph Stakeman has examined the question of whether Blacks in late nineteenth- and early twentieth-century Maine were the fugitive slaves of the 1850s and their descendents. Using the 1850 and 1880 censuses, Stakeman found that Blacks who came to Maine from outside the state were born in Canada, Massachusetts, and New Hampshire, with Blacks from New Brunswick and Nova Scotia comprising the largest immigrant group.[49]

> It is impossible to tell for sure whether these blacks were the descendents of [L]oyalist blacks who had been resettled in Canada by the British after the revolution, descendents of runaway slaves or freedm[e]n who had emigrated to Canada, or fugitive slaves who were claiming Canadian birth as a ruse to hide from bounty hunters. The 1880 census shows the birthplaces of the parents of individuals and several of the Canadian born people in that post Civil War census list parents who were born in the southern United States. This suggests that at least some of the Canadians were the descendents of runaway slaves and freedmen.[50]

Herbert Heughan grew up near Bangor, in Hampden. Some of his ancestors were the very fugitives who came through Maine en route to Canada. Heughan, in an interview with Randall Kenan, recalled his family's history:

> My family came from Canada. New Brunswick. Both my father and mother. . . . My mother's people came through on the Underground Railway. . . . She remembers her grandfather talking about it. But my father, his people, they won't say anything. We don't know where they came from. They just say 'don't know, don't know anybody. . . . My mother said that a lady brought my great-grandfather in her arms and they wouldn't talk about where they came from or anything. They picked up the culture of Fredericton. Or New Brunswick, I guess. And that was it. Lost all track of anything else.[51]

Based on New Brunswick census data for 1891 and 1901, however, many of the Blacks who immigrated to Bangor in the late nineteenth and early twentieth centuries had family lines dating back to the early 1800s; several went back as far as the Loyalist era of the 1810s. The majority of Blacks who left New Brunswick and shaped Black Bangor were not the fugitive slaves of the 1850s or their children, but were more likely the descendents of eighteenth- and nineteenth-century-era Blacks—possibly free or enslaved Loyalists.

Some Maritime Blacks who helped comprise Black Bangor left as early as the 1860s and 1870s. Georgia Talbot, wife of Bangor barber Alvin A. Talbot, was born in Canada in 1847, and moved to the United States in 1864. She married Maine-born Alvin Talbot three years after her arrival in the country; together they had eleven children, eight of whom were living in 1900. Georgia Talbot, whose parents had also been born in Canada, was at least a second-generation Canadian.[52] David and Rebecca Willis, who had been born in Canada in 1855 and 1860, respectively, left Canada in the mid-1870s. They each made separate sojourns to the United States before they were married, and by 1900 each had lived in the United States for more than twenty years. They lived in Bangor with David's mother, Susan, who had left Canada in 1899. Susan and Rebecca Willis were at least second-generation Canadians; David Willis was at least a third-generation Canadian.[53]

Based on immigration data found in the United States census, most of Black Bangor's Canadian-born population moved to the United States in the twenty-five years between 1885 and 1910. Fannie Saunders was born in Canada in March of 1869 and immigrated to the United States when she was approximately sixteen years old. By June of 1900, Saunders had been in the United States for fifteen years; she was married and had a teenaged son.[54] David MacKenzie was born in 1867, and his wife, Bessie, was born just a few years later in 1870. They married in 1885, and the following year they immigrated to the United States. In 1900, David and Bessie MacKenzie were living in Bangor with their two children, Sadie and Barbara. Both of the MacKenzies' daughters were born in Maine.[55]

Samuel and Harriet McCarty were both at least second-generation Canadians who left New Brunswick the year after David and Bessie MacKenzie. Born in the mid-1850s and married around 1881, they moved to the United States in the late 1880s when their eldest daughter, Addie, a third-generation Canadian, was six years old. Living in Bangor by the spring of 1900, the McCartys had four more daughters—Nora, Pearl, Myrtle, and Esther—all of whom were born in Maine.[56] William and Harriet Alberts were born in Canada, as were each of their parents. In the late 1880s, William immigrated to the United States without Harriet, because she either was preparing to have or had recently delivered their first child, daughter Elizabeth. Both Harriet and baby Elizabeth immigrated to the United States in 1889. Once in Maine, the Alberts had another child, son Percy, in early 1893.[57]

The 1890s brought more Blacks Canadians from New Brunswick to the United States and to Bangor. Carpenter Enoch Hardling and his wife, Ella, were both at least second-generation Canadians who moved to the United States in the mid-1890s. Their daughter Hazel was six years old in June of 1900, and appears to have been born in Maine shortly after her parents' arrival in the state. The Hardlings' son, Harold, also had been born in Maine, and he was one year old at the time of spring 1900 census.[58] Boarding with the Hardlings were several men ranging in age from twenty-one to thirty-nine years. Enoch Ervin, John Nelson, Herbert McCarty, and Arthur Waters were all natives of Canada who migrated to the United States between 1897 and 1899. Ervin tended horses, while McCarty, Nelson, and Waters all worked for one of the local lumber companies. Another boarder, Abraham Holmes, immigrated to the United States from Canada around 1890, and in 1900 was working in Bangor as a gardener.[59]

The clustering of Blacks from Fredericton, Kingsclear, and Woodstock was not coincidental. Blacks sought better economic opportunities for themselves, and took advantage of the opportunities that Bangor and the surrounding area had to offer them. Labor agents for the Bangor area's booming lumber industry recruited laborers from New Brunswick and Nova Scotia, and were directly responsibly for at least some Black relocation to the area. Companies needed river drivers to sort and move logs cut from interior sites, and down the Penobscot River to waiting sawmills. When lumber production shifted to pulp and paper production, workers still were needed to supply emerging paper giants like the Great Northern Paper Company and the International Paper Company with the necessary raw materials, even as the industry moved further north and west of Bangor.[60]

The opening decades of the twentieth century witnessed the movement of more New Brunswick Blacks. Ford and Rosalie Peters Clark were born in Canada and had their first child, Isabelle, in 1899. A few years after Isabelle's birth, the Clarks left Canada for the United States. Ford left first, in 1903, and Rosalie and Isabelle followed in 1904. By the spring of 1910, the Clarks were both thirty years of age and had added two more children to their family. Son Ford, Jr., was almost two years old in April of 1910, and daughter Avis was a two-month-old infant. Both Ford and Avis Clark were born in Maine.[61]

The Dymonds were among the most prominent families to immigrate in the early 1900s. Sterling Dymond and his wife, Janie Simmons Dymond, both came from New Brunswick (illustration 6). Earl Dymond, his older sister Blanche, and his younger sister Vera, all left Canada in 1913, and were living in Bangor by 1920. It appears that Earl's wife, Nora Cox Dymond, moved to the United States in 1918 — the same year that Earl Dymond was naturalized.[62] Tephy Leek also immigrated to the United States in 1913, and in 1920, she and husband, Wallace Leek, had two very young children, two-year-old Galen and one-year-old Daphne. Wallace Leek left Canada during the previous decade and, like Earl Dymond, was naturalized in 1918.[63]

James Alexander Beale (also Beal), and his wife, Ida Holmes Beale, migrated to the United States in 1914, and by 1920 they had two Maine-

ILLUSTRATION 6. Janie Simmons Dymond migrated to Bangor from New Brunswick. *Gerald E. Talbot Collection, African American Collection of Maine, Jean Byers Sampson Center for Diversity in Maine, University of Southern Maine Libraries.*

born daughters, three-year-old Christina and two-year-old Loretta. Violet Holmes, Ida Beale's sister, also lived in this Bangor household. Harold and Daisy Cromwell immigrated to the United States in 1917, only a few years after the Beales. In 1920, Harold was a woodsman, while Daisy worked as a domestic.[64]

The manuscript census of 1930 is the last United States census currently available to provide specific information on the individual and familial im-

migration of Black Bangor's Canadian population. It reveals that the movement of Canadian-born Blacks to the city had slowed considerably as compared to previous decades. In fact, very few Black Canadians living in the city
in 1930 had immigrated to the United States between 1920 and 1925 and apparently none had immigrated between 1926 and 1930. Sisters Mamie and
Elizabeth O'Ree were ten and nine years old, respectively, in 1930. They left
Canada in 1925 and lived in Bangor with their uncle and aunt, Ford and Rosalie Peters Clark.[65] Elma Bernard, wife of Maine native Harry Bernard and
daughter-in-law of Henry and Lena Bernard, immigrated to the United
States from Canada in 1920. She married in the mid-1920s and by 1930 had
three children born in the state—Irene, Lebaron, and Eugene.[66]

Blacks from New Brunswick were not the only ones from Maritime Can-
ada to immigrate to Bangor. A few Nova Scotians also made the move to
Maine. Steamboat waiter Henry Elias was born in Nova Scotia in February
of 1871 and moved to the United States in the late 1880s. Coal laborer Sandy
Gordon was born in Nova Scotia in December of 1865 and immigrated to the
United States in the early 1870s. In 1900, he was a husband and the father of
three children. Henry Elias and Sandy Gordon were two of the very few
Blacks in Bangor who had been born in Nova Scotia.[67]

Census record information on immigration suggests that many Black
Canadians resisted or were passive about United States naturalization. And
while Earl Dymond and Wallace Leek were naturalized in 1918 within approximately ten years of their arrival in the United States, several others were
not. Blacks such as Lena Bernard, John Nelson, Andrew Burtt, James and Ida
Beale, and Abner and Emma Peters all remained in alien status more than
twenty years after leaving Canada. This seeming persistence of Canadian
identity was also one of the hallmarks of New Brunswick migrants settling
in Bangor.[68]

### The West Indians

In addition to those Blacks born in the United States and Canada, Bangor
had a very small Caribbean population. Between 1900 and 1930, they averaged 5 percent of Black Bangor's foreign-born population. They accounted
for an even smaller proportion of the overall Black community. From 1900
through 1930, West Indians comprised an average 1.8 percent of Black Bangor.[69] Despite their meager numbers, West Indians were a relatively hetero-
geneous population, drawn from various islands across the Caribbean basin.

Born in the West Indies in the early 1870s, Charles Burt was probably in his late teens when he immigrated to the United States in 1890. By 1900, Burt was living in Bangor with his Canadian-born wife, Sophia, and their eleven-month-old daughter, Beatrice. During the next decade, the Burts would have four more children, sons Charles and James and daughters Florence and Helen. Despite having been settled in Bangor through two decennial censuses and for the birth of at least four of their five children, the Burts' time in the city appears to have been short lived. They appear to have left Bangor by 1920.[70] Henry Bernard was also from the West Indies and, like Charles Burt, he immigrated to the United States in 1890. In Bangor, Bernard married and raised a family; he worked as a watchman, later as a janitor, and owned an employment and real estate agency.[71]

The case of Hubert Scott illustrates the ability of census documents both to provide and to obscure nativity information. The 1920 census, for example, records that Hubert Scott was born in the Bahamas, British West Indies. The next decennial census reports that Scott had been born in Grenada and that his parents had been born in Nassau and Venezuela. Local lore reports that Hubert Scott was actually born in Trinidad, and that he ran away from the British island colony when he was in his early teens. Scott appears to have immigrated to the United States in 1899 and was an American citizen by 1930.[72]

Like Scott, William Stewart was also from the West Indies. He moved to the United States in 1892, and by the time he appeared in the Bangor census of 1910, he had become a naturalized citizen. Sources also disagree on Stewart's birthplace. The 1920 census records that he was born in Martinique, while the 1930 census records his birthplace as Puerto Rico. While whether Stewart's actual birthplace was Martinique or Puerto Rico remains unclear, the census does indicate that Stewart did not come to Bangor directly from the Caribbean. Instead, Stewart resided in Massachusetts—possibly Boston—for several years before appearing in Bangor sometime between 1903 and 1910 with his wife of fourteen years, Lenora, and their three children, aged six to twelve.[73]

Edith Delaney Johnson's migration story has complications and contradictions similar to those of Hubert Scott and William Stewart (illustration 7). The 1910 census records that Delaney was born in the Danish West Indies, but the 1920 census reports a birthplace of Haiti. The 1930 manuscript census only reports that she was born in the West Indies.[74] More details of Edith Delaney Johnson's background were illuminated when, in January 1963, the *Bangor Daily News* celebrated her ninetieth birthday with an extensive article.

ILLUSTRATION 7. Elizabeth Delaney Johnson and one of her children. *Gerald E. Talbot Collection, African American Collection of Maine, Jean Byers Sampson Center for Diversity in Maine, University of Southern Maine Libraries.*

The newspaper chronicled her early years and confirmed Johnson's birth in the Danish West Indies, known after 1917 as the United States Virgin Islands.[75] The newspaper reported:

> The former Edith Mae Delaney, she was born on St. Thomas Island in the Virgin Islands on January 26, 1873. When she was 10 years old, her family left the Islands to come to the United States. They traveled, for three weeks, on a three-masted sailboat, landing first in Boston. Mrs. Johnson was 12 years old when she came to Bangor. She spoke French as a child.[76]

Johnson's profile is one of the most detailed public accounts available of Black migration to Bangor at this time. Based on the article's timeline, Delaney probably arrived in Boston 1883 and moved to Bangor in 1885. When she arrived, her future husband, William A. Johnson, was already in the city and had established his clothes-cleaning business.

Dijon Piris and Fred D. Matheas were two exceptions to the Canadian and Caribbean profile of Bangor's foreign-born Blacks. Born in 1864 in Cape Verde, a Portuguese colony off the western coast of Africa, Dijon Piris immigrated to the United States in the late 1880s. By 1900, he was living in Bangor and working as a seaman. Fellow Cape Verdean Fred D. Matheas was Piris' contemporary. While actually Portuguese nationals, Cape Verdean residents were counted among the city's Black population.[77]

Just as the interstate movement of native-born Blacks to Bangor should be considered in light of the Great Migration, the movement of Canadians and West Indians was part of a larger increase in the United States' foreign-born Black population. The United States Census Bureau found in 1910 that the Black foreign-born population in the United States had virtually doubled since the previous census. In that year, there were more than forty thousand foreign-born Blacks in the United States; of these, more than thirty-three thousand Blacks came from throughout the Americas. More than twenty-four thousand came from Cuba and the West Indies (except Puerto Rico) and almost seven thousand came from Canada and Newfoundland. New York State saw the largest increase in its foreign-born Black population from 1900 to 1910, with an increase of more than nine thousand people over the previous decade. The next largest increases were seen in Massachusetts and Florida, each with an increase of more than two thousand. New Jersey and Pennsylvania each saw an increase of more than one thousand.[78]

In 1910, the foreign-born Black population was concentrated heavily in northern states, and while the Middle Atlantic region of the country had the largest number of foreign-born Blacks, New England had the largest proportion of foreign-born Blacks as part of their total Black population.[79] Nationally, the number of Caribbean-born Blacks in the United States was almost four times that of Canadian-born Blacks, yet in Bangor, that ratio was completely reversed. The number of Canadian-born Blacks easily and dramatically outpaced that of Caribbean-born Blacks. This is largely because many from the Caribbean probably came through and settled in or near large port cities such as Boston and New York. There they would have settled with other Caribbean-born Blacks and established organizations like New York's West Indian Product and Improvement Company, an enterprise that imported tropical fruits and vegetables, manufactured condiments and preserves, and served as an opportunity for investment. Located at 150 Nassau Street, the company had three branch offices and two agencies around the city.[80]

⚬⚬⚬

Black Bangor was produced by the movement of three distinct cultures of people along two migratory streams. Americans from Massachusetts to Florida moved northward, Canadians from New Brunswick and Nova Scotia moved southward, and West Indians arriving in any number of port cities in the United States probably fell into the existing, domestic migration stream. The core movement of people evolved over the course of the thirty years from 1880 to 1910, although the population continued to climb through 1930. This complex mix of people, histories, and cultures ultimately made Bangor's African American population more cosmopolitan than either its size or its geographic location might suggest. Once in Bangor, Black women and men faced the task of finding employment. For some, the search appears to have been easy; for others, steady, gainful work would prove to be elusive. The Bangor market place offered different opportunities for women and men, opportunities that would help shape the conditions and opportunities for themselves, their children, and even their grandchildren.

*Chapter 2*

ᑦᕆᕐᖕᕐ

# EARNING A LIVING

## Laboring Men and Women

Thomas G. Brown was born in Virginia in the early 1800s and took up residence in Bangor as early as the late 1820s. At one time a Bangor merchant, Brown became one of the city's first doctors. At his Main Street office he specialized in treating diseases of the blood and advertised his services in the *Daily Whig and Courier*. Although Brown's early investments in land speculation had erratic results, he did build a three-story double house for himself and his family on Third Street (illustration 8). When Brown died in October of 1887 at the age of eighty-two, he was one of the city's "oldest and best known citizens."[1] Fred D. Matheas joined Bangor's Union Hose Company No. 1 when he was in his early twenties, starting a thirty-six-year career as a fireman. Fred Matheas also operated his own moving business, and his van, "with its strikingly original legends [was] a famous Bangor institution."[2]

In the early 1890s, Carrie Dymond was a twenty-eight-year-old wife and mother of three who worked in her Bangor home as a dressmaker. Dymond's work life changed considerably over the next two decades. By the time she was in her forties, she was a widow responsible for an extended household. No longer a dressmaker, Dymond was a servant at busy Union Station. She later retired from Union Station and shared her house with her youngest daughter, LaRue, a stenographer.[3]

Maine native Josephine Smallwood was a well-known member of the Bangor community. Originally a restaurant cook, Smallwood used her culinary skills to her own advantage, and after her husband's death began catering parties out of her Manners Avenue home. Dymond and Smallwood were

ILLUSTRATION 8. Thomas Brown's double house at 72–74 Third Street. *Collections of the Bangor Museum and Center for History.*

widowed around the same time, but unlike Dymond, Smallwood had no children to support.[4]

As the gateway population of migrants settled in and made their livings, strong similarities and distinct differences emerged in the working lives of these African American men and women. Both groups had occupations that spanned the labor spectrum, but very few belonged to the professional class. Working men were visible to the community as barbers, porters, teamsters, and general laborers; most laboring women juggled the demands of productive and reproductive labor. Despite having a variety of skills, they often had to settle for or eventually move into some form of domestic employment. During Black Bangor's history, the American labor marked changed and expanded. Some changes helped and other changes hindered African American laboring pursuits in the city.[5]

### The Transformation of American Labor

Between 1880 and 1950, the American labor market underwent unprecedented change. Increased industrialization, the proliferation of labor unions, the increase of women laborers, and federal labor reform all combined to transform the means by and the conditions under which Americans made a living wage. By the turn of the twentieth century, as Howard Zinn described it, "steam and electricity replaced human muscle, iron replaced wood, and steel replaced iron."[6] Changes through mid-century included the dominance of the Pullman railroad company, the rise of the American auto industry, and the continued increase in the number and variety of manufactured food, clothing, and appliances. The garment industries continued to draw women into the workplace, as did the widespread commercial use of the telephone and the typewriter and the labor demands of World Wars I and II. The New Deal era of the 1930s brought both the Social Security Act of 1935 and the Fair Labor Standards Act of 1938. The former legislation included provisions for aiding the elderly and dependent children; the latter introduced a forty-hour work week, a twenty-five cent minimum wage, and restrictions on child labor. For the country's most vulnerable workers, those men and women who worked as agricultural workers or as domestic servants, the Fair Labor Standards Act did little to improve their lot.[7]

The railroad was a significant marker of American industrialization. By 1900, there were more than 190,000 miles of railroad track in the country, moving people and products to their various destinations. Not only were African American men fixtures in the railroad industry, they were the key to success for one major company—the Pullman Car Company. Begun in 1876 as the Pullman Palace Car Company, the Pullman Company served twenty-six million passengers annually at its peak in the 1920s. Black porters were critical to the success of the Pullman Company, as they were on constant call to the company's patrons as they boarded and disembarked from the trains, as well as when they ate, drank, slept, or needed any creature comfort or personal service. Propelled by the market value of the porters' service, the wage and policy discrepancies between Black porters and White conductors, and his own belief in organized labor, A. Philip Randolph successfully organized the International Brotherhood of Sleeping Car Porters and Maids in 1925 and unionized Black workers in an unprecedented fashion. Despite the significance of the Brotherhood, it was not until 1937 that the union gained official recognition from the Pullman Company.[8] African American women were less successful in their labor struggles, and many Black women living in northern states remained confined to private domestic service work.

### Black Professionals: The Elusive Few

Professionals comprised Black Bangor's smallest socioeconomic class. Thomas G. Brown was probably the community's only African American doctor from 1880 through 1950. Brown was born in Virginia in 1805, and moved to Bangor sometime in the next two decades. In 1828, Brown married Belinda Douglas of Prospect, Maine, and the couple soon started a family. In 1834, Brown operated a store at or near Strickland Block, in which he sold sundry goods including jewelry and musical instruments. Declining fortunes led Brown to barbering, after which he operated as a druggist at his Exchange Street apothecary. A physician for many years, Brown "practiced medicine in the treatment of special complaints."[9]

Thomas Brown promoted his medical practice in the local newspaper. Some more extensive than others, Brown's advertisements lauded his ability to cure general debility, local weakness, irregularity, and all diseases affecting the purity of the blood. Brown furnished patients with medicine at his 45 Main Street office. His workdays were long—beginning at 8:30 A.M. and ending at 8:30 P.M., with an hour off each for lunch and dinner. Those who could not call upon the doctor in person were invited to consult him by mail.[10]

Black Bangor's single most identifiable professional was Milton Roscoe Geary. Milton Geary graduated from the University of Maine Law School in 1913, and was admitted to the Maine Bar that year. For Geary, the road to becoming an attorney was a test of determination, not only because of the rigor of the discipline, but because of financial obstacles. He arrived in Bangor with twelve dollars, which he spent on a room, food, and books. He soon began work at a local box factory to cover the law school's fifty-dollar tuition—the relative affordability of which having been the decisive factor in choosing the institution. Geary continued to work his way through law school by shining shoes at Union Station and studying between trains (illustration 9).[11]

Geary's career was marked by various milestones, including his June 1925 appointment to the National Memorial Association's board of commissioners. The Washington, D.C.–based organization was creating a memorial to Black soldiers and sailors who had served in the country's wars. Geary joined a highly professional group on the board of commissioners that included other lawyers, doctors, clergy, businessmen, and professors. Given the board's highly professional profile, Geary was a natural choice. Governor Ralph O. Brewster wrote to the National Memorial Association's secretary of his appointee:

> Mr. Geary has been actively identified with things that are of civic concern and I am sure will be able to be helpful in connection with the interest with which you are concerned.[12]

ILLUSTRATION 9. Union Station and Engine 470 at mid-century. *Collections of the Bangor Museum and Center for History.*

Governor Brewster's appointment of Geary is somewhat ironic given the fact that Brewster had ties to the Ku Klux Klan in Maine. His campaign for the state's highest position was controversial in that the Ku Klux Klan highly supported his candidacy. The Ku Klux Klan was very active in Maine during the 1920s, with chapters across the state and a reported membership of several thousand people.[13] In his 5 June 1925 letter accepting the governor's nomination, Geary responded:

> I am keenly sensible to and deeply appreciative of the honor you have conferred upon me by your appointment as the representative of our State to serve as a commissioner on the Board of the National Memorial Association.
>
> I am proud to serve our State, and of this opportunity to serve my people. I assure you that I accept the appointment with the resolution to so discharge any and all duties that may be entrusted to me that your confidence shall not have been in vain.[14]

Geary concluded his letter very cordially:

Kindly accept [my] felicitations for the continued success of your administration, and your own personal welfare.

Thanking you for your thoughtful interest in me, I am,

Yours very truly,

M. R. GEARY.[15]

In October of 1927, Milton Geary expanded his professional standing by becoming a minister. Admitted to the Baptist conference, Geary assumed the pastorate of West Hampden Baptist Church, a predominately White church located just outside of Bangor. On the event of Geary's ordination, the *Bangor Daily News* described this new highlight in an already accomplished professional career:

> An examination of the candidate as to his qualifications to enter the ministry was held in the afternoon before the church council and after a very fine showing he was unanimously elected to the office of minister of the Baptist church. The paper read by Mr. Geary to the council was one of the ablest and best prepared documents of the kind ever presented to the council, showing a thorough knowledge of the bible, creeds, and doctrines of the Baptist church. He was warmly congratulated by members of the council for his success with the examination.
>
> The council organized with Rev. Aubrey M. Winsor of Bangor as moderator and Rev. Howard M. Welch of Brewer as clerk. The business of the council was transacted in the afternoon and the report was made at the church service at night when the ordination to the ministry was held.[16]

Geary was in high demand as a minister. At the peak of his pastoral life, he delivered sermons at as many as five churches per Sunday. During his later years, he preached primarily by invitation. Because Geary was a man of small stature, members of the public referred to him as "the little minister." At little more than five feet tall, Geary was noted more for his size than for his skin color.[17]

African Americans in Bangor continued to call upon Geary for his legal services after his ordination, and local records indicate that he was involved intricately in settling the estates of various African American families. Geary witnessed the Warrant and Inventory of William A. Johnson's estate after his 1913 death and of Charles A. Talbot after he died in 1934. Geary also helped settle the estates of Fannie Talbot and Pearl Leek after they died in 1934 and 1957, respectively.[18]

Fifteen months before Milton Geary's own death in 1964, the *Bangor Daily News* marked the fiftieth anniversary of his admission to law practice in Maine. At the time, he still was considered the state's only Black lawyer and the only attorney also ordained as a minister. The *Daily News* described Geary as follows:

> His two professions he terms predestined, law was a matter of competing with a fellow student in Marlboro, and he felt called to the ministry. He maintains that they harmonize[,] pointing out that he sometimes makes spiritual contacts through his legal work. "God expects some men to perform unusual feats" is his way of summing it all up, although by now, he does not view it as anything out of the ordinary.
>
> His law clientele is white by a large percentage. Over the years he has achieved success by insisting on right, and by his willingness to pass up large fees to settle as many of his cases as possible in his office rather than in court. He recalls the early years when his study light burned far in the morning hours as he prepared his legal cases and, equally important to him, his sermons.[19]

As the only African American attorney in the city during his lifetime, Geary's ability to practice law for more than fifty years was not a small feat. He could not have survived by serving the Black community exclusively, and clearly the White community was not averse to contracting his services.

Many other men worked in the profession and offered Bangor residents alternate sources of legal advice. In 1920, for example, the *Maine State Register* identified more than ninety lawyers in Bangor. In 1950, that number had dropped significantly, but there were still more than fifty other lawyers in the city besides Milton Geary. One of the many other Bangor attorneys was Oscar Walker. Attorney-at-law, notary public, and justice of the peace, Oscar Walker operated his practice at 155 Hammond Street. Geary and Walker may have been friends; Walker was the executor of Geary's estate and was the default executor of Fahy Geary's estate in the event that Milton predeceased his wife.[20] In total, Milton Geary spent more than fifty years as a lawyer and more than thirty-five years as a minister. His death in June 1964 was front-page news in the city's local newspaper and an indication that an important chapter in the professional history of Black Bangor had closed.

Fred W. Matheas distinguished himself as a railroad engineer. Matheas earned a diploma in civil engineering from the University of Maine in 1907. After receiving his degree, Matheas left his job as a teamster, and began work as a railroad engineer.[21] Another professional, W. Alonzo Johnson, played with the Bangor Symphony Orchestra for more than twenty-five years (illus-

ILLUSTRATION 10. W. Alonzo Johnson, a member of the Bangor Symphony Orchestra for more than twenty-five years. *Courtesy Earl R. Johnson Collection.*

tration 10). He studied violin and viola, and joined the orchestra in 1912. Johnson played second-chair violin, then viola, and finally became principal of the viola section a few years before his death in 1937. In addition to his Symphony Orchestra tenure, Johnson was a violinist at one of the city's premier places of entertainment, the Bijou Theatre. With three of his siblings, Doris, Julia, and Vivian, Alonzo Johnson formed a quartet that provided

music for the Nickel Theatre, one the city's most popular houses of entertainment.[22]

Black professional women included Linda Brooks Davis, the only child of
Frank and Sarah Brown Brooks and the granddaughter of physician Thomas
Brown. Linda Brooks attended the renowned New England Conservatory of
Music. In her late twenties in 1900, Brooks worked nine months of the year
as a music teacher. Brooks married Charles L. Davis; they had a daughter,
Dorothy, in October of 1905. A failing marriage and the support of her young
child were probably behind Davis' decision to leave teaching for a more reliable, yet less prestigious, source of employment. So, despite her conservatory
training, Linda Brooks Davis took a job as a matron — a ladies' restroom
attendant — at Union Station when it opened in 1907.[23]

Davis' days at the station began at eight o'clock in the morning — sometimes earlier — and she never knew what any given day might bring. Once,
a female passenger accidentally left her infant child at the station. In the
meantime, Davis returned from her lunch break "to find a wailing infant[,]
and railroad officials trying in vain to quiet it." As a woman and a mother
herself, it may have been Davis' job to take care of the child until officials
located the mother, who was soon "returned to Bangor and her baby" (illustration 11).[24]

Over the course of more than thirty years at Union Station, Davis found
that she encountered two general types of patrons. She reported to the
*Daily News:*

> I have found that the average traveler is courteous and appreciates any service
> one renders — but of course there are exceptions. Most women are careful
> about spilling their powder when making up in rest rooms, but others appar-
> ently feel that it is a public place and doesn't matter.[25]

Davis' criticisms were rooted in class more than race. Her interview relates
classist impressions: the courteous patron was usually a seasoned traveler;
the discourteous one was often a woman who just dropped into the station
to use the bathroom. Davis may have been being diplomatic, but her failure
to comment on racist experiences suggests that she was generally comfortable with the travelers who crossed her path, and she with them.

When Davis retired from Union Station in 1940, it seems to have been
with an overall satisfaction with her work experience. She reflected, "The
years have passed quickly and happily, and I leave with pleasant memories
and kind thoughts of my employers and fellow workers, who have been very

ILLUSTRATION 11. Linda Brooks Davis, Union Station matron. *Collections of the Bangor Museum and Center for History.*

kind to me." Linda Brooks Davis moved to Washington, D.C., after her retirement, but in 1969 returned to Bangor, where she lived out what would be the last two years of her life.[26]

Callie Mills Peters may have been Black Bangor's only public school teacher. Born in Maine in the late 1890s to George and Mary Mills, Callie Mills Peters was a divorced mother of one son. Peters and her son, Paul, resided with her widowed mother and her older sister, Gladys, at 186 Washington Street. As a divorced African American woman, Callie Peters' position as a school teacher seems to have defied the conventions of her day, when neither divorced nor African American women were the classroom ideal (illustration 12).[27]

Maine's teaching culture was generally inhospitable to African Americans. Of the more than 6,500 female schoolteachers in Maine in 1930, only two were African American. Callie Peters was one of them. No Black men were recorded among the more than 1,100 male teachers in Maine that year. The 1930 census illustrates the surface disparity in the number of Black female professionals between northern and southern New England. Four Black female school teachers were reported for Maine and New Hampshire combined, while Rhode Island, Massachusetts, and Connecticut had a combined total of more than ninety. However, further investigation reveals that the proportion of Black women teachers in each New England state relative to the state's total population was roughly the same. The only exception is Vermont, which recorded no Black female school teachers in 1930.[28]

Published and unpublished interviews with African Americans who went to high school and university in the state corroborate what seems to have been an unwritten rule in education. The convention was that despite their post-secondary training, African Americans could not teach in Maine. For some, this meant that they would have to complete what were often mandatory teaching internships outside of the state; for others, it meant that they realistically could not hope to pursue teaching careers in the state after receiving their bachelor's degrees. This policy prompted Blacks to do one of two things—change their vocation or teach outside of the state. James and Elizabeth Jackson Warner's daughter, Beryl, earned her bachelor's degree in mathematics from the University of Maine in 1935. She did her student teaching in Orangeburg, South Carolina. Herbert Heughan received his University of Maine degree in mathematics in 1940. He soon left the Bangor area for Virginia's Hampton Institute. About the experience Heughan ex-

ILLUSTRATION 12. Teachers and students of the Pond Street School. The teacher on the middle left could be Callie Peters. *Collections of the Bangor Museum and Center for History.*

plained, "I determined that I'd just have to work in the South anyway because I was a teacher. They didn't have any [B]lack teachers up here."[29]

Teaching was one of the few professional occupations available to African American women in the early decades of the twentieth century. Many Black women across the country in 1930 taught in historically or predominately Black schools created by the Reconstruction-era establishment of historically Black colleges and universities (HBCUs) and expanded by the institutional segregation of the nation's public schools. As Bangor did not have racially segregated schools, the opportunities for Black women and men to teach were reduced significantly. Had Bangor area schools freely allowed Black women and men to teach, Black Bangor's professional class would have been enlarged. When Blacks were hindered or denied opportunities to teach, therefore, they were not only robbed of employment and satisfactory wages, they also lost a reliable avenue to the general public esteem that comes with professional status.[30]

*Proprietors*

As self-employed workers, Black Bangor's proprietors risked economic failure and its impact on their families, but at the same time enjoyed more autonomy than average wage laborers. William A. Johnson was one of Black Bangor's most famous entrepreneurs. Originally from Norfolk, Virginia, Johnson moved to Maine from Boston in the late 1870s and started Johnson's, a clothes-cleaning and pressing business. He opened his business at 25 Franklin Street, and relocated again before occupying his space at Broad Street (illustration 13).[31] By the time that he moved to the corner of Broad and Water Streets, Johnson had long expanded from cleaning and pressing clothes to renting costumes and selling a variety of second-hand merchandise, including tools, reconditioned logging boots, and even musical instruments. Edith Johnson's contribution to the family business included mending costumes. This was in addition to raising ten children and making their clothes.[32]

After William A. Johnson's death in 1913, his two eldest sons, Alonzo and Cecil, took over the family business. Cecil Johnson died three years after his father, leaving Alonzo as the business's sole proprietor. Johnson's continued to be such a commercial success that locals embraced their slogan, "See Johnson First." The adage and local press coverage directed Bangor consumers to consult the Broad Street business for "everything from a needle to an anchor."[33] Alonzo Johnson was highly esteemed for his knowledge of goods and his personal service, and received high praise from the local press:

> The personal attention of Mr. Johnson is given to every sale as well as purchase. If he doesn't have it, he will soon find it. All he asks is that you give him a try.
>
> To retrieve all articles which are still of service at a very low cost, "See Johnson First." Mr. Johnson has worked hard to make his business a success. He occupies the whole building in which he has his store and his willingness to advise and help at all times has won for him a warm spot in the hearts of Bangor people.[34]

In 1937, Alonzo Johnson died, and Johnson's, after more than half a century of business, closed permanently.[35]

However, the commercial prominence of the Johnson family was not over. Edith Johnson's youngest and only surviving son, Earl, operated his own business. He established Earl's Radio Service at 137 Broad Street before his thirtieth birthday. Of his business, the *Daily News* reported that Earl's Radio

ILLUSTRATION 13. William A. Johnson's Broad Street business was a Bangor institution. *Bangor Daily News photo; Courtesy Earl R. Johnson Collection.*

Service "was complete with modern equipment with which he [was] enabled to give the most satisfactory service on all types of radio for home and automobiles." Prior to opening his own shop, Johnson worked at various local music and radio businesses, including Andrews Music House, Hartford Battery, and the Home Radio Company.[36]

Another example of African American entrepreneurship was Henry and Lena Bernard's business, the Bernard Employment Agency and Real Estate Company, which they ran from their home at 42 Lane. The Bernards advertised their services in the local city directory using the slogan, "Why not list your property with us to sell or rent at modern cost?"[37] Employment and real estate agencies played valuable roles in helping newcomers settle into new towns and cities, and assisting current residents locate new or improved work and housing. Myra Young Armstead's research on African Americans in Newport, Rhode Island, reveals that job networking, including through employment agencies, was important in placing Blacks in local jobs. This was especially true for southern migrants and the city's seasonal resort workers. In

Newport, three Black women, Virginian Mildred Winston, Pennsylvanian Susan Cradle, and Georgian Sara Ellen Owen offered employment services or operated formal employment agencies, most of them in their own homes.[38]

Despite providing what would have been valuable services, Henry and Lena Bernard were not able to live solely off the proceeds of their business. They both took outside employment. In 1900, for example, Henry Bernard worked as a watchman at Union Iron Works, and by 1910 he was working as a janitor at a private building. Between the 1890s and 1910, Lena Bernard had seven children, four of whom would survive to adulthood. With all of her children working in the 1920s, Lena Bernard took up domestic work and became a housekeeper. By 1930, the Bernard Employment Agency and Real Estate Company ceased operations, perhaps a casualty of the Great Depression. In her early sixties in 1930, Lena Bernard still performed domestic work—this time doing laundry for a private family.[39]

Not much is known about the operation or relative success of the Bernards' company. In 1900, the Bernards rented their home for an undetermined amount of money, but by 1910 they seem to have been made some financial gains. They had purchased their residence at 42 Lane and by 1930 had completely paid off the mortgage. It simply may have been that the revenues of the business alone were not enough to cover the mortgage and day-to-day familial expenses. Perhaps Bangor's African American population was insufficient to support their business. This might be true particularly if White patrons bypassed them in favor of one of the city's other such companies, including the Penobscot Employment and Real Estate Agency, the Great Northern Employment Company, or the various offices operated by Charles Bernstein, William Bragg, and Timothy Conners, and clustered on downtown's Exchange Street.[40]

Other African American proprietors in Bangor included Nova Scotian James Alfred Cromwell, who owned Al's Barber Shop at 197 Ohio Street for more than forty-five of the sixty-three years he lived in the city.[41] Black barbers and hairdressers held significant social and cultural status in the African American community, but barbering alone did not confer proprietary status. Barbers who owned their own shops moved up the ladder from skilled/semi-skilled labor to proprietary labor, one category below the professional.[42]

Not all of the Black entrepreneurs had formal offices or shops from which they could sell their products or offer their services. For many, their homes were their offices and their vehicles—and their reputations in the city—were their calling cards. Known as teamsters, expressmen, truckmen, or just movers, they seem to have seen brisk trade in the growing city. As Bangor consumers enjoyed the general prosperity of the 1920s and purchased more and more manufactured goods, people like Charles A. Talbot, Fred D. Matheas, Frank Matheas, Fred O'Ree, Charles O'Ree, and William R. Stewart were there to transport them.[43]

Literally building his business on horses and wagons, Charles A. Talbot established a highly visible and seemingly profitable delivery business in the city. Bangor records document some of Talbot's transactions as he secured and also disposed of delivery-related equipment. In August of 1904, Talbot purchased for thirty dollars a double wagon, a double team harness, blue running gear, and other sundry fixtures. In 1915, he purchased "one horse long sled," for which he arranged to pay ten dollars and 7 percent interest. In 1918, Talbot purchased a twelve-year-old black horse for twenty-five dollars. The next year, Talbot sold two of his own horses—one brown and one bay. Sterling Dymond, Jr., remembers Talbot as "a shrewd old man" who, in addition to his horses, kept a cow in his pasture. The cow that Sterling Dymond remembers may well have been the red and white cow that Talbot purchased in 1927 for twenty-five dollars.[44]

In 1900, brothers Fred D. and Frank Matheas worked as teamsters, as did Frank's son, Fred Walter Matheas. Furniture mover Fred D. Matheas owned several horses and wagons along with assorted moving equipment during his lifetime. In the ten-year period between 1901 and 1911, Matheas was in ownership of at least three horses—one black horse about six years old; one bay horse, "Baby"; one gray mare, "Sis." In addition, he owned at least two covered, wheeled moving wagons and one covered moving sled.[45] Fred D. Matheas continued in this work until he died in 1912. By 1910, however, his nephew, Fred Walter, had received his bachelor's degree in civil engineering and was working in his field for the railroad.[46] Fred D. Matheas's death and Fred Walter Matheas's graduation reduced the number of African American teamsters in Bangor, a void that brothers Fred and Charles O'Ree helped fill. In 1917, Fred O'Ree purchased from Brown & White a Gilson express wagon, with yellow gear and a dark body. For it, O'Ree agreed to pay seventy-five dollars, to be paid over the next year at the rate of ten dollars per month for the first six months, and the balance within six months at 6 percent interest. Ten years later, O'Ree purchased from the S. L. Crosby Company a Ton Truck with Warford Transmission. For the automobile, O'Ree would pay

$325, and an additional $39 for collection and insurance. The terms of the sale required O'Ree to make an initial down payment of $109 and twelve monthly payments. In 1920, William R. Stewart was in his early twenties and had also entered Black Bangor's work-a-day world as an express man.[47]

## Managers and Clerks

Black managerial and clerical workers were generally few in number in the early twentieth century, but did increase over the decades leading up to mid-century. One of the most prominent men in this class was Connecticut native James H. Warner, who was a steward at Bangor's exclusive Tarratine Club for more than ten years and a steward for the Bangor and Aroostook Railroad for more than thirty years.[48] John H. Mason holds the distinction as Bangor's only Black mailman at the turn of the century. Mason held the position at the time of the 1900 census, and continued to hold it a decade later in 1910.[49]

Sarah Brooks, mother of Linda Brooks Davis, was one of the few early women whose worked qualified as managerial. In 1900, Brooks was a fifty-eight-year-old stewardess (food service manager). By the next decade, Brooks appears to have left the workforce. At sixty-nine years old, she lived on her own income, the exact nature of which is unclear. She died in 1916.[50]

As more women entered the workplace of the 1920s and 1930s, Black women made some employment gains by entering clerical positions. Nationally, however, it would be several decades before Black women would make significant wage and occupational gains as compared to their White counterparts. In Bangor, Gladys Davis was a laundry clerk. Edith Johnson's daughter, Evelyn, was a stenographer at a local automobile shop. Carrie Dymond's daughter, LaRue, worked as a stenographer at Sampson Insurance Agency on Central Street.[51]

## Skilled/Semi-Skilled Laborers

Skilled and semi-skilled laborers comprised a significant proportion of the Black male population. These occupations included auto repairmen, barbers (without their own shops), chefs, gardeners, masons, and painters. In Bangor, barbers were particularly prominent in 1900, when there were six different African American men in that profession. Paris (also Parris) O'Ree was a Bangor fixture. He worked at 3 Pickering Square as early as 1880, and by

1900 had moved to 38 Harlow Street. Frank O'Ree barbered at 142 Haymarket Square and George O'Ree worked at 94 Pickering Square. Daniel H. Mason worked at 20 Hammond Street and John H. Mason was employed at 80 Central. Alvin A. Talbot also barbered.[52]

Whether Black Bangor was too small to sustain six barbers or whether White patrons refused to patronize them, the number of Black barbers in the city dropped significantly after 1900, leaving George O'Ree, Frank O'Ree, and Daniel Mason the only barbers still listed in the *Maine Register*. By 1930, James Alfred Cromwell had established his Ohio Street barbershop; Daniel Mason remained at 20 Hammond, and Frank O'Ree worked at 209 Broad Street. During the following decades, James Alfred Cromwell became the last of the group still barbering in the city. He appears in the *Maine Register* for 1940 and 1950, still working on Ohio Street.[53]

Skilled or semi-skilled jobs for Black women included hairdressing, catering, dressmaking, and tailoring. Louise Mahoney, probably Black Bangor's only hairdresser, was well known to the African American women of the community. She operated her salon in her apartment at 16 Post Office Square (16 Harlow Street); located in the city's downtown core, her shop was convenient to women who came to run household errands, to shop, or to socialize. Unlike the White-owned Elite Beauty Shoppe, located one story below Louise Mahoney's salon, Mahoney's did not have an official name, and was less formal than other shops of its kind. Louise Mahoney continued to operate her business into the early 1930s. However, when she died in 1934, she and her husband were living at 58 Division Street and she was no longer in the beauty business.[54]

Louise Mahoney was part of a small group of Black women hairdressers in Maine. The 1930 census reports that only five Black women worked as barbers, hairdressers, or manicurists in the entire state during that year. This official number may be artificially low; some Black women simply may have worked informally out of their own homes, earning money doing the hair of family and friends. The hardships caused by the Great Depression induced frugality, and the spread of hair care products, like those produced by Madam C. J. Walker, gave African American women more options for taking care of their own hair at home.[55]

Technical changes in the marketplace affected Carrie Dymond, the dressmaker introduced at the beginning of the chapter. The increased production and affordability of manufactured, ready-to-wear clothing, combined with competition from the city's other more formal tailoring businesses, probably made it increasingly difficult for Dymond to make a living with her at-home business. Her husband's death between 1910 and 1920 and the need to support her family probably made it more expedient for her to find steadier, though lower paying employment. Carrie Dymond became a servant at Union Station. At the busy train station, Dymond would have seen, talked to, and even commiserated with Davis, the station's matron, on a regular basis.[56]

Nettie O'Ree also worked at home as a dressmaker in the early twentieth century. By 1920, O'Ree had not moved down the economic ladder, but had made something of a lateral move by working as a ladies' tailoress for Edward I. Morris. Morris, a tailor and furrier for both women and men, operated his shop at 27 Central Street. His establishment was one of the two shops in the city that specialized in tailoring for women. Fahy Heughan Geary, wife of lawyer-minister, Milton Geary, also worked at a tailor shop, although it is not clear where she worked. It may have been with Nettie O'Ree at Edward Morris's establishment; it may also have been for Morris's competitor, M. Hecht. Located at 148 Main Street, M. Hecht was convenient to Geary's residence at 36 Main.[57]

In 1930, there were reported to have been forty-three Black dressmakers and seamstresses in the state of Rhode Island. In Newport, Rhode Island, Mary Dickerson, wife of grocery store proprietor Silas Dickerson, operated a dressmaking business on busy Bellevue Avenue. In New Haven, Connecti-cut, jobs as dressmakers and seamstresses comprised the third-largest source of employment for Black women in 1900, 1910, and 1920. After 1930, however, the number of Black women in this trade declined dramatically as more of such work was done in factories and Black women found themselves ex-cluded from factory jobs. In Massachusetts, almost two hundred Black women worked in the trade, a far cry from the one reported for Vermont and the two reported for Maine.[58]

Nettie O'Ree and Fahy Geary's tailoring work required precision, skill, and manual dexterity. Hairdressers like Louise Mahoney were highly es-teemed for their ability to make women beautiful in an era when the main-stream market strongly adhered to a European model of femininity and beauty. But the most revered Black laboring women may well have been the caterers. Caterers turned everyday domestic labor into profitable ventures, marketing their skills to some of the most elite members of Bangor society. The worlds of Blacks and wealthy Whites in Bangor did revolve on different axes, and caterers had entrée, if only temporarily, into the private worlds of elite society, as they catered private parties for owners of local industry, transportation, and entertainment.

Panzy Talbot and Josephine Smallwood were two such women. Panzy Talbot actually held down two catering positions. She catered meals in the dining hall of the Kenduskeag Canoe Club, situated on the edge of the Penosbcot River in nearby Hampden. In addition, she catered such private functions as weddings and teas for some of the city's social and business elite, including the owners of the Bangor Opera House and the Bijou Theatre.[59] Talbot seems to have received significant financial compensation, periodic gratuities, and small gifts, as well as the esteem of those who contracted her services.

> Popular accounts report that Panzy Talbot was a rather well-to-do woman by all accounts. Each year [or two] she bought a new Plymouth; she gave away free theatre tickets she had been given by her employers; in her home was a library full of books.[60]

Whether by design or by coincidence, the life of caterer Josephine Smallwood seems to have been simpler than Panzy Talbot's. Although she was born in Maine, Smallwood's parents were both born in Kentucky; one or both may have been enslaved. Smallwood operated out of her simple home at 52 Manners Avenue, but "catered many gatherings and parties for the money people" and "could prepare meals fit for a king."[61] A lesser remembered contemporary of Smallwood and Talbot was Adell Johnson. A native of New York, Johnson was in her early fifties when the 1900 census recorded her occupation as a caterer. Precious little is known about her.[62]

Caterers had the power to affect the lives of their patrons. The success of their food products and the timeliness of their service had the potential to make or break their patrons' functions. Continued patronage by the wealthy elite demanded that Talbot and Smallwood offer consistent, high-quality products and service. At the same time, Talbot, Smallwood, and Johnson's work freed their patrons from the drudge work of food preparation and clean up, allowing them to focus on entertaining and receiving the accolades of their guests.

Chefs, like stewards and barbers, distinguished themselves by the longevity of their careers and by the clientele they served. Perhaps the two most famous African American chefs in the city were father and son, Charles Raynsford and W. Edgerton Talbot. Charles Raynsford Talbot worked as a chef on a railroad dining car before becoming a chef at the city's distin-

ILLUSTRATION 14. The Bangor House employed various Black men as cooks and stewards. *Collections of the Bangor Museum and Center for History.*

guished Bangor House Hotel (illustration 14). In 1930, when his father was at the Bangor House, Edgerton Talbot worked as a dining car cook. Edgerton Talbot eventually followed his father to Bangor House, before taking a position at the Allen House Hotel by 1950.[63] Edgerton Talbot's position at the Bangor House afforded him particular status within the African American community, but, as his teenage son, Gerald, observed, it sometimes required him to accept a "dressing down" from hotel management.[64]

Bangor's love affair with the automobile and the brisk business enjoyed by local automobile dealers opened up employment opportunities for young men to work in vehicle maintenance and repair. In 1920, Harry Bernard, the seventeen-year-old son of Henry and Lena Bernard, was a garage repairman. Hiram Simmons was a mechanic in 1930 at the popular Henley-Kimball Company located at the corner of May and Summer Streets.[65] Other sundry workers in the category of semi-skilled labor included Hubert Scott, who worked as a meat cutter at Broad Street's C.H. Rice Company; electric lineman Arthur Washington; John Lawrence, a plumber at the Union Bottling Company; and Joseph Sickles, an apprentice printer at the Bangor Publishing Company on Exchange Street.[66]

### Unskilled/Service Workers

Because of the diverse nature of unskilled and service work, and because African Americans consistently were relegated to servile labor, this category comprised the largest group of Black Bangor's male workers. Particularly vulnerable to economic swings, this group included bootblacks, janitors, cooks, waiters, railroad porters, and general laborers. Unskilled and service workers—cooks, domestics, maids, matrons, washerwomen, and general servants—made up the single largest group of Black female laborers in Bangor as well. They, too, worked for some of the wealthiest families in the city, but, unlike caterers, their positions did not confer on them significant status from either the Black or the White community. Some domestics lived in their employers' homes, but the majority lived out.[67]

Mabel O'Ree was born in Maine in the mid- to late 1870s, and in 1920 she was in her forties and earned a living doing laundry at the Bangor Children's Home at 218 Ohio Street. Ten years later, O'Ree was in her fifties and had become a live-in maid for George and Mary Hopkins. George Hopkins was the president of Penobscot Savings Bank, and he and his wife lived in a ten thousand dollar home at 54 Ohio Street, down the street from O'Ree's former place of employment.[68] Florence Dymond was twenty-two in 1930 and worked as a live-in maid for Sumner and Ruth Hopkins at 213 French Street. Sumner Hopkins was another prominent businessman who managed the investment banking company Worthen and Company, Incorporated, located at 6 State Street.[69] Annie Russell was a live-in servant who worked for Hattie Patterson, proprietor of Rockaway House, a boarding facility in the city.[70]

Other women in Bangor had housekeeping arrangements with individual families and worked on a live-out basis. In the spring of 1900, Mary Pratt was a forty-year-old widow who worked as a laundress to support herself and her two children, George, seventeen, and Lucy, fourteen, both of whom were in school.[71] Other domestics in 1900 included kitchen girls like fifteen-year-old Carrie Hardling, nineteen-year-old Prudewell Burt, and twenty-one-year-old Ida Jenkins, all of whom were from Canada. Burt and Jenkins had been in Bangor for less than one year at this time, and domestic service was probably the work most readily available to them.[72]

Domestic work, in all its forms, continued to be the dominant employment for Black women for much of the twentieth century. Daisy Good (also Goode) did washing at home, as did her widowed mother, sixty-seven-year-old Margaret A. Halfkenny. Another widow, Jane Eastman, worked as a washerwoman for a private family. Theodosia Hoyt worked as a laundress on her own account. Women like Good, Halfkenny, and Hoyt were able to work without the supervision of their employers. Because they were related, Good and Halfkenny probably worked cooperatively to complete their work. Lilly Sunth, a mother of seven, worked as a housekeeper for a private family, as did widow Hannah Mason. Eliza Taylor, wife of laborer Enoch Taylor, worked as a servant in a private house. Women like Sunth, Mason, and Taylor who worked inside their employers' homes had more stringent supervision and may have been subject to sexual harassment.[73]

Other second-generation women still labored in jobs traditionally pre-scribed for women of color, positions that in 1930 were still essentially servile. Helena Dymond, daughter of Sterling and Janie Simmons Dymond, was a nurse girl to a private family, as was eighteen-year-old Lucille Johnson, daugh-ter of William and Edith Delaney Johnson. William and Lenora Stewart's daughter, Sophie, was a private housekeeper and Marion Peters' seventeen-year-old daughter, Marion, did general housework after school and on weekends.[74]

The same increase in manufactured clothing that had probably made it difficult for women like Carrie Dymond to maintain home-based sewing businesses also increased the already heavy workload of washerwomen. As Tera W. Hunter has argued,

> Unlike cooking, laundry work became more demanding as a result of indus-trialization. Manufactured cloth expanded individual wardrobes and the wider availability of washable fabrics such as cotton increased the need for washing. Laundry work was the single most onerous chore . . . and the first chore . . . hire[d] out whenever the slightest bit of discretionary income was available.[75]

The work of laundering was demanding not only because of the amount of work entailed; it was also onerous because the work of laundering often began on Monday and continued until all laundry was washed, dried, ironed, and delivered by Saturday.[76]

Of all Black female unskilled and service workers, matrons—who attended any number of the city's restrooms—were perhaps the most public type of female service workers. In addition to Linda Brooks Davis, who spent more than thirty years as a matron at Union Station, other matrons included Mary A. Mills and Alice Wheary Hoyt. Born in Maine in the late 1870s, Mills was

ILLUSTRATION 15. The Bijou Theatre, one of the premier cultural institutions in the city. *Collections of the Bangor Museum and Center for History.*

in her early fifties in 1930. A widow at that time, Mills worked as a matron at the Bijou Theatre at 164 Exchange Street (illustration 15). New Brunswick native Alice Wheary Hoyt, wife of coal teamster, Cecil C. Hoyt, worked as a matron at the city's telegraph office.[77]

Domestic service was a double-edged sword. Housekeeping and general service provided Black women with a predictable, but often low-paying income. This employment could also keep them from their families for extended periods of time. For women with young children, their domestic work may have been flexible enough to allow them to take their children with them. It may also have required them to leave small children in the care of older children, with neighbors, or with relatives. In addition to requiring Black women to reorder their own private lives, domestic work required Black women to do some of the least desirable and unrewarding work in the marketplace, including cooking, cleaning, laundry, and supplementary child care of their patrons' children.

While not as diverse as Black men's labor, Black women's work tended to be steadier. Women, who tended to be domestic laborers, saw lower wages, but generally had the security of year-round employment. As a group, Black men's labors were more stratified, but tended to be less secure. In 1910, for example, Black women who worked as domestic workers on either a live-in or live-out basis reported being employed for the entire duration of the previous year. Those Black men who did odd jobs, general service, or seasonal work saw more weeks without work.[78]

In several cases, like those of Mary Mills, Linda Brooks Davis, Lena Bernard, and Carrie Dymond, Black women's move from professional or semi-skilled labor to unskilled/service work was often preceded by some major change in the family's composition and wage structure. Death and divorce not only wreaked havoc on Black women's personal lives, they also took away the family's primary wage earner. For widowed and divorced women, domestic work functioned as a consistently available means by which they could enter or reenter the workforce. Although not necessarily an attractive employment option, domestic work helped support various women and their children.[79]

Not only was domestic service Black Bangor women's dominant form of employment in the early to mid-twentieth century, it was also their default occupation. It was the work that Black women did or were forced to do when other work, even professional work, was not open to them or proved unable to sustain their families. The effects of this change varied. The local marketplace lost access to the skills of some highly trained and skilled women. The local community lost the women's potential contributions. Black women themselves lost or were greatly reduced in their own self-fulfillment and their claim to a higher socioeconomic status.

Not all African American women worked outside the home or had home-based businesses. For some women, like Harriet McCarty and Janie Dymond, the reproductive labor involved in raising their large families was their sole work. In 1900, Harriet McCarty had five children—all daughters—between the ages of three and eighteen years. Her husband, Samuel, worked as a day laborer and apparently earned enough to support the family on his wages alone. Fredericton native Janie Simmons Dymond was another woman who did not work outside the home. Her husband, Sterling Dymond, was a manager for the Great Northern Paper Company and after many years of working in the woods around Millinocket, he took a job with the city of Bangor's public works department. Whether her husband was working far away or within the city, Janie Dymond did not work outside the home.[80]

Like men in other occupations, bootblacks often were tied to the railroad industry, shining shoes for departing passengers who waited for their train's arrival or for passengers arriving after a long trip. Several bootblacks were in their late teens and early twenties, suggesting that this type of work allowed them entrance into the workplace during or after high school as well as in college. Lawyer and clergyman Milton Geary recounted how he had shined shoes at Bangor's Union Station while a student at the University of Maine during the 1910s. In 1930, eighteen-year-old Donald Wise, the nephew of George Leek; Arnold Watters, the nineteen-year-old son of Annie Watters; and Robert Wise, the eighteen-year-old son of John and Lenta Peters Wise, all held jobs as bootblacks.[81]

The position of railroad porter was one several of Black Bangor's men held over the years. In 1910, Edward Ambrose, Edgar Buck, and Edward Palmer all worked as porters. In 1920, William H. Derricks and William Campbell were both porters, and in 1930, Alyson Wise was a railroad station porter and J. Robert Mahoney worked as a private porter for the Bangor and Aroostook Railroad. [82] In the African American community, portering was generally one of the more prestigious nonprofessional and nonproprietary jobs open to Black men. Portering allowed men to travel to various parts of their home state, across different regions, and even coast to coast. Long hours, mandatory deference to passengers, and lower wages than their White counterparts were their rewards.[83]

In 1916, the porter's monthly wage averaged $40.00; by 1924, it had risen to an average of $81.75 plus tips on tourist trains, like those in Maine. After A. Philip Randolph organized the Brotherhood of Sleeping Car Porters and Maids in 1925, the minimum monthly pay for porters rose to $89.50, although a sixty-hour work week was still the standard. Nonetheless, portering gave Black men access to some of the wealthiest and most prestigious men in the area, and contacts that they could parlay into generous tips or future job placement. Despite their occupation's long hours, Black Bangor's porters likely enjoyed the same advantages as porters outside of Maine. Interstate travel allowed exposure to new cities, new contacts brought awareness of other Black communities, and the evolution of the Brotherhood helped protect Black jobs while modeling the power of organized, industrial labor.[84]

Future Morehouse College president Benjamin E. Mays worked as a Pullman porter during the latter part of 1920, after graduating from Maine's Bates College and before beginning his graduate work at the University of Chicago. His testimony sheds light on the type of conditions that Black porters had to endure. In his biography, *Born to Rebel,* Mays recounts his portering experiences and how his work for the Pullman Company took him from the Boston district where he was stationed, down the east coast, and as far west as Chicago. Mays soon was dissatisfied with how work was assigned and, like other porters across the country, he had to deal with being subordinate to the train's conductor. Ultimately, Mays' tenure as a porter was ended by a disagreement with a Pullman conductor and by an earlier suspicion that he had fraudulently generated and submitted his own time slip.[85]

Black men filled other positions in the railroad industry, including cooks, waiters, janitors, railroad car cleaners, and general laborers. William Shears, Earl Leek, Edgerton Talbot, Albert Martini, and Bedford Peters all worked as railroad waiters and cooks at some time in their lives. William Derricks, Harry Bernard, and George (or Randolph) Dymond worked cleaning railroad cars in their later years, the average monthly pay for which was approximately fifty dollars in 1915. In 1930, John Nelson, Earl Dymond, Peter Hart, Sandy Gordon, William Alberts, and Ralph Gordon all worked as janitors for either the Bangor and Aroostook Railroad or the Maine Central Railroad. Seemingly occupying jobs for older men, the group had an average age of fifty-three years.[86]

There was a noticeable, but not exclusive concentration of native-born Blacks in portering, while Black Canadians, who had been recruited into the region's timber industry, frequently worked as river drivers, woodsmen, and pulp and paper mill workers. Several Blacks, including Canadian natives Earl Dymond, Wallace Leek, Harold Cromwell, and Reginald Small, worked in the paper industry. Dymond drove a lumber truck, Leek drove truck for a paper mill, Cromwell was a woodsman, and Small was a paper mill laborer.[87]

Sterling Dymond, Jr., was born in Bangor and knows quite well the history of the Blacks in the timber drive:

> Back in the 1800s, early 1900s, they worked in the woods, they were woodsmen. And on the timber drive, [of] course the drive came down into Bangor with the pulp, and a lot of them stayed here, and made their homes here. [Bangor] was a big wood port. And they used to go up in the woods and work. . . . And they built homes and they lived here and had families here.[88]

Dymond's father, Sterling A. Dymond, worked for many years as a manager for the Great Northern Paper Company in Millinocket. According to Helena Dymond George, the eldest Dymond child, her father's work of coordinating the delivery of supplies to the lumbering camps kept him away for long periods of time. It did, however, allow him to return home on holidays.[89]

## Other Workers

The manuscript census is littered with individuals whose only job description is "odd jobs" and "laborer." In 1900, Canadian natives Samuel McCarty, Charles White, David Willis, John Peters, David MacKenzie, Clifton Half-kenny, and Banyon Halfkenny all worked as laborers. In 1910, Abner Peters, Ford Clark, Harry O'Ree, Nelson Peters, Henry Peters, Charles Burt, George Wetters, Thompson Hoyt, and Enoch Taylor were among those who performed odd jobs for a living. The prosperity of the 1920s appears to have resulted in a significant drop in the number of men who got by working odd jobs; in 1930, Austin Gordon, Cecil G. Hoyt, and Sterling Dymond were a few of the men who, at some point in their lives, performed odd jobs or general labor for a living.[90]

The type of labor that Black men performed in Bangor not only dictated their presence or absence from their families and the larger community. It was also a factor in whether they were able to maintain steady employment or whether they were subject to seasonal fluctuations in demand. The manuscript census reports the number of weeks during the previous twelve-month period that a particular worker was unemployed. From early 1909 through early 1910, for example, thirty-year-old Ford Clark performed odd jobs and had been without work for nine weeks. For that same period, Clark's nineteen-year-old nephew, Stanley Peters, who also performed odd jobs, had been without work for only one week. In a more extreme example, eighteen-year-old Thompson Hoyt had been without work for twenty weeks during the previous year and his twenty-nine-year-old cousin, Harry Close, had been out of work for ten weeks. Sterling A. Dymond, whom the 1910 manuscript census records as performing odd jobs, had worked without interruption during the previous twelve-month period.[91]

Despite the general prestige that they enjoyed within the Black community, porters in Bangor found that their work schedules could be as uncertain as that of less skilled workers. Porter James Warner had twelve months of uninterrupted employment, as did his stepson Edward Ambrose. Porter Edward Palmer, however, was not as fortunate. In 1910, Palmer, a twenty-nine-year-old husband and father of two young children, had been without work for twenty weeks—some five months—during the previous year.[92]

Maritime and agricultural labor was not highly reported in the increasingly urban city of Bangor. In 1900, Cape Verdean Dijon Piris worked as a seaman and George Walker worked as a deck hand; in 1920, Austin Gordon worked as shipbuilder. In 1910, Herbert McCarty worked as a farm hand; in 1920, Lee Leplayne worked as a farm truck driver; and in 1930, Russell Payne worked as a farm laborer.[93]

Cape Verdean Dijon Piris's relationship with the sea was indicative of the type of work done by Cape Verdeans in late-nineteenth-century New England. By the 1880s, Cape Verdeans were prominent in the whaling and sealing industries of New Bedford, Massachusetts. A few decades later, however, changes in the whaling industry brought Cape Verdeans back inland, where they entered the mills of New Bedford and the fruit orchards and cranberry bogs of southern New England.[94]

⁓☙⁓

Blacks' experiences in the Bangor workplace varied widely. At their best, Blacks were highly esteemed professionals and entrepreneurs who created comfortable lives. At their worst, Black workers were trapped in a makeshift economy that required them to piece together unskilled or service labor at different phases of their lives or from season to season.[95] The labor market for Black men seems to have been relatively fluid, as Black men moved in and out of jobs, often ascending the ranks of a particular industry as younger men and descending those same ranks as older men. This is particularly visible in the railroad industry, as some Blacks were able to progress from being porters to stewards, but then moved into janitorial and general laboring duties in their fifties and sixties. But the diversity of Black women's labor in no way matched that of their male counterparts. Although some women escaped domestic service, many women did not achieve their full potential. Women such as conservatory-trained Linda Brooks Davis and teacher Callie Mills Peters prepared for greater things than becoming washroom attendants, but had to settle for dreams deferred for the sake of their children.

*Chapter 3*

⚬⚬⚬

# DAILY LIFE

## *Rhythms of the Community*

In 1930, laborer and World War I veteran Dean Davis, his wife, Marianne, and their two sons, George and Dean, Jr., lived at 186 Washington Street in Bangor's first ward. Located in a rather industrial section of the city, the Davis home was flanked on one side by the Eastern Fuel Company's scrap yard and on the other side by a junk yard owned by neighbor Jacob Dresner. Directly across from the Davis' house stood a fifteen-foot wall, behind which lay the tracks of Maine Central Railroad. Beyond the tracks ran the Penobscot River. For their Washington Street residence, the Davises paid a monthly rent of fifteen dollars, a median rate in Bangor at a time when Blacks paid anywhere from a very low eight dollars a month to an above average thirty dollars.[1] Across the city, in Ward 3, stevedore Ford and Rosalie Clark lived at 106 Walter Street, with their six children and two young nieces. For their modest, one-and-a-half-story house, the Clarks had paid the median home cost of one thousand dollars; other Black-owned houses cost or were valued at up to six thousand dollars.[2]

African Americans took up residence in virtually every ward in Bangor (illustration 16). They did cluster, however, in a western portion of the city, known popularly as the Parker Street neighborhood, and distinguished by its concentration of African American renters and homeowners. In their day-to-day existence inside and outside the Parker Street neighborhood, Blacks lived typical life cycles of birth, marriage, sometimes divorce, and death. They immortalized themselves in photographs, and were part of a growing

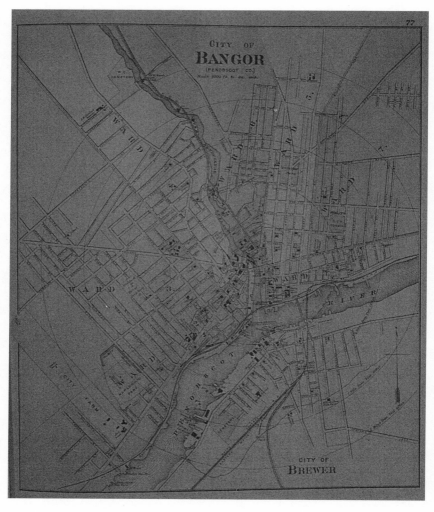

ILLUSTRATION 16. Stuart's Map of Bangor, 1902. Most Blacks in Bangor lived in Wards 3 and 4.
*Courtesy of the Osher Map Library, University of Southern Maine.*

American consumer culture that demonstrated an appetite for modern conveniences and middle-class status symbols like pianos and automobiles.

## City-wide Residency

Bordered on the north by State Street, on the west by the Kenduskeag Stream, on the south by the Penobscot River, and on the east by the city limits, Bangor's first ward was home to a mix of commercial and residential buildings. Widow Mary Mills lived in this ward at 186 Washington Street. While not a double house in a formal sense, the multi-level structure was partitioned and allowed Mills, her two daughters, and a grandson to occupy one side of the house while the Davis family, mentioned above, occupied the other. Mills, who worked as a matron at the Bijou Theatre at 164 Exchange Street, rented the Washington Street home for eight dollars a month—less than one hundred dollars a year—and for approximately half of what Dean and Marianna Davis paid to rent their portion of the building. This was a relatively low-rent area, as other homes on Washington Street had rents of ten to fifteen dollars.[3]

Oak Street ran north from Washington Street and was situated a few blocks east of the Kenduskeag Stream. On this small street lived William and Eunice Shears, both in their early forties in 1930, and Eunice's teenage daughter, Katherine. A two-story frame house with a two-story stable, 98 Oak Street was also home to chauffeur Carlton Cromwell, who boarded with the Shears family and probably contributed toward the household expenses. Up the street from the Shears were a number of businesses, including the Northern Oldsmobile Company and Rogan's Granite and Marble Works at 81 and 58 Oak Street, respectively. Like Dean Davis, railroad chef William Shears paid fifteen dollars a month to rent his family's Oak Street home.[4]

Hotel cook George Jones, his wife, Alvilda, and their son, Arthur, lived nearby at 1 Frazier Street, where they paid eighteen dollars a month to rent the family dwelling. Also residing at 1 Frazier was World War I veteran Oakley Patterson and his wife, Elizabeth. The Pattersons, like the Joneses, paid a monthly rental fee of eighteen dollars. Walter O'Ree lived next to the Joneses and Pattersons at 9 Frazier Street. Several woodsmen, including New Brunswick-born Alton Leek, took lodging at a rooming house on nearby Exchange Street.[5] Overall, the number of African American households located in Bangor's first ward was minor.

The boundaries of Bangor's second ward comprised Union Street, Sec-

ILLUSTRATION 17. The Bangor Opera House. *Collections of the Bangor Museum and Center for History.*

ond Street, the Penobscot River, and the Hampden town line. The number of Black families living in the city's second ward was significantly higher than that of the first ward, and included some of the African American community's and the city's most well-known residents. Lawyer and clergyman Milton Geary, his wife, Fahy Heughan Geary, and their son, Milton R. Geary, Jr., lived at 36 Main Street. The Gearys lived on the third floor of the four-story brick building where Geary also operated his legal practice. As the address suggests, 36 Main Street was in the heart of the city's downtown sector, and was located near such notable businesses as the F. W. Woolworth department store at 57 Main, Freese's Department Store at 80 Main, the *Bangor Daily Commercial* at 81 Main, and the Bangor Opera House at 131 Main (illustrations 17 and 18).[6]

Railroad waiter Earl M. Leek and his wife Mary lived at 10 Patten Street with their three young children. This residence was a large, frame dwelling with one-and-a-half stories on the front and two stories on the back. The building housed two families, and the Leeks rented their portion of the structure for fifteen dollars per month.[7] Five doors down the street, at 34 Patten, lived William and Mabel Derricks, and lodger, William Jolley. Both men worked for the railroad, Derricks as a janitor and Jolley as a waiter. The Derricks' one-and-a-half-story home cost eighteen dollars per month, and was one half of a double house, adjoined to the 36 Patten Street residence of Earl and Nora Cox Dymond. Like his neighbors, Earl Dymond worked for the railroad. Although the rents on this double house did not vary much, the Dymonds paid a slightly higher monthly rate of twenty dollars.[8] The concentration of railroad employees on Patten Street suggests that the houses may have been owned by the railroad as places for Black employees to live.

Dutton and Pleasant Streets also were located in the second ward. In 1930,

ILLUSTRATION 18. Main Street at night. *Collections of the Bangor Museum and Center for History.*

Peter and Pearl Patterson Hart were in their fifties and thirties, respectively. They resided at 33 Dutton Street with their four children. Peter Hart's work as a railroad laborer was sufficient to allow him to purchase the family's one-and-a-half-story, two thousand dollar home.[9] Lucius and Evangeline Wickers lived nearby at 8 Pleasant Street. Lucius worked as a garage laborer and supported a growing family of five children. The Wickers lived in a two-story double house, and by paying twelve dollars per month in rent, they paid less than $150 per year for housing.[10]

Ward 3 began at the intersection of Second and Union Streets, followed Union Street to the city limits, continued along the western city line to Second Street, and returned back up Second to Union. Much of the ward comprised a maze of relatively small and seemingly quiet streets. Nestled in this area in 1930 were more than twenty-five Black families. These families accounted for more than one hundred men, women, and children—almost half of the city's total Black population—and made the third ward the most densely populated part of Black Bangor. Much of this area had been known as "Paddy Hollow" in the 1850s, because of its high concentration of Irish residents.[11]

Hersey Avenue was home to additional Dymonds and Leeks. Carrie Dymond lived at the corner of Hersey Avenue and Bryant Street with her daughter, LaRue, a stenographer. Fortunately, Dymond, who had been widowed between 1910 and 1920, did not have to pay a mortgage and had owned her home for at least the previous ten years. Her two thousand dollar home at 33 Hersey Avenue stood one-and-a-half stories high and had an attached garage of equal height.[12] Goodridge and Pearl Simmons Leek lived a few doors down the street from Carrie Dymond at 61 Hersey Avenue. Goodridge Leek, who had his own trucking business, also owned his house, which was valued at the median one thousand dollars. Also living in the Leek home were Goodridge and Pearl's two sons as well as Pearl's elderly father, widower James Simmons.[13]

John and Lenta Wise's home at 94 Patten Street was still further up Patten Street from the Derricks and the Dymonds. John Wise was a restaurant cook and Lenta did housework for a private family. The Wises' standard one-and-a-half-story home also housed eight children, who in 1930 ranged in age from three to eighteen years. Like most other Black families on the street, the Wises did not own their home; they rented it for a below-market cost of eleven dollars per month when other Patten Street rentals fees were as high as twenty-two dollars. James Alfred and Grace Cromwell and the couple's three children lived next door to the Wise family. Not only was Cromwell, the proprietor of Al's Barber Shop, the only African American on Patten Street to own his home in 1930, he had the most expensive house on the street. Valued at eighteen hundred dollars, the one-and-a-half-story home included a basement garage in which the Cromwells would have parked their car.[14] The Wises, Cromwells, Leeks, Derricks, and Dymonds all lived on the same street, separated only by the invisible boundaries between Wards 2 and 3.

William and Lenora Stewart lived at 108 Parker Street with their daughter, Sophie, and Sophie's infant daughter, Teresa. William Stewart worked as a carpenter, Lenora did private housework, and Sophie also kept house for a private family. To rent their two-story home, the Stewarts paid twenty dollars per month, the median rent on that street. Four doors down at 118 Parker Street lived widow Louise Elms, who worked as a housekeeper and paid an above-the-median rent of twenty-two dollars per month. Parker was a solidly middle-class street, with several homeowners, although few of them Black. House values started at two thousand dollars and rose as high as six thousand dollars.[15]

Parker Street intersected Third and Fourth Streets. George Leek lived at 148 Third Street, in one half of a double house that stood on the corner of Third and Parker. Several children and extended family members lived in the household, including the Leeks' three children, George's mother-in-law, Helen Wise, and George's two nephews. George Leek was a yardman. The Leeks rented their home for twenty dollars a month, which was located at the higher end of the rent scale for African Americans.[16]

At 133 Fourth Street lived Sterling and Janie Simmons Dymond and their nine children. The Dymond house was an impressive, multi-level structure, which, at two thousand dollars, seems to have been a bargain.[17] Coal laborer Jesse Hudlan (also Hudlin) lived on nearby Sixth Street, at house number 180. Hudlan owned his three thousand dollar house, and his sister, Annie, occupied it with him.[18]

The African American families on Carroll Street lived very much in the heart of the third ward. They lived among various other families, several of them Irish, and both owners and renters. Rents generally ranged from fifteen to twenty-five dollars per month; owned homes generally were valued between one thousand and two thousand dollars, with the most valuable being a four thousand dollar home. Most people on the street were laborers and truckmen; a few were tradespeople.[19]

At 12 Carroll Street lived Mrs. Abbie Peters. Her house, the mortgage of which had been paid since at least 1920, was a long one-and-a-half-story house with a separate one-story auto garage in the rear. Next door, at 18 Carroll, lived Charles Raynsford and Panzy Dymond Talbot. Both in their early forties in 1930, Charles Raynsford was a chef at the Bangor Hotel and Panzy catered private parties. Son Edgerton was a dining car cook and son Vincent was a student at Bangor High School. The Talbots owned their one-and-a-half-story frame house, valued at one thousand dollars.[20]

Next door to Charles Raynsford and Panzy Talbot, at 22 Carroll, lived Union Station matron Linda Brooks Davis (illustration 19). Fifty-nine years old and widowed, Davis paid twelve dollars per month to rent her home. Next door to Davis at 24 Carroll Street lived Charles Raynsford Talbot's parents, Charles A. and Fannie Saunders Talbot. At seventy years of age, Charles A. Talbot still made a living as a truckman, and like his son, he owned his one thousand dollar home. The Carroll Street residences of Linda Davis and Charles and Fannie Talbot comprised a sizeable two-storied double house. In the rear of the lot was a two-story, shingled stable that appears to have belonged to the Talbots, but may well have been used by the Davis household as well.[21]

Two streets southwest of Carroll, on nearby Vine Street, lived the Hudling and Buck families. Widower Enos Hudling (also Hudlan) lived at 63 Vine. Well advanced in years by 1930, Hudling was one of several homeowners on the street. Edgar Buck's longtime employment with the Maine Central Railroad—as a porter and then as a janitor—provided the income that allowed him to purchase his home across the street from the Hudlings at 66 Vine. Valued at thirty-five hundred dollars, the Bucks' home was one of the most expensive houses on the street and also one of Black Bangor's more expensive homes.[22]

Hammond Street was and remains one of Bangor's more prominent commercial and residential thoroughfares. Beginning in the city center, it runs west, crossing busy Union Street and bisecting the third ward. Seamstress Nettie O'Ree lived at 498 Hammond Street, with her brother Albert. At almost seventy years of age in 1930, Nettie O'Ree appears never to have married. She did, however, own the Hammond Street house in which she lived, and it was a formidable home. The large one-and-a-half-story frame house and attached garage sat on a large diamond-shaped lot. Worth five thousand dollars, Nettie O'Ree's home had the second-highest value among Black-owned houses in the city.[23] Several blocks down and across the street at 903 Hammond lived plumber John D. Laurence, his wife, Hester Dymond Laurence, and their three children. Despite being on a major street—or perhaps

ILLUSTRATION 19. The Brooks/Davis home at 22 Carroll Street was in the heart of the Parker Street neighborhood. *Collections of the Bangor Museum and Center for History.*

because of it—the Laurences rented their home for a mere eight dollars a month, the lowest monthly rent among Blacks.[24]

Railroad steward James H. Warner, and his wife, Elizabeth, resided at 192 Fourteenth Street with their two daughters, Beryl and Helen Althea (illustration 20). The Warners' six thousand dollar house had been paid off for at least a decade before the 1930 census, and was the single most expensive home in Black Bangor at the time. Based on the values of their neighbors' homes, the Warners lived in a distinctly middle-class neighborhood. Their neighbors included a post office clerk, a retired U.S. Navy lieutenant, a railroad inspector, and a locomotive engineer. All but a few of the homes on Fourteenth Street were valued at a minimum of five thousand dollars.[25] At nearby 31 Manners Avenue lived laborer Austin Gordon, his wife, Rhoda, and their three daughters. The Gordons also owned their home, which was valued at twenty-three hundred dollars. The Manners Avenue home was a small one-story house with a shingled roof and a one-story garage in the rear of the property. Austin Gordon's parents, Sandy and Annie Gordon, lived nearby in the five thousand dollar house they owned at 27 Thirteenth Street.[26]

Not all Black families in Ward 3 lived in close proximity to one another; some lived in other parts of the ward, and often as the only African Ameri-

ILLUSTRATION 20. The architectural style of the Warner family's Fourteenth Street home was common to Black Bangor. *Courtesy Dr. H. Althea Warner Mandel Collection.*

cans on their particular street. John H. and Maude Nelson lived at 27 Dexter Street, with their niece, Arvella McIntyre, in a very comfortable home worth four thousand dollars. Andrew and Margaret Burtt owned their home at 48 Perkins Street—mortgage free. The house was a modest one-story structure valued at one thousand dollars. Andrew Burtt continued to work as a private coachman, and his daughter, Clara Burtt, worked as a stewardess managing the food service on a steamboat. Farm laborer Russell Payne boarded on Fuller Road while Claude C. Hoyt lived on Odlin Road, with his wife, Alice Wheary Hoyt, and their son, Cecil. All of the Hoyts were working in 1930. Claude was a teamster for a coal company, Alice was a matron at the telegraph office, and Cecil was a general laborer who did odd jobs. The Hoyts' industry probably contributed to the ownership of their thirty-five hundred dollar home, which was more than three times the median value of Black-owned homes.[27] It is unclear whether Black residency outside Black Bangor's more densely populated area translated into negative race relations.

The boundaries of Bangor's fourth ward ran the length of Union Street from the mouth of the Penobscot River to the city line, along the city's outer limits, and back along the length of the Penobscot. Fourth ward residents included James and Ida Beale and W. Alonzo and Villas Johnson. James and Ida Beale lived with their three children at their 10 Highland Court home. James Beale worked as a laborer for a private family and purchased their thirty-five hundred dollar home. The Johnson family at 24 Kossuth Street also owned their spacious four-thousand-dollar home, one of only three Black-owned houses of this value in 1930. Most people on Kossuth Street owned their own homes, which ranged in value from three thousand to sixty-five hundred dollars, and worked as machinists, architects, insurance salesmen, and proprietors. Built by William A. Johnson before his death, the Kossuth Street home continued to house an extended Johnson family. William Johnson's widow, Edith; Alonzo Johnson; his wife, Villas; and their three children all lived in the house. So did William and Edith's three other adult children.[28] The Beales and the Johnsons comprised the very few African Americans in the fourth ward. The 1930 census also locates a minute number of Blacks in the city's fifth ward.

Ward 6 was on the opposite side of the Kenduskeag Stream from the city's fourth ward; it was bounded by the water on one side and by Center and State Streets on the other. The Mahoneys, the Martinis, and the Watters all made their homes in this section of Bangor. John Robert and Louise Mahoney lived downtown, on the third floor of a four-story stone building at 16 Harlow Street. Living at the top of Post Office Square, the Mahoneys were surrounded by various commercial and governmental offices. The Post Office and other federal offices stood at 73 Harlow Street. The Graham Building at 84 Harlow housed the Bangor and Aroostook Railroad offices.[29] Bangor and Aroostook railroad cook Albert Martini and his wife Bessie, a general housekeeper, lived at 5 Willow Street. They owned their one-and-a-half-story frame home. At a very modest three hundred dollars, it was Black Bangor's least expensive residential property.[30]

Blake Place was home to a few other local families. At 3 Blake Place lived thirty-four-year-old Marion Peters, a cook for a private family, and her daughter, Madeline, a Bangor High School student and general worker. A two-story frame dwelling with a basement, 3 Blake Place was one half of a double house. A few doors down the street, at 15 Blake Place, lived Annie Watters, a housekeeper who shared her home with two adult children and a young grandchild. Across the street from the Watters, at 14 Blake Place, lived Hannah Mason and her adult son, Charles. Peters and Watters both paid the median rent of fifteen dollars, while Mason's rent was below the median at ten dollars per month.[31]

Comparatively few Blacks lived in the city's seventh ward. Garage mechanic Hiram Simmons, his wife, Pearl, and their daughter lived at 191 Pearl Street in the family's four thousand dollar home, a one-and-a-half-story frame house with shingled roof and a one-and-a-half-story shingled garage in the rear. A few streets over from the Simmons, at 175 Parkview Avenue, lived the Smiths. Coal worker Raymond Smith and his wife, Elsa, paid thirty-three dollars a month to rent their Parkview Avenue home, a two-story house with an attached one-story auto garage. Finally, Hubert and Alta Dymond Scott lived at 189 Palm Street. Scott worked as a meat cutter at a wholesale meat market, and supported his wife, their five children, and Alta's widowed mother, Florence Dymond. The Scotts owned their twenty-five hundred dollar home.[32]

Approximately half of the African American homes in Bangor in 1930 were rented and the other half owned. Blacks paid a median rent of fifteen dollars a month, slightly higher than the national rate of just over thirteen dollars that Blacks elsewhere paid to rent non-farm homes. The 1930 census does not provide the median value of non-farm, Black-owned homes for Bangor, but the national median value of such dwellings was just over thirteen hundred dollars. The manuscript census reveals that the median value of Black Bangor's homes was approximately one thousand dollars, with a small number of homes valued below that mark and a greater number valued above it.[33]

### Parker Street Close Up

The Parker Street neighborhood comprised Parker, Vine, Walter, Carroll, lower Fourth, Third, Patten, and Warren streets, most of which were confined to the third ward; some portions of Parker, Patten, and Walter streets, however, were located in the second ward. In 1930, Parker Street neighborhood residents included the Stewarts and Elms on Parker Street, the Hudlans and Bucks on Vine Street, and the Clarks on Walter Street. On Carroll Street lived the Peters, Davis, and Talbot households, while the Dymonds lived on Fourth Street. Patten Street, like Carroll, saw various families, including two Leek households, the Derricks, Dymonds, Wises, and Cromwells. An additional Leek household was to be found on Third Street. Of the streets in the Parker Street neighborhood, Patten Street had the highest number of individual African American households in 1930, but its residents were predominately renters rather than owners.[34]

African American homeownership ran close to 50 percent in the Parker

Street neighborhood, as it did for Black Bangor as a whole. Of the fifteen Parker Street area households identified above, seven were owned and eight were rented. James Alfred Cromwell, Sterling Dymond, Charles A. Talbot, Charles Raynsford Talbot, Enos Hudling, Edward Buck, and Ford Clark were all homeowners in 1930, and their houses ranged in cost from one thousand to thirty-five hundred dollars. John Wise, Earl Leek, William Derricks, Earl Dymond, George Leek, Linda Davis, William Stewart, and Louise Elms all rented their homes for fees that ranged from eleven to twenty-two dollars per month.[35]

Parker Street was perceived as a rough neighborhood made famous by the separate murders of a city policeman and an elderly Black woman in her Carroll Street home. Despite the concentration of Blacks in the area, a 1988 newspaper retrospective wrote that

> it was still a predominately white neighborhood and there was prejudice, if not open, then surely just below the surface. But all in all, the families lived in peace. The youngsters, both black and white, were pretty tough kids. Rawboned, young men honed their street-fighting skills at the drop of a hat. . . . Out of these chaotic skirmishes came a few amateur and professional boxers to the rings of Maine and New England. . . . Occasionally the "Parker Street gang" would engage its crosstown rival, the "Hancock Street gang" but these "meetings" were mostly for bravado.[36]

The newspaper also described the neighborhood as an active, almost self-contained area:

> [M]ost of the neighborhood family shopping was done at Gallagher's Market at Third and Warren, where Jimmy Gallagher had a tab for about every family. There was also the First National Store on Third between Warren and Parker and Julia Haley operated a "candy store" at Patten and Third. Later there was Ruby Donovans on Patten Street.[37]

Black residency within the Parker Street neighborhood was not fixed. African Americans moved in and out of various neighborhoods, up and down various streets, and into residences formerly rented or owned by other Blacks in the city. For example, Annie Huddlin lived at 133 Fourth Street in 1914, but by 1923 this was the home of Sterling and Janie Dymond. Harry V. Hill boarded at 54 Parker Street in 1901, but the next decade finds him living in his own house at 93 Fourth Street. Mary Dymond boarded with Jane Eastman at 78 Parker in 1914 before moving to board at 189 Palm. Zarah and

Theodosia Hoyt lived just down the street from Eastman at 74 Parker. Further down and across the street lived William and Lenora Stewart. The Stewarts lived at 83 Parker when William worked as a janitor; they later moved further down the street to 108 Parker.[38]

To some degree these moves probably reflected changes in Black families' size and economic status. It also raises the question, however, of whether this pattern is a subtle marker of racism in Bangor's housing industry. It is unknown whether Blacks, who clearly had access to and achieved homeownership, faced restrictions on what houses they could own in particular areas. Further, the conversation returns to the question of the Bernard Real Estate Agency. Did they serve a predominately or even exclusively African American clientele? Did they help facilitate transferring property from one Black family to another? Without records or a clearer picture of the company's work, these questions remain unanswered.

African Americans' experiences with housing in late-nineteenth and early-twentieth-century Bangor were comparable to those in other New England cities, most notably Newport, Rhode Island. In the late nineteenth century, many Blacks in this resort town clustered in "New Town," on the city's west side, in a manner highly similar to that of Black Bangor's Parker Street neighborhood.[39] The expansion of the west-side sector continued through 1920, and the homes in this highly African American enclave, renamed "West Broadway," shared the structural features of the Parker Street neighborhood as the "one- and two-family units . . . were rectangular, simple, and most commonly 1 ½ or 2 ½ stories tall."[40] West Broadway was not the only part of Newport that saw clustering of African Americans. Blacks resided in significant numbers in an area around the northern end of Bellevue Avenue; in 1925, nearby Filmore Street was home to more than a dozen African American families. Blacks also lived on other streets in the city, most notably Edgar Court and De Blois Street. Proximity to work on Newport's waterfront and to highly valued institutions, including several of the city's Black churches, were significant considerations that helped shape African American residency patterns in this Rhode Island city.[41]

Black housing patterns in New Haven, Connecticut, were less similar to Bangor, with African American households located predominately in the western half of the city, and with many Blacks clustered in large areas northwest and southwest of Yale University, an institution that employed several of the city's Black citizens. In an arrangement comparable to that of Bangor's third ward, almost one-half of Blacks in New Haven resided in Ward 19. The nineteenth ward, in combination with others in the southwestern portion of the city, accounted for almost three-quarters of the city's entire African American population.[42]

In the early twentieth century, Blacks in New Haven's Ward 19 generally paid ten to fourteen dollars per month to rent a four- or five-room dwelling capable of housing a small family. In poorer neighborhoods, rents could be as low as eight dollars per month. Blacks did cluster, in some degree, along lines of class and national origin. Black professionals and proprietors of the middle class moved to Prospect Hill, near the university, but as the turn of the century brought increasing numbers of immigrants and poorer Blacks, this section of the city's middle class moved again to more ideal locations. West Indians and Cape Verdeans, found in large numbers in New Haven, formed some enclaves in the southwest part of the city. Over time they scattered across the city as cultural alliances eventually broke down and they married outside of their respective populations.[43]

For the poorest of New Haven's Black population, tenement living was the norm. In 1930, houses with the modern conveniences of running water and toilets, (but no baths), averaged fifteen dollars per month; those with presumably shared water closets averaged twelve to thirteen dollars a month, while those on the very poor Eaton Street were considerably less. The slum conditions that Blacks had to cope with stood in sharp contrast to the affluence and prosperity symbolized by adjacent Yale University, many of whose ivory towers were easily visible from the ramshackle buildings that many Blacks called home. It was not until the late 1930s that Blacks living in New Haven's slums saw the prospect for change, when 2.5 million dollars in federal housing monies were committed to building a housing complex to accommodate more than 450 African American families.[44]

Blacks in Bangor achieved homeownership with significant success. Not only did they convey the lessons of homeownership and its value, many passed on the material legacy to the children who would occupy family homes after they passed away. Within the walls and beneath the roofs of these coveted structures, the joys and sorrows and quotidian events of life played out.

### Birth and Death

Although migration had played a central role in creating Black Bangor, migrants themselves established families that played pivotal roles in its expansion and history. Most families conceived at least three children, while several had at least five; some had nine or more. For example, Ford and Rosalie Clark, Abner and Emma Peters, Sterling and Janie Dymond, and William and Edith Johnson all had large families, with between seven and ten children.[45]

Family growth was not without its contractions, and few families were spared the loss at least one child. In Maine in 1930, the White mortality rate was 13.1 per 1,000 people, while that of Blacks was significantly lower at 9.3 deaths per 1,000. However, in Maine cities with ten thousand residents or more, the Black mortality rate went up by more than 50 percent. The White mortality rate was 14.8 per 1,000 people, and the Black rate was 15.7. The infant mortality rate nationally in 1930 was 64.6 for every 1,000 live births. For Blacks, it was a much higher 99.5 and for Whites it was a lower 59.6.[46]

On New Year's Day of 1895, Andrew and Maggie Burtt lost their eight-year-old daughter, Lydia Agnes. The Burtts appear to have married young and were only in their early twenties when they buried their first child. Lydia Burtt was survived by her five-year-old sister, Clara. Perhaps Andrew and Maggie Burtt never recovered emotionally from losing their eldest child, for they had no more children.[47] Charles and Fannie Saunders Talbot had an experience quite similar to that of Andrew and Maggie Burtt. The Talbots had been married for fifteen years by the time the January 1900 census was taken. At that time, they had lost one of their two children. Like the Burtts, Charles and Fannie Talbot would have no more children.[48]

The loss of just one child would have brought immeasurable pain and loss, but some parents and families experienced this trauma multiple times. David and Bessie MacKenzie were both in their early thirties in 1900. By that time, they had had six children, but only two of them, twelve-year-old Sadie and nine-year-old Barbara, were living. By 1900, barber Alvin Talbot and his wife Georgia had lost three of their eleven children. Watchman Henry Bernard and his wife Lena lost two of their five children by 1900; their three remaining children—James, Randolph, and A. Bertina—were all less than ten years old. Daniel and Jennie Mason had three children in 1900, but had already buried four other children by that time.[49]

Some deaths among Bangor's Blacks garnered significant public attention. On 14 July 1939, the *Bangor Daily News* reported the death of Murray V. Scott, the twenty-one-year-old son of Hubert and Alta Dymond Scott. A popular member of the community and a graduate of Bangor High School only three years prior to his death, Murray Scott reportedly had committed suicide. The newspaper summarized the incident as follows:

The body of Murray V. Scott, 21, was found yesterday morning in a small room in the basement of a local church, by the pastor who entered the building about 8 o'clock. Dr. Herbert C. Scribner, medical examiner, gave as his verdict, following an examination, suicide by means of gas.

Scott had been missing from home since Wednesday morning, when he left before 7 o'clock for his place of employment. When Scott did not return to dinner, relatives learned he had not been to work during the morning, and the police were asked to aid in locating the missing man.[50]

Gas was also the culprit in the accidental deaths of Albert and Bessie Martini; they died of asphyxiation in their 5 Willow Street home in February 1946. As in the 1939 death of Murray Scott, individuals became alarmed when Albert Martini failed to show up for work. Martini's body was found at the foot of the stairs on the ground floor of his house. Investigators speculated that he was trying to trace the source of the leak when he was overcome by gaseous fumes and soon died.[51]

According to the local newspaper:

Three employe[e]s of the gas company . . . were investigating the leak when they knocked at the door of the Martini residence. There was no response but they could hear a radio playing inside and, becoming alarmed, forced an entrance through the cellar.

Upon finding Martini dead and Mrs. Martini unconscious, they notified Dr. C. E. BoDine, who in turned called an ambulance and police. Dr. BoDine ordered Mrs. Martini to the hospital.

Meanwhile James A. Cahners, manager of the gas company, ordered an investigation into the source of the leak and his crew discovered that the gas was escaping through the main under Willow Street, directly in front of the Martini residence. He reported the leak was immediately repaired.[52]

At the time the newspaper went to press, it reported that Bessie Martini, who originally had been found unconscious in her second-floor bed, had been taken off the hospital's danger list. However, Bessie Martini died in Bangor's Eastern Maine General Hospital on 26 February, three days after her husband died and the day after the newspaper printed the story.[53]

Both Albert and Bessie Martini's deaths were considered "instantaneous," and because the couple left no heirs "for whose benefit a cause of action could have been brought under Section 10 of Chapter 152 of the Revised Statutes of Maine," the Bangor Gas Company was only liable for the couple's funeral expenses. In this case, the compensation due was $1,145 per person. The gas company settled the entire Martini claim for $2,290, on the condition that Panzy Dymond Talbot, administratrix of the Martini estate, brought no further action against the company.[54]

The deaths of Albert and Bessie Martini must have sent shock waves through Black Bangor and through the city at large. Albert Martini had worked for the Bangor and Aroostook Railroad for years, and was widely known among its patrons. Martini had strong professional ties to railroad management, as he had served as the personal porter and chef to the railroad's general manager, William K. Hallett. No other Willow Street residents were seriously injured by the gas leak, but Mrs. Jerome Green, who lived across the street from the Martinis at 8 Willow, received medical attention after she complained of feeling ill. Ironically, Albert and Bessie Martini had narrowly escaped death the previous year when firemen rescued them from a fire that engulfed their home and overcame both of them with smoke.[55]

### Marriage and Divorce

By 1900, when Blacks were moving to Bangor in significant numbers, many of the couples making new lives in the city had already been married for many years. In 1900, Samuel and Harriet McCarty had been married for nineteen years. Laborer David Willis and his wife, Rebecca, had been married for twenty years. Charles and Fannie Talbot, George and Annie Winslow, and David and Bessie MacKenzie had all been married for fifteen years when the 1900 census was taken in June of that year.[56]

Other Blacks married in Bangor started what would prove to be very long-lasting marriages. Sterling and Janie Simmons Dymond, for example, had a marriage of considerable longevity. Married in Bangor in November of 1901, they celebrated their golden anniversary in November of 1951 with an afternoon and evening open house covered by the local newspaper. When Sterling Dymond died in August of 1954, he and Janie had been married for more than fifty-two years.[57] Yet, other African Americans in Bangor saw their marriages cut short by the death of a spouse. Josephine Smallwood, Elizabeth Jackson Warner, Edith Delaney Johnson, and others went on to live a considerable number of years after their husbands' deaths. Smallwood lived more than a decade after the death of her husband, Charles; Warner lived more than ten years after her husband, James, died; Edith Johnson lived in Bangor more than five full decades after her husband, William, died in 1913.[58]

Despite the general longevity of Black Bangor's marriages, divorces did take place in several of the community's families. At least two marriages begun in the late 1880s were terminated by the mid-1890s. Frank and Emma O'Ree were married for only five and a half years before they were divorced in April 1894. George and Elizabeth O'Ree divorced in October 1895 after nine years of marriage. Adultery played a role in the dissolution of both O'Ree marriages. After more than thirty years of married life, "cruel and abusive treatment" caused Lena Bernard to divorce her husband, Henry, in 1924; Stanley and Marion Watters Peters' marriage ended in 1923 for the same reason. The 1920s saw the dissolution of several other marriages as well. In 1930, poultry farm laborer Albert O'Ree was divorced, as was Sophia Hudling. Coal worker Jesse Hudlan divorced his wife, Jane, in November 1928. Living in St. Mary's, New Brunswick, at the time of the divorce ruling, Jane Hudlan apparently had deserted her husband. Finally, Ernest and Callie Mills Peters may have had Black Bangor's shortest marital union. Married in January 1920 and divorced less than four years later in November 1923, Callie Mills Peters charged her husband's "gross and confirmed habits of intoxication" with ruining the marriage.[59]

Economically speaking, divorce weighed more heavily on women than on men. No longer able to rely on their husbands' labor to provide for them or to supplement their own income, divorced women, like those who were widowed, had to look critically at their ability to care for themselves and any dependent children they may still have. As the previous chapter illustrated, the need to enter or reenter the workplace usually meant taking on some type of domestic or service-oriented work, even if it was less lucrative than what they had been accustomed to or had been trained for. Marion Peters worked as a cook for a private family, Annie Watters did housework, and Lena Bernard earned money doing laundry for a private family.[60]

## Foodways

The consumption and celebration of food is something that bound Bangor's Black community together regardless of its national or regional roots. Based on the cultural backgrounds of Bangor's population, the foodways of Black Bangor would have included southern, New England, Canadian Maritime, Caribbean, and Cape Verdean culinary traditions. While we may not be able to say with absolute certainty the degree to which various culinary traditions persisted in Bangor, some salient information can be found in interviews with surviving members of the community.

The details of Sunday dinner figured central in the recollections of local residents. Memories of the day-to-day culinary routine may fall by the wayside, but those of Sunday—for many, the week's capstone dining experience—remain crystal clear. Sterling Dymond, Jr., remembers:

> Sunday dinner was either you had roast chicken or you had roast pork. We had roast of beef. And you had the whole works, potatoes, and you had vegetables and dessert and the whole nine yards. See, Canadians, we have a breakfast, then we don't eat again till about four o'clock in the afternoon. Only two meals for the day. Yeah, that's all we ever had. And, you'd eat your breakfast and go to church, and you'd come back and you might have a doughnut or glass of milk or something like that to hold you 'till dinnertime. And I still have the same thing.[61]

Holiday meals were also integral parts of the Dymond family traditions.

> And holidays, you know, always had the big meal. Thanksgiving, when I was a kid, we had chicken. We didn't have turkey supper. People didn't decide to have turkey around here 'till during the war. Turkey was more like a rich man's dinner. Because we raised our own chickens, when we was young. Right up to, I think about 1945, we stopped raising chickens.[62]

In the Dymond household, Christmas brought a cross-section of North American and British traditions to the table.

> And Christmas was the same thing. We had roast of pork and you had roast of chicken. Then you'd have mashed potatoes, you'd have squash. You'd have carrots, and green beans that were put up, preserved for the winter. And then you'd have your plum pudding. And your pies, apple pie and squash pie. Then afterwards, later on, you would always have made these cakes during the fall and we'd have them all winter long. Fruitcake. And tea, later on in the evening.[63]

The celebration of and with food continued into the new year.

> New Year's Day. Mother would generally have either fricasseed chicken or something like that, you know. With the full meal. Mince pies. Always had mince pie and squash pie and apple pie and pumpkin pie. Because Easter was for ham and eggs, always. Had the big ham.[64]

Dymond's discussion of the Fourth of July is an interesting fusion of American patriotism and Maritime Canadian tradition. Sterling and Janie Dymond were both born in New Brunswick, and maintained at least some of their Canadian foodways. At the same time, they lived in the United States, and their children, all born in Bangor, were American citizens.[65] Fusing Canadian and American cultures seems to have worked well:

> Fourth of July we always had salmon. Atlantic salmon. Well, that's what the Canadians always had. We would have steam salmon and potato salad or else we'd have the new potatoes, and we would have the egg sauce over the salmon. Then we'd have green peas, always had new peas. Then we had fresh strawberries and strawberry shortcake. And I have the same thing right today. Got to keep my kids into that tradition. I like traditions.[66]

Herbert Heughan's recollection of life in nearby Hampden illustrates that southern foodways also persisted in the Bangor area, if only selectively.

> My mother raised a lot of chickens. . . . We ate the hens, the ones that weren't laying. We kept the laying ones, you know, to sell eggs. But when they got a little older and tougher, we killed them. Ate them boiled. Then we always had a pig, cooked, killed for the winter. We had most of the vegetables that they eat in the South. We didn't have chitlins. We didn't bother with all that stuff. Pig's ears, and . . . pig's feet, and all that stuff.[67]

By taking some southern traditions that served their needs and their tastes, while discarding others, African Americans like Heughan created their own hybrid food tradition. These southern traditions appear to have been further hybridized by the addition of New England staples like baked beans:

> Well, my mother made head cheese. She made the loaf, you know. I guess the kidneys she must have thrown away. But we ate a lot of potatoes, baked beans, that was a staple, still is with me. I have baked beans every Saturday. Even now, I take baking beans when I go back. And cucumbers, and we raised just about everything they raise in the South. We didn't use much rice or things of that sort. A lot of pies, cakes. And in the wintertime, we couldn't get in to town. We had barrels of flour in the pantry, and barrels of sugar, and that sort of thing. And most of us could cook.[68]

The exact degree to which there was a confluence of Maritime, southern, and New England food traditions is unclear, but indications are that Blacks actively preserved them.

More challenging than the question of southern influence, however, is the problem of placing Caribbean and Cape Verdean foodways in the culture of

Black Bangor. Did West Indians such as Edith Delaney Johnson and Hubert Scott and Cape Verdeans such as Dijon Piris abandon their own traditional foodways? Were they able to secure ingredients necessary to continue their culinary traditions? Or did they adapt Caribbean and Cape Verdean food traditions to the New England foodstuffs available to them in Bangor?

For those men and women who served as cooks in restaurants, in railroad dining cars, and in private homes, food was also a part of the larger culture of service through which Blacks earned their livings, purchased and rented their homes, and even sent their children to college. For women like Josephine Smallwood, Panzy Talbot, and Delia Murray, food was a centerpiece in the larger enterprise of entertaining, and their work of catering confirmed their employers' position in the social elite.

Given what is known about the cultural backgrounds of Blacks in Bangor during the late nineteenth and early twentieth centuries, it is likely that some degree of acculturation took place. African Americans who traveled from the southeast, for example, had to become accustomed to the traditions of Maine. At the same time, they probably were influenced to some degree by the customs of Blacks who had come from Canada and the Caribbean.

### Consumer Appetites

Though comparatively small in number and clearly removed from larger U.S. cities, African Americans in Bangor were part of the growing consumer culture of the twentieth century. Not all Blacks had significant amounts of disposable income, but some clearly had middle-class tastes. City records reveal that Blacks patronized local stores, acquiring the goods necessary to furnish their homes and make their lives comfortable.

William and Edith Johnson were one of the most prominent Black couples in Bangor. In February 1898, they had a considerable inventory of goods in their 8 Spring Street home, predecessor of the family's permanent home at 24 Kossuth Street. In their kitchen were a table with four chairs, a Kineo Range for cooking, a refrigerator, a set of silverware, and a set of tableware. The Johnsons' acquisition of appliances, particularly the refrigerator, at an early time in the manufacture of such domestic products indicates their solid financial position. In the parlor, the Johnsons had a parlor set, a wood stove for heating, and two easy chairs. The dining room sported a dining table with six chairs and a sideboard. The family's bedroom furniture included a crib, a cot, two beds, and two ash chamber sets, suggesting that they did not yet have indoor toilet facilities. Elsewhere around the house, the Johnsons had carpets, several framed pictures, a hat tree, a clock, a Wheeler and Wilson sewing machine, a towel rack, at least one mirror, and assorted vases and bric-a-brac. By 1899, William A. Johnson also acquired an Amesbury open buggy, a Portland-made sleigh, and a two-wheel cart. By 1904, he had added a Hallet and Davis piano—seemingly to support his family's love and penchant for music—and a hunting silver-cased watch.[69]

Local records also reveal that in 1904 Annie Gordon's home contained, among other things, two French bedsteads, a hair cloth sofa, one willow and one camp rocker, a mantel mirror, eight framed pictures, and a Dirigo cooking range.[70] In 1907, Josephine Smallwood purchased a Crown Kineo furnace for $110 that included four registers and a return air pipe. Given the long and difficult winters typical of central Maine, Smallwood's purchase must have been a welcomed addition to the home.[71]

Some of the local merchants with whom African Americans consistently did business were Central Street's Noyes and Nutter, which manufactured and sold furnaces, ranges, and stoves. They also did brisk business with Exchange Street's Hodgkins and Fiske Company, a supplier of home furnishings and kitchen cabinets, and with the Eastern Furniture Company. From 1913 to 1916, dressmaker Carrie Dymond added to her Hersey Avenue home a parlor stove, a hoosier kitchen cabinet, a refrigerator, and a couch hammock, all purchased from Hodgkins and Fiske. Perhaps Dymond was drawn to Hodgkins and Fiske's advertisements in the *Bangor Daily News*. The company advertised that the "easiest way to buy your refrigerator" was to join their "'50' Refrigerator Club, and have any Refrigerator in our stock put into your home at once." Patrons were required to make a down payment of five dollars and then make weekly payments of one dollar. The company's top-selling refrigerators cost between twelve and sixty-six dollars. At $16.50, Dymond's refrigerator was actually at the lower end of the price scale.[72]

Blacks in Bangor also frequented Hodgkins and Fiske Company for various home goods. Edgar S. Buck purchased a Glenwood range for his Vine Street home from the company in November 1911 for forty-eight dollars. A year and a half later, Buck returned to Hodgkins and Fiske and purchased a refrigerator for twenty dollars and eighteen yards of stair carpet at the price of one dollar per yard.[73]

In September 1927, Abner Peters bought from Noyes and Nutter a King Kineo Tank and Steel Closet stove for $121.25.[74] Around the same time, Lenora Stewart, at 17 Fourth Street, purchased a kitchen cabinet, two unfinished chairs, a rug, and a pool table, from the Eastern Furniture Company for $126.17.[75] Clearly a luxury item, Stewart's pool table affirms her middle-class tastes, which, as the 1920s progressed, afforded growing opportunity for and put increased emphasis on the culture of leisure. The pool table allowed friends and family to gather, to be entertained, and to separate themselves from the demands of work. It was also a symbol that they had "bought into the signs and symbols of an improved standard of living."[76]

Earl Leek and J. Robert Mahoney also were making significant purchases in the late 1920s. In February 1928, Leek purchased a Glen N. Range with mantel coal fixtures, a brass bed, a cotton mattress, and a bedspring from Eastern Furniture Company, probably to help furnish his 10 Patten Street rental. City records reveal that in December 1927, John Robert Mahoney purchased a $105 Universal Range from the Bangor Hydro-Electric Company.[77]

City mortgage records also reveal to some degree how Blacks stocked the interiors of their businesses. As a lawyer and a minister, Milton R. Geary was quite probably the most accomplished Black professional in Bangor in the early decades of the twentieth century. In January of 1914, Geary owned a Monarch typewriter, a 1905 copy of *The Revised Statutes of Maine*, a 1905 copy of *The Laws of Maine*, and "a diamond ring set with two red stones in a gypsy setting."[78] In March 1915, Geary had a Monarch typewriter worth $37.50. Several years later, Geary purchased a $115.00 Remington Typewriter from the Remington Typewriter Company, an expensive piece of equipment for his time.[79]

In 1927, Edward Buck ordered a fifty-eight dollar register from the National Cash Register Company of Dayton, Ohio. The register, which had standard keys and an oak finish, was for his shoe shine business.[80] For his shoe shine business, Charles Mason purchased a more expensive mahogany-finished cash register. Also from Ohio's National Cash Register Company, the machine cost seventy-five dollars.[81]

Blacks in Bangor were highly engaged in local commerce beyond their basic functional and decorative furnishing needs, and they regularly and actively acquired two distinct symbols of middle class status: pianos and new automobiles. Newspaper advertisements clearly linked the ideas of success and piano ownership, and appealed to the American middle class's interest in appearing upwardly mobile and cultured. According to Craig H. Roell,

> Piano advertisements by the 1920s depict a complex mythology. . . . Throughout the decade ads concentrated on stylish grand pianos and automatic in-

struments. They emphasized the family, a fashionable home, a social life, and the piano as a symbol of respectability and cultural refinement.[82]

In Bangor, African Americans' interest in acquiring pianos and other musical instruments brought them through the doors and into the showrooms of stores distinctly different from Noyes and Nutter and Hodgkins and Fiske. These new vendors included the Andrews Music Company and Steinert and Sons, both on Main Street, as well as S. W. Bridgham on Columbia Street. J. Robert Mahoney had business dealings with the Andrews Music Company. In June 1911, he leased a Sterling piano from Andrews for $285. At the end of his thirty-nine-month payment schedule, Mahoney had the option to purchase the piano for an additional penny.[83] Six years later, in December 1917, Mahoney returned to the Andrews Music Company and leased a Remington Player Piano for the Grand United Order of Odd Fellows and its women's auxiliary, the Household of Ruth. The twenty-nine-month lease was for $185 with a one-cent purchase option. In that same month, Mahoney traded in an existing piano and leased an Angelus player piano for $375. Highly marketed in the early 1900s, the Angelus allowed the player to "render the most difficult compositions in a manner possible to only the most accomplished pianists."[84]

In October 1906, Charles A. Talbot paid local musical instrument merchant Steinert and Sons thirty-three dollars for the rental of a Victor Talking Machine made by the Victor Talking Machine Company. The Victor Talking Machine Company had only been founded a few years before Talbot's purchase, and in 1905 sold more than sixty-five thousand phonographs. The company introduced the internal horn phonograph that retailed for two hundred dollars.[85] The next month, Talbot traded in his existing piano for fifty dollars and leased an Allrecht piano from local merchant M. H. Andrews for three hundred dollars. Around this time, Talbot also acquired from Noyes and Nutter a Kineo Grand complete stove for his 24 Carroll Street home for $44.80.[86]

In April 1908, Charles Raynsford Talbot rented a Victor made by the Victor Talking Machine Company from Steinert and Sons.[87] In June 1913 Edward Buck purchased a $450 Ricca and Son player piano from S. W. Bridgham. Four years later, he returned to Bridgham, where he purchased a $150 phonograph.[88] In 1925, Claude C. Hoyt purchased a Victrola and twelve records for a total of ninety-nine dollars.[89]

As the traditional pianos of the nineteenth century gave way to player pianos in the opening decades of the twentieth century, the stigma that playing piano was for women, and, therefore, effeminate, gave way as well. The player piano had a novelty traditional pianos did not: it did not take long to master and it gave immediate gratification. Unlike traditional pianos, the introduction of new models of player pianos encouraged consumers to trade in and trade up for newer, better models.[90] The need for instant gratification, increasing market competition, lack of permanence, and overall consumption of early-twentieth-century player pianos, phonographs, and radios are likened to the place of the automobile in turn-of-the century culture:

> Whatever its similarity to the traditional piano, the mechanical player was a product not of the Victorian age, but of the machine age of immediate gratification. As such, it had much more in common with the motor car, the phonograph, and the radio than with its manual predecessors. . . . They were all objects to consume, all easily replaced by newer models, all in competition with endless numbers and kinds of other products. Permanence found no place in the philosophy of consumption.[91]

The general prosperity of the 1920s combined with increased automobile production and the pursuit of leisure activity among the middle class all combined to foster an American love affair with the automobile. Bangor became a "Motor Center," not just because the city's Chamber of Commerce encouraged tourists to drive through en route to the Maine woods and waterways, but because it had more than twenty-five different dealers of new and used automobiles by 1920. Several automobile vendors did brisk business in the city; many of their clients were the leading men and women of Black Bangor.[92]

Foley Chevrolet was a local car company that served various members of Bangor's Black community. Between May 1927 and April 1930, Claude Hoyt was involved in three separate transactions with Foley Chevrolet. In 1927, he purchased a 1927 Chevrolet Landau for a cost of $820 and a related financing charge of $79. Two years later, in August 1929, Hoyt acquired a 1929 Chevrolet Sedan for $385 at 6 percent interest. Less than twelve months later, in April 1930, Hoyt purchased a new, six-cylinder Chevrolet Sedan.[93] Hoyt's activity in the local automobile marketplace is quite exceptional, with the purchase of three different Chevrolets in the space of three years.

In a fashion similar to that of Claude Hoyt, Charles Raynsford Talbot made several transactions involving automobiles. Between 1920 and 1930, Talbot purchased four vehicles, three cars and one truck. In July 1920, Talbot acquired an Atlas 1,000-pound truck for $450 at 6 percent interest from Utterback-Gleason Company.[94] Two years later, Talbot purchased from the Neil E. Newman Company, a National Twin Six, seven-passenger touring car; the price was $600. By the end of the decade, Talbot had acquired a 1927 Dodge Deluxe Sedan; three years later he owned a $1,300 1930 Dodge DA Six Sedan.[95]

W. Alonzo Johnson purchased a Moon Touring car in September 1926 from the J. M. Morris Motor Company. Wallace Leek purchased a used 1926 Model T Ford Truck from the Foley Chevrolet Company for a modest forty-four dollars in May of 1930. Alton Leek bought from P. I. Gould a used Studebaker touring car for $75.20. In August 1927, Shenton Peters acquired from the Hall Motor Company at 725 Broadway a used 1926 Essex Coach for a total cost of $421.80.[96]

Goodridge Leek made a few automobile purchases in the late 1920s. In April 1927, he purchased from the S. L. Crosby Company, for a total of $674, a new Ford Ton Truck Closed Cab with Warford Transmission. In April of the following year, Leek purchased from the Henley-Kimball Company a 1927 Dodge Sedan, "accepted in present condition," for $495.[97]

Women did not sit on the sidelines and watch the automobile revolution pass them by. They also purchased cars of their own. In July of 1923, tai-loress Fahy Heughan Geary purchased a Ford Sedan from S. L. Crosby; she paid $737.25.[98] The hundred dollar down payment and the forty dollar monthly payments were each larger than the thirty dollars per month that Fahy and Milton Geary paid to rent their Main Street apartment. Caterer Panzy Talbot also is reputed to have purchased a new car for herself every one or two years.[99]

Although participation in the consumer culture of musical instruments and motor cars demanded financial commitment on different scales, what appears to have been Black Bangor's brisk trade in pianos and automobiles symbolizes its growing middle-class tastes, if not its expanding middle-class status. In general, Blacks in Bangor seem to have enjoyed the 1920s prosperity seen in towns and cities across the United States. They purchased the necessities for furnishing their family homes and conducting their businesses, but even some of these goods seem to have been extravagant. More indulgent purchases, such as player pianos and pool tables, signified the desire for more luxurious, durable goods that would offer entertainment and leisurely respite from the demands of the working world. Blacks purchased automobiles, some even as frequently as once every year or two. Interest rates generally were reported at 6 percent, but were as high as 10 percent. Blacks put down as much as 50 percent of the purchase price and arranged for monthly payments that in various cases were equal to or greater than the family's monthly rent. If we consider the porter's monthly minimum pay of ninety dollars per month, the median rent of fifteen dollars per month accounted for 17 percent of the monthly income. This did allow for monthly car payments that were usually between twenty and thirty dollars per month, and payments on household appliances and musical instruments of between eight and twenty dollars per month. Making the rather large initial payments on cars or instruments, however, would have required significant savings.

Black Bangor's purchasing power probably derived from two additional sources other than base pay: tips and investments. Porters, stewards, bootblacks, matrons, and general workers all stood to increase their wages through the gratuities of their patrons. Blacks knew that good service translated into good tips, and good tips supplemented what were often meager wages. For some, tips may have represented disposable income that could be saved and then spent on material indulgences. Blacks also had investments that may have provided additional revenue. When Albert and Bessie Martini died in 1946, they had furniture, a fur, jewelry, more than thirty-six hundred dollars in cash, and six twenty-five-dollar U.S. War Savings Bonds.[100]

### Photographs

Through the mid-twentieth century, representations of African Americans revolved on the axes of docility, brutality, and tragedy. Not only were antebellum constructions of Blacks not lost, they were adapted and even longed for. Between 1909 and 1927, for example, Hollywood created at least five different film versions of Harriet Beecher Stowe's 1852 novel, *Uncle Tom's Cabin*, "in which the tale of the good Christian slave was again made the meat of melodrama."[101] In early movies and on local stages, minstrelsy infused the docile Tom (or Sambo) and his female counterpart, Mammy, with new, modern life. The coon archetype, which operated under character names like Rastus, Uncle Remus, and Stepin Fetchit, constructed, as Donald Bogle describes, "unreliable, crazy, lazy . . . creatures good for nothing more than eating watermelons, stealing chickens, shooting crap, or butchering the English language."[102] Typically a female character, the tragic mulatto became a vehicle for the complications of and prevailing wisdom against miscegenation. Various films in the 1910s and the 1934 *Imitation of Life* all contemplated interracial relationships, identity, passing, and the tolls they took on the individual, the family, and society at large. These hostile and damaging images of African Americans penetrated the spectrum of American culture, including advertisements, music, games, and children's books.[103]

African Americans in Bangor lived within this same culture of stereotype and caricature, and were subjected to a variety of highly offensive, formulaic images. As early as 1901, local advertisements bombarded Blacks with damaging images. Park Street's M. Lynch and Company used the slogan "All Coons Look Alike" to promote sales of personal and commercial safes (illustration 21). Using the logic that the average person could not tell law-abiding African Americans from dangerous, predatory ones, the advertisement preyed on American suspicion of Blacks. The company appealed to the coon stereotype to persuade the local public to buy their products. While not original to Bangor, the concept was an enduring one. Advertisements were printed in the Bangor city directory, giving the merchant—and the stereotype—substantial readership.[104] Widely available from druggists and grocers, Sanfords Ginger advertised in the *Bangor Daily News*, and used an even more archaic stereotype to sell its product. Sipping what could be ginger tea, a figure with stereotypically nappy hair and bulging eyes exclaimed, "Gosh! But It's Good."[105]

While those around them consumed and even reproduced damaging stereotypes of Blacks, African Americans in Bangor produced (or, rather, had produced for them) dignified, studio-generated photographs. Various photographers operated in the late nineteenth and early twentieth centuries, including Frank C. Weston, C. L. Marston, George Lansil, J. F. Gerrity, and F. C. Chalmers, but two of the oldest were Lansil and Weston. In the late 1880s, Lansil was described as a "painstaking, thorough artist" and one of the city's finest photographers. A Maine native, Lansil established himself as a photographer in the early 1860s and by the mid-1880s occupied a studio at 4 Main Street. At that time, he employed five assistants and occupied three floors and eight rooms for the operation of his business. Maine native Frank C. Weston established himself as a photographer in the late 1870s. He occupied two floors at Hammond Street's Smith's Block and employed three artists. Weston's prices were reportedly "dictated by a spirit of moderation," and may explain why he had extensive African American patronage in the city. Of all the city's photographers, Weston may have been Black Bangor's preferred photographer.[106]

Photographs taken in Bangor, such as one that may be Florence Dymond (or another member of the Dymond family; illustration 22), call into sharp

# All Coons Look Alike

to some people and the same might be said of Safes. When you want a safe, come to us and we will show you that there is a great difference in them. We are agents for several manufacturers and will be pleased to explain the merits of different safes.

We still continue to Repair Locks and Keys, and are ready at any time to send a man to any part of the state to open safes, doors, trunks, etc.

## M. LYNCH & CO.,

9 PARK STREET,        -        -        BANGOR, MAINE.

ILLUSTRATION 21. "All Coons Look Alike" was a popular advertising slogan in Bangor. *Bangor city directory, 1901.*

ILLUSTRATION 22. This woman's identity remains elusive, but her beauty is unforgettable. She may be a member of the Dymond family. *Gerald E. Talbot Collection, African American Collection of Maine, Jean Byers Sampson Center for Diversity in Maine, University of Southern Maine Libraries.*

relief the fallacy of prominent Black caricatures and replaces them with images of beauty and sophistication. This was the New Negro:

> The New Negro was self-defined. . . . Self-understanding, self-direction, self-
> respect, self-dependence, and self-expression supplanted the self-pity that is
> the sole emotion with which the Old Negro seems to have been entitled.[107]

It illustrates how, according to Deborah Willis and Carla Williams,

> the medium of photography offered black subjects a sense of self and self-
> worth within their communities. The photographs constructed a visual image
> of the so-called "New Negro" that accompanied the optimistic revision of
> nineteenth- and twentieth-century African American experience that the
> New Negro movement represented.[108]

This woman's flawless skin, stylishly coiffed hair, and engaging eyes all speak
of incredible beauty. In addition, her fur collar intimates middle-class status.
In sum, the photograph is reminiscent of James VanderZee's Harlem photographs of the 1920s and 1930s.[109]

At the same time, Claudia Brush Kidwell and Nancy Rexford point out
that a studio photograph is formulaic: that as the object of consensus between photographer and subject, it is, to some degree, a rearranged reality
and a manufactured truth. The poses, the painted backdrops, the props, and
even the subjects' choice of clothing all manipulated reality and generally followed the convention of how one should appear in a photograph.[110] The
photograph of young Dorothy Davis supports the photo formula (illustration 23). Wearing a white dress, white stockings, and a hair ribbon, Davis
reinforces the idea of childhood innocence and of middle-class propriety.
The porcelain-faced doll—Davis' own—suggests a childhood of privilege.
At the same time, Davis' photograph suggests a departure from a formula.
Rather than sitting in a fine chair or on a stool—as the child in the other
photograph—she stands, her body suggesting the movement of a precocious
little girl (illustration 24).[111]

Whether mounted on walls or catalogued in family albums, photos were
significant in countering mainstream constructions of African Americans.
Cultural critic and Black feminist theorist bell hooks explains the significance of photographs to domestic, familial spaces:

> When we concentrate on photography, then, we make it possible to see the
> walls of photographs in black homes as a critical intervention, a disruption of
> white control of black images.[112]

ILLUSTRATION 23. A young Dorothy Davis with her doll. *Collections of the Bangor Museum and Center for History.*

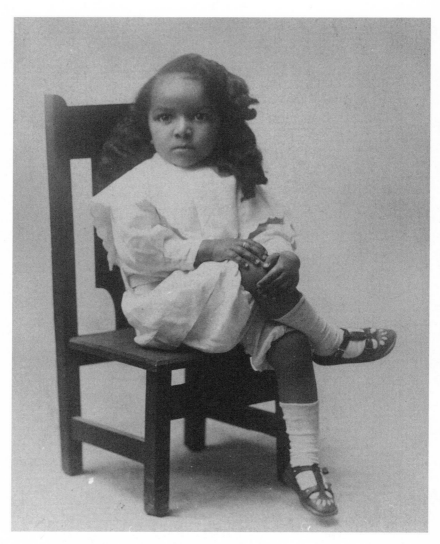

ILLUSTRATION 24. This child's clothing and jewelry suggest membership in an affluent family. *Gerald E. Talbot Collection, African American Collection of Maine, Jean Byers Sampson Center for Diversity in Maine, University of Southern Maine Libraries.*

hooks continues to define the taking and displaying of photographs as acts of resisting domination:

> Most southern black folks grew up in a context where snapshots and the more stylized photographs taken by professional photographers were the easiest images to produce. Significantly, displaying those images in everyday life was as central as making them. The walls and walls of images . . . were sites of resistance. They constitute private, black-owned and -operated gallery space where images could be displayed, shown to friends and strangers.[113]

Although hooks reflects on her own southern experiences, her points speak equally to the experiences and resistance of Blacks nationally.

◌⁊◌

Census materials, mortgage records, newspaper announcements and advertisements, photographs, and interviews all provide a collective glimpse into the daily life of Black Bangor. While they cannot replicate the breadth or the depth of the socially intimate experiences of African Americans at the time, surviving written and visual records serve as signposts that direct attention to some of the questions that may be asked about this experience and specific examples that help answer them.

# FEELING THEIR TWONESS

## Black Bangor's Institutional Maturation

Sterling Dymond, Jr., was born in Bangor and has lived there all his life; he graduated from the city's public high school in 1938. Bangor High School was an integrated institution, and Black and White students seem to have attended classes and sporting events with equal ease. However, in social situations that were not distinctly school related, the same two groups self-segregated. As Dymond explained it, "When you went partying, we went to a party by ourselves, [and] they went to a party by themselves."[1]

In the 1940s, World War II magnified the social distance between Blacks and Whites in Bangor when the local United Service Organization (U.S.O.) Center denied access to African American military personnel stationed at Dow Air Force Base. Local residents attributed this unprecedented affront to newly introduced southern attitudes and protocols. Members of Bangor's Black community, however, were not content to lay blame, and immediately took up the servicemen's cause. With individuals like Milton Geary, Shenton Peters, and Gertrude Buck playing particularly active roles in its administration, African Americans established an alternate center for the enjoyment of Black servicemen and their families.[2]

In 1903, W. E. B. DuBois published *The Souls of Black Folk* and introduced to the United States, in particular, and to the world at large a new racial discourse. Central in this discourse was the concept of the "double consciousness" that African Americans had both as persons of African descent and as American citizens. While well removed from the southern Black Belt about which DuBois wrote, Blacks in Bangor also felt their twoness. They were integral parts of the city's established institutions, but felt the need to create other voluntary institutions to satisfy their own personal, recreational, or civic needs. Black Bangor's greatest achievements were in the creation of their institutions, from the highly formalized fraternal organizations to the loosely organized neighborhood clubs. It is within its history of institutional maturation that the defining history of Black Bangor lies. It is also here that the community's decline would be most deeply felt after the 1940s.

## The Double Consciousness

As the leading Black intellectual of the first half of the twentieth century, DuBois articulated the experiences of African Americans with a discourse and a precision that had not been seen before. Occupying a central place in the racial discourse was DuBois' articulation of Black double consciousness. He explained:

> The Negro is a sort of seventh son, born with a veil, and gifted with second-sight in this American world,—a world which yields him no true self-consciousness, but only lets him see himself through the revelation of the other world. . . . One ever feels his two-ness,—an American, a Negro; two souls, two thoughts, two unreconciled strivings.[3]

Published after the United States Supreme Court decision in *Plessy v. Ferguson* (1896), which sanctioned racial segregation, and before Alain Locke's anthology on *The New Negro* (1925), DuBois' *Souls of Black Folk* gave voice to Black experiences nationally, experiences that took place (even) in Bangor. It provided a framework for examining and, ideally, improving relationships between White and Black Americans.

## The Church

Because they were few in number and because they were rooted in a variety of religious denominations, African Americans in Bangor did not have a Black church. In fact, the absence of an historically or predominately Black church is a hallmark of Black religious life in the city. As Sterling Dymond, Jr., explained in Randall Kenan's *Walking On Water*,

> No, we never had a [B]lack church, not what [Portland] had. They went to all different churches. I'm Episcopalian. They had a Baptist church and Methodist

church and some went to the Pentecostal church. They never all went to one church. Never crossed our minds. Never thought about having a church of our own. Not until we got grown up, you know, after the war, that's when they first encountered [B]lack churches. But Portland always had a [B]lack church.[4]

One of the glaring differences between Black Bangor's religious life and that of Blacks in comparable New England cities is the absence of a historically or predominately African American church. Newport, Rhode Island, hosted four historically or predominately Black churches: Union Congregational Church, Mt. Zion A.M.E. Zion Church, Shiloh Baptist Church, and Mt. Olivet Baptist Church. Typical church activities included strawberry socials, picnics, and other engagements designed to broaden the imagination and cultivate the mind.[5]

By 1940, New Haven had more than a dozen Black churches of various sizes, histories, and wealth. The largest churches historically have been the Immanuel Baptist, the Dixwell Avenue Congregational, and St. Luke's Episcopal churches. Other churches of note in 1940 were the Union American Methodist Episcopal Church and the Church of God in Christ. As in Newport, New Haven's churches were tight-knit institutions that regularly engaged in fundraising practices and had significant influence on Black parishioners.[6]

In Portsmouth, New Hampshire, People's Baptist Church was organized in 1892 as an affiliate of Middle Street Baptist Church until it became an independent entity in 1908. Seven years later, People's Baptist took ownership of an old church on the corner of Pearl and Hanover Streets. It stood there for more than half a decade, before closing in the early 1960s. Another church of note was the African Methodist Episcopal Church.[7]

Although Blacks in Bangor did not have their own churches, when they traveled out of state and visited Black churches in their same denominations, they did not necessarily prefer them nor find their own churches lacking in comparison. Sterling Dymond, Jr., explained:

> I was in Washington, D.C., way back in the '40s. Visit my sister, and went to her church, and heck, she goes to the Episcopal church, and it was just the same as the service I had here. I was very disappointed. Just like being in my own church here.[8]

In Bangor, African Americans attended churches across Protestant denominations, from the quiet Episcopal to the more stirring Congregational and Pentecostal. Most Blacks attended St. John's Episcopal, Grace Methodist Episcopal, All Souls Congregational, Hammond Street Congregational, and Columbia Street Baptist Church. There is no indication that they were un-welcome or that they were relegated to any particular part of the church, whether in the back, along the sides, or in the galleries. Church membership tended to be dictated by family background and residential location, more than by race or class. The church may well have been the institution in Ban-gor where Blacks were treated with the greatest sense of equality.

St. John's Episcopal Church, at 225 French Street, was organized in 1835 and dedicated two years later in 1837 (illustration 25). Considered "one of the most influential Gothic Revival churches in America," St. John's was planned by Richard Upjohn, who went on to design New York's Trinity Church. St. John's wood construction made it vulnerable to fire, and it was consumed in the Bangor fire of 1911; only the church's lectern and baptismal font survived. St. John's Episcopal was rebuilt by the end of that decade by Hobart B. Upjohn, Richard Upjohn's grandson. Built of limestone-trimmed granite rather than the original wood, the post-1911 St. John's Episcopal Church had plaster and stucco interiors that gave it "a mechanical quality," but its "delicate pointed arches" and "handsome stained glass windows" fos-tered celebration of its new spatial composition and natural light.[9]

Sterling and Janie Simmons Dymond worshipped at St. John's Episcopal Church. Their attendance both reflected and continued their Canadian-rooted religious traditions. Other local Blacks to attend St. John's were Charles Raynsford and Panzy Dymond Talbot, Edgerton and Arvella McIntyre Tal-bot, Hubert and Alta Dymond Scott, and Herbert and Frances McCarty. Goodridge and Pearl Simmons Leek also attended St. John's Episcopal, where Goodridge was a vestryman. Other attendees included Linda Brooks Davis and Andrew and Maggie Burtt. Subsequent generations of Africans Americans continued to choose St. John's Episcopal as their home church. Sterling and Janie Dymond's daughter, Helena Dymond George, and her husband, Edson, attended St. John's, where Helena was a member of the Altar Guild. The Dymonds' son, Sterling Dymond, Jr., and his wife, Dorothy McIntyre Dymond, also attended the French Street church. Because of the high concentration of Black Canadians in Bangor and because of their roots in the Episcopal Church, St. John's had some of the highest Black attendance rates in the city.[10]

Situated at 195 Union Street, Grace Methodist Episcopal Church organ-ized in 1847, only two years after the organization of Columbia Street Baptist.

St. John's Episcopal Church, Bangor, Maine

ILLUSTRATION 25. St. John's Episcopal Church was the place of worship for many Black Canadians. *Collections of the Bangor Museum and Center for History.*

It was built from 1854 to 1855 by Maine native Harvey Graves. The structure cost fifteen thousand dollars to erect. It was 75 feet long and 48 feet wide; it had eighty-four elliptically arranged pews and a black walnut pulpit. It was lit by gas and warmed by portable furnaces. The church's spire, considered at its completion to be the best in the entire city, stood 143 feet high. Edith Delaney Johnson faithfully attended Grace Methodist Church for seventy years.[11]

Broadway's All Souls Congregational Church was formed in 1913 by the merging of two congregational parishes destroyed by the 1911 fire, First and Third (Central) Congregational Societies (illustration 26). Ralph Adams Cram designed the church, and the new construction incorporated the salvaged ruins of both of the previous churches. More than 126 feet long, more than 64 feet wide, and approximately 100 feet high at its tower, All Souls' elevation and location at the corner of Broadway and State streets made it a highly discernable, even dominating, landmark on the cityscape.[12] Ralph Adams Cram is said to have had a "reverence for the wood structure of the English Gothic Church," as exhibited by the dark wood exposed in All Souls' trusses, vaults, and rafters. The church, noted for its tripartite stained glass windows, cost $110,000 to build, a sum that rose as additional stained glass windows were added through the 1940s. Comparatively fewer Blacks attended All Souls.[13]

Second (Columbia Street) Baptist Church was organized in September of 1845 after separating from the First Baptist Society earlier that year. The congregation met at different halls before opening in 1853 at 63 Columbia Street, just one block from the city's busy Main Street. The church, designed by William G. Morse, cost approximately $15,000 and was paid for through support from Bangor, Boston, and New York.[14] Shenton and Alice Gosman (also Gasman) Peters attended Columbia Street Baptist Church. Shenton held various positions at the church, including president and pianist for the Danforth Class and member of the Oratorians. Abbie O'Ree Peters, wife of John J. Peters, also attended Columbia Street. Viva F. Dymond joined Columbia, as did her sister, Blanche O. Dymond, who was a member of the Mary Ellen Sunday School Class. Florence Dymond was a highly esteemed member of the congregation and Mabel Derricks attended Columbia Street until her death in 1953.[15]

Hammond Street (Congregational) Church was built at the corner of Hammond and High streets. It was organized in 1833 by more than sixty members of the First Congregational Society as a response to that church's problem with overcrowding. A brick structure measuring 65 by 90 feet and

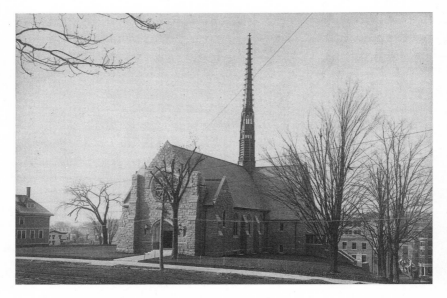

ILLUSTRATION 26. Some Blacks also attended All Souls Congregational Church. *Collections of the Bangor Museum and Center for History.*

standing 30 feet high, it had a four-column portico and two square towers.[16] The Hammond Street Church was remodeled in the early 1850s as designed by architect John Towle and at a cost of eighteen thousand dollars. The extensive remodeling comprised "raising of the walls about six feet, lengthening of the entire building, removal of the two towers and portico, substitution of one tower, and the installation of a completely new interior, including new pews, a new organ, the minister's study, and new vestries."[17] Alice Wheary Hoyt was a long-time member of Hammond Street Congregational Church.[18]

The more recent history of Bangor's churches includes the short-lived establishment of the Church of God in Christ, founded in Bangor in the late 1940s by Bishop Richard D. Williams, Jr., and the first of its denomination to be established in Maine. Shortly after establishing the Bangor church, however, Williams relocated to southern Maine and established a church there. Initially located on Lancaster Street in Portland, the congregation moved to Franklin Street in 1957. It would move again to Wilmot Street before building on its current, permanent site on Terrace Avenue. The church, which originally had been named Christ Temple, was designated Williams Temple in honor of Bishop Williams.[19]

Sunday services, baptisms, marriages, and funerals were all points where the lives and activities of Bangor's African Americans intersected with their respective churches. There was no absolute way of predicting which churches Blacks would attend. Those of Canadian birth or parentage, for example, may have kept to Methodist or Methodist Episcopal congregations, but they were also members of other denominations.

## *Elementary and Secondary Education*

Bangor's children attended a variety of elementary schools. In 1890 alone, the city was home to two grammar schools, thirteen intermediate schools, eighteen primary schools, and twelve suburban schools (illustration 27). Not all the intermediate and primary schools were in separate buildings; often they shared the same complex.[20] When students were old enough for high school, however, all roads led to Bangor High School, the city's only secondary institution until John Bapst Catholic High School opened in 1928. Bangor High School began on Prospect Street in 1837 as an eight thousand dollar,

ILLUSTRATION 27. Before entering high school, various students attended the Hannibal Hamlin School. *Collections of the Bangor Museum and Center for History.*

gable-end brick building.[21] In 1879, the school reached a milestone: water closets—three in total—were installed in the basement. Other improvements were made in subsequent years. The high school was devastated by fire in February of 1882; it was rebuilt, only to be destroyed completely in the fire of 1911.[22]

Rebuilt after the second fire, the high school was deemed to be "the largest and finest in all Maine." Removed to Harlow Street and convenient to the adjacent public library, the new structure was made of brick and stone. It measured 160 feet by 200 feet and was three stories high; it had sixty rooms and an auditorium capable of seating one thousand people. The first floor housed offices, classrooms, study rooms, and the auditorium; the second floor hosted the library and additional classroom space; the third floor supported commercial, typewriting, and scientific instruction. The manual training and domestic science departments were in the basement, as were the gymnasium, cafeteria, toilets, and lockers. The high school's other features included one thousand lights, fifty-four telephones, and electric clocks. Given both the institution's and the city's experiences with devastating fires, the school was wise to include its twelve fire alarm boxes.[23]

Just as Bangor High School's exterior changed over time, so did its curriculum. In 1894, for example, Paris O'Ree's daughter, Maud, was in her freshman year at the high school. At that time, her high school day began at 8:00 in the morning and concluded at 12:30 in the afternoon; there were three terms in her school year. Also at that time, there were four courses or tracks for students: English-Latin, English, College Preparatory-French or German, and College Preparatory-Greek. Students followed a strict schedule of recitations determined by the course of study, the day of the week, and the particular hour of instruction.[24]

By the turn of the century, the secondary curriculum had added a commercial course of study. While the school still offered instruction in language, mathematics, history, and science, the commercial course of study included instruction in commercial law, commercial geography, and commercial arithmetic. It also incorporated bookkeeping, stenography, typing, and economics.[25]

The high school catalogue urged students intent on going to college to identify the college of their choice as early as their sophomore year and to determine exactly that institution's admission requirements. Students in the college preparatory course began their high school years with Latin, algebra, history (Greek and Roman), and English. The next year's study was of Latin, Greek, German or French, geometry, English, and college literature. The students' junior year required Latin, Greek, German or French, algebra, geometry, English, college literature, and history (Greek and Roman). The senior year of study again required Latin, Greek, geometry, trigonometry, English, college literature, and possibly physics or chemistry.[26]

The school's commercial course, while still very intense, was designed to offer students a different type of rigor and develop a different type of competence. Freshmen students following the commercial track were to have four recitations of algebra, five of English, and three of commercial arithmetic. Penmanship, spelling, and bookkeeping were also required. The next year's course of study required three recitations each of commercial arithmetic and bookkeeping, with additional recitations in commercial law and history. During this year, students could begin taking electives in German, French, geometry, Latin, stenography, and typing. The junior year required three recitations of bookkeeping, with additional classes in commercial geography and commercial English. Electives continued as in the sophomore year, with the addition of an elective in chemistry. The senior year, which required a minimum of seventeen recitations per week, called for five recitations each of political economy and civics, with additional courses in office work and banking and securities. Electives remained the same as the previous year, with the exception that physics took the place of the chemistry elective. The school assured both students and parents that the commercial department was adequately equipped and that its branches of instruction were thorough and in the tradition of the best commercial colleges.[27] The High School Catalogue of 1904–1905 advised that the "selection of studies is subject to the approval of parents and principal, and whenever necessary, of the superintendent." Students desiring to change their courses of study could do so only with permission from the superintendent.[28]

At the time that the 1904–1905 catalog was published, there were two schools of thought concerning African American education. The Washingtonian model emphasized industrial education and vocational training, while the DuBoisian paradigm called for education according to ability. Bangor High School's rigid system of tracking students may have limited the potential of some students, subjecting them to the decisions informed by prevailing race, gender, and class stereotypes.[29]

By 1910, the high school's courses of study expanded further. The classical course provided "an all-around Academic Course, strong in language" and "prepare[d] for any College." The scientific course was designed for students who sought admission to technological schools and to college-level science departments. The technical course, which provided an "all-around Technical education" also prepared students for scientific and technical schools.[30]

The remaining courses of study—the general, commercial, industrial, and household arts—were not necessarily designed for students who intended to move on to college, but for those who would move more directly into the workplace. Designed to enable the student "to make himself of greater value along industrial lines," Bangor High School's industrial course stressed subjects such as English, mathematics, drawing and shopwork, and bookkeeping. Subjects like French, german, physics, and chemistry were some of the many electives available, but students were only allowed to take one or two per year.[31]

The household arts course was designed for young women, and was described as being "of a practical character," emphasizing "such studies as would be useful in a well ordered home." Students took English each of their four years in high school and some limited courses in algebra, science, Latin, and history. The mainstay of their instruction was in cookery, sewing, sanitary science, dressmaking, millinery, household physics, household chemistry, home management and laundry, dietetics, home decoration, and home nursing. One of the high school's most inflexible courses of study, the household arts track allowed students only one opportunity for elective study. In their sophomore year, students were able to choose one elective from among Latin, French, German, and geometry.[32] While the household arts track prepared all female students to meet the demands of being wives and mothers, it also helped ensure that the next generation of Black women was equipped to serve the local demand for domestic servants.

In 1919, the Reserve Officers' Training Corps (ROTC) was established at Bangor High School and the first army personnel instructors arrived. Having the mission "to awaken in the student an appreciation of the obligations of citizenship and qualify him for positions of leadership in time of national emergency," the ROTC afforded "practical training in organization, leadership, and discipline which will be of value to graduated students in an industrial or professional career."[33]

The 1953–1954 Bangor High School catalogue contained this history of the ROTC in Bangor:

> In 1919, the Reserve Officers' Training Corps was organized and and became compulsory. In the spring of each year, staff of the United States army officers makes a formal inspect of the R.O.T.C. battalion at Bangor High School.

This consists of reviewing the complete battalion in drill and also the inspecting of a typical classroom scene. If the standards of the work are satisfactory, the school receives a red star, the symbol of an Honor School in the R.O.T.C. program. It is now one of the five high school corps in New England. Many times during its history it has received this Honor School rating. It received this honor in 1952.[34]

All boys with sophomore status were required to enroll in ROTC, after which time it was voluntary. At the ROTC's annual Field Day, each cadet company commander chose a girl to be "honorary cadet captain of the company," and the honorary captain of the winning company became the honorary lieutenant colonel.[35]

As photographs of senior class members became a standard feature of high school yearbooks, so did the descriptions of their extracurricular activities and their post-secondary aspirations. A review of individual profiles also illuminates how Blacks were esteemed by their White classmates. Ada V. Peters was a senior in 1923, and her yearbook caption read:

> "A" is certainly the proper way to begin Ada's name, for she gets A in everything she sets out to do. Ada is the pride of the Senior class.[36]

A member of the Orchestra, Dramatic Club, and a finalist in the Junior Exhibition, Ada Peters appears to have been a popular, highly regarded student.[37]

The 1920s continued to see a number of children from well-known African American families advance through their high school years. LaRue V. Dymond, affectionately known as "Dimples," graduated in 1926.

> Little, but oh my—!
> Just watch those merry eyes, and
> Those two big dimples come, and go—
> Yes, she's popular, is our Dimples.[38]

A member of the Dramatic Club, the History Club, the Commercial Club, and a "semi-semifinalist" in the typewriting contest, LaRue Dymond was clearly active in her school. Her skills served her well, as she became a stenographer after graduation.[39]

Albina McCarty graduated with Dymond. Appearing equally well liked, McCarty's photo had a caption that suggested comraderie among and esteem from her peers:

Here is a girl we all know well
We wish you the best of all the luck
And we will remember the days we spent
In the good old, good old B. H. S.[40]

Several more African American seniors appear in the *Oracle*, including Florence Dymond, Edgerton Talbot, Earl Johnson, and Clifford Clark (illustration 28). With a yearbook photograph reminiscent of a 1920s Hollywood starlet, Florence Dymond had no extracurricular activities attributed to her, but did garner the praise of her peers:

Full of fun!
Bright as the sun.
We'll all miss you Flo
For-get-us-not.[41]

Edgerton Talbot, whose activities included ROTC and wrestling, was known for having a fine voice that pleased his music teacher, Adelbert Sprague (illustration 29).[42] Earl Johnson, who also had been in ROTC, was in the rifle club, the high school orchestra, and the high school band that took the state championship that year.[43] Earl, or "Jack" as he was nicknamed, was as astute with a rifle as he was with a trombone:

On the rifle range with Winchester true
We can bank on [Earl] for a bullseye or two,
And in the band with a jazzy round tone,
We will miss him playing his brass trombone.[44]

The 1930s saw a significant number of Blacks graduate from high school. They included Beryl Warner (1931), Stanford Peters (1932), John Hartt (1933), Harold Nelson (1934), Helen Heughan (1935), Margaret Cromwell (1937), Arline Peters (1937), Elizabeth Simmons (1937), Sterling Dymond, Jr. (1938), William LeBarron Wise (1938), James Reginald Clark (1939), James Oliver Cromwell (1939), Muriel Irene Hartt (1939), and Roxie Anna Peters (1939). While most students excelled in sports or music, they often also were distinguished academically. Both Beryl Warner and Margaret Cromwell were members of the National Honor Society. Arline Peters planned to be a nurse, Elizabeth "Betty" Simmons had aspirations of becoming a famous dress designer, and William "Flash" Wise prepared to attend Maine State College. Stanford Peters and James "Reggie" Clark were both in ROTC.[45]

ILLUSTRATION 28. Florence Dymond, as she appeared in her 1927 senior class photograph. *Courtesy of Bangor High School.*

ILLUSTRATION 29. Edgerton Talbot, as he appeared in his 1927 senior class photograph. *Courtesy of Bangor High School and the Patricia Pickard Collection, Special Collections, Bangor Public Library.*

While the Bangor High School catalogue previously had provided course information, it was not until the mid-1940s that high school yearbooks revealed which students took which particular tracks. The class of 1942's Ronald "Dragger" Smith, for example, followed the school's general course. The graduating class of 1946 included Madaline "Maddie" Gordon, who followed the school's business course and hoped to become a telephone operator. Galen Leek followed the high school's general course, but missed his 1946 senior class picture because he was serving in the Army. According to the *Oracle*, Leek, who was a member of the Rifle Club, desired to become a general.[46]

Daisy Mae Nichols was one of the comparatively few African Americans in Bangor to graduate from John Bapst High School. Also a member of the 1946 senior class, Nichols had only been "lent" to the school for her high school years. She intended to complete her education at a college in New York. Nichols, an attractive young woman with shoulder-length hair, had a profound yearbook quote, "The more I see of other countries, the more I like my own."[47]

Finally, the early 1950s witnessed further Black excellence in school leadership and athletics. Joseph Bernard was college-bound in June 1950 with an accomplished record of activity. During his high school years, Bernard had been a member of the Student Council and was Sergeant-at-Arms in the Alpha Hi-Y Club. The club's purpose was "to create, maintain, and extend throughout the school and community high standards of Christian character." A class officer in his junior year, Bernard was president of his senior class.[48]

Elaine Talbot graduated with Joseph Bernard. Talbot had a record of activity and accomplishment as impressive as Bernard's record, and it included Athletic Honor Council, Junior Chorus, Girls' Field Hockey, All-Bangor Hockey, Girls' Basketball, and Girls' Volleyball. Talbot served as captain of the volleyball team during her junior year and as captain of the basketball team her senior year. Talbot's membership on the All-Bangor team witnessed to her athletic prowess, since eligibility was earned by two or more years of field hockey and a vote "for the most outstanding girl in each position."[49] The *Oracle* records that Elaine Talbot's ambition was "to be a gym teacher and she has the ability to be a good one. Her favorite school activity is sports—what else?"[50] Beverly "Bev" Talbot was "a whiz in any sport and a sport always." Like her older sister, Elaine, Beverly Talbot was active in many sports. Most notable was the fact that she captained the girls' field hockey team to victory and was voted to the All-Bangor girls' team.[51]

Socially speaking, high school was an experiment, a microcosm for testing and defining what were becoming increasingly adult social relationships along and across racial lines. African American students' minority status in the city crystallized in the classroom. Sterling Dymond recalled:

> After we got to high school, we always had our own little parties. Dances all the time, so it didn't seem strange to me at all. I was surrounded in high school, six blacks graduated in my high school class. And year before and year after that was six more. When I went to high school, there was at least a dozen blacks in the school. Well, over a thousand kids in the high school probably.[52]

Blacks' minority status was so commonplace and perhaps, so germane to their life in Bangor that what African Americans in larger cities would call a negligible number of fellow Blacks students, those in Bangor in considered substantial. Dymond's contention that he was "surrounded" by twelve Black students, students who constituted 1 percent of the student population, reflects this minority framework.

Black and White students also lived in two different, although often overlapping, worlds. Drawn together by commonalities like education and sports, the worlds of Black and White students diverged when it came to those events that were fundamentally social. Dymond continued,

> Well, we didn't socialize together after that. When you get to high school, that's when, you know—you may go to the same places, see everybody there, but you really didn't socialize that much with each other. You all went to school and back together, or basketball games, football games and what all. But when you went partying, we went to a party by ourselves, they went to a party by themselves.[53]

African American narratives denote two distinct lines of demarcation between Black and Whites in Bangor. The first was when students moved from school-related to purely social activities on a daily or weekly basis. The second took place at the end of students' high school careers, when graduation took Blacks and Whites in different directions socially and, often, academically (illustration 30).

### Post-Secondary Education

The city of Bangor was home to several post-secondary institutions, including Shaw Business College, Beal's Business College, and Bangor Theological Seminary. Just north of Bangor, in nearby Orono, was the University of Maine,

ILLUSTRATION 30. The Bangor High School Orchestra. *Collections of the Bangor Museum and Center for History.*

the state's land grant university. With its programs in law, engineering, science, and later, education, the institution had the potential to increase and transform Black Bangor's professional class. From 1880 to 1950, however, relatively few Blacks pursued degrees there.[54]

Frederico Walter Matheas was one of Black Bangor's earliest and most impressive university alumni (illustration 31). After graduating from Bangor High School, Matheas continued his studies at the University of Maine. A member of various varsity teams including basketball and track, Matheas graduated with a Bachelor of Science degree in civil engineering in 1907. The next year, he married Hazel O'Ree, started a family, and began work as a transit man at Maine Central Railroad. According to his alumni profile, Matheas worked in South America as an assistant engineer for the Medeirrra Mamoré Railroad from 1909 to 1910. Matheas ultimately removed his family from Bangor to Philadelphia, where he had a notable career. In 1949, the mayor of Philadelphia appointed Matheas as the city's assistant director of public safety. At his death in January of 1970, Matheas had spent more

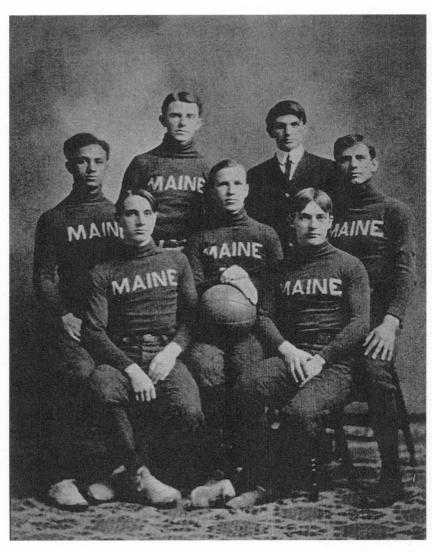

ILLUSTRATION 31. While earning his degree in civil engineering, Fred W. Matheas (rear, left) played basketball at the University of Maine. *Prism Yearbook, 1905, University of Maine, Orono, Maine.*

than thirty years working for the City of Philadelphia in the Department of Public Works' Bureau of Water.[55]

Although he did not grow up in Bangor, well-known lawyer and minister Milton R. Geary earned his Bachelor of Law degree at the University of Maine in 1913 and was admitted to the state bar in the same year. Geary had practiced law for more than fifty years when he died in Bangor in June of 1964. Alonzo Johnson also attended the University of Maine. He earned his bachelor's degree; he also attended classes at the Law School, but does not appear to have completed his course of legal study.[56]

A few African American women earned degrees from the University of Maine. Sisters Beryl and H. Althea Warner each went on to earn a bachelor's degree from the institution after graduating from Bangor High School. Beryl Warner studied mathematics at the University of Maine and received her Bachelor of Science degree in June of 1935.[57] H. Althea Warner, the younger of the two, majored in home economics and was a member of the Home Economics Club. She received her Bachelor of Science degree in 1940 and went on to graduate study at Howard University in Washington, D.C.[58]

Like Beryl Warner, Herbert Heughan also earned a bachelor's degree in mathematics from the University of Maine. He matriculated in 1936 and graduated with a bachelor's degree in 1940. He went on to earn his graduate degree at Virginia's Hampton Institute, and became a mathematics professor at North Carolina Agricultural and Technical (A&T) State University in Greensboro, North Carolina.[59]

While they successfully pursued their degrees at the University of Maine, Blacks found certain aspects of student life off limits. As chapter 2 illustrated, African Americans such as Heughan and the Warner sisters could not student teach in Maine. This marginalization, coupled with the practical training they received student teaching out of state, were probably critical factors in their decisions to leave Maine after graduating in the 1930s and 1940s. In addition to being locked out of teaching systematically, Blacks did not join university fraternities. There were not enough Blacks at the university at one time to establish any one of the several Black fraternities and sororities founded nationally during the early 1900s. Many Black students did not reside on campus. Some preferred to live in private housing, near—but not on—the University of Maine campus. This may have been an economic decision, but some Blacks found the University hostile and were uncomfortable with the idea of campus living.[60]

For Blacks like Sterling Dymond, Jr., college represented an opportunity for a new direction in life. Dymond graduated from Bangor High School during the Depression and went directly into the workforce. After several years in the workforce, Dymond matriculated at the University of Maine and earned an engineering degree. He later joined the Soil Conservation Service, where he worked as an engineering technician until his retirement.[61]

### The Military

Several Blacks served in the military during World War I, including laborer Dean Davis, chauffeur Carlton Cromwell, plumber John Laurence, Oakley Patterson, and Galen Leek. Laurence enlisted in the army when he was eighteen years old. He saw no overseas service and received an honorable discharge in February of 1919. Oakley Patterson was a private. He did not see overseas service and was honorably discharged in December of 1918. However, Private First Class Dean Davis saw overseas action in France from August 1917 to January 1919. Charles Raysnford Talbot was one of the fewer Blacks in Bangor to serve in the U.S. Navy.[62]

While the effects of World War I were removed from Bangor, those of World War II came very near. Many non-Maine Blacks were stationed at Bangor's Dow Air Force Base, and they were subject to racial segregation in ways that Blacks in Bangor probably had never experienced or witnessed. Racial segregation at Bangor's Dow Air Force Base was not considered organic to the city or to the state, but rather a product of southern laws and conventions that had been carried north. Blacks were housed separately from White military personnel. A distinct U.S.O. unit was established on Columbia Street for the recreation of Black troops, and separate housing was constructed in the city.[63]

According to Sterling Dymond,

> We never had no trouble until after World War II started, when they had a lot of Southern soldiers, white Southern soldiers come here. And that started a lot of the problems here. When they came in. And it seemed the black soldiers that were there had hard times getting rents. But I blame that on the commander of the base. Then they built a place for the GI's to live, so they didn't have a problem after that.[64]

Blacks' experiences with military segregation and discrimination were strikingly similar to those of African Americans stationed at the Portsmouth, New Hampshire, Naval Shipyard. In Portsmouth, the U.S.O. segregated its events and periodically offered "colored night" events, particularly dances. As in Bangor, local Blacks in Portsmouth were active in making servicemen and their families feel comfortable in their new surroundings.[65]

The U.S.O. Center established on Columbia Street became an important social center for native Blacks and those serving in the military. African Americans such as Milton Geary, Shenton Peters, Gertrude Buck, Mabel Derricks, Alice Peters, Goodridge Leek, Grace Cromwell, and others played important roles in the administration of the center, particularly after Geary was named its director in July 1944. Local Blacks formed property, program, hostess, housing, refreshment, and general administrative committees that collectively kept the center filled with activity and assisted Black soldiers and their wives in making the transition to Bangor.[66]

Weekends and holidays were particularly popular and crowded at the Columbia Street Center. Jitterbug dancing, pool, ping pong, piano performances, and singing were features of the weekend activities that regularly drew between eighty and one hundred people. At Christmas, more than one hundred people gathered to dance, enjoy refreshments, and exchange gifts, while New Year's Eve celebrations drew 250 people to welcome in another year with singing, dancing, and traditional noise makers (illustrations 32 and 33).[67]

The obituaries of various members of Bangor's Black community document their family members' continued military affiliation after World War II. At the time of Sterling Dymond's death in August of 1954, his son, Paul, was stationed in Japan with the U.S. Air Force. By the time of Janie Dymond's death less than five years later, Paul Dymond had been reassigned to Loring Air Force Base in Limestone, Maine. George Leek died in the Togus, Maine, veterans hospital in January 1945. Also a veteran of World War I, Leek left behind his wife and three children, including Army Corporal William Leek, who was then stationed in France. David J. Sickles, who died in Waterville, Maine, in February of 1967, had served in World War II. When Mabel Derricks died in a nearby Hampden convalescent home, she was survived by her two children and by her grandson, Sergeant Philip McAuley, who was then stationed in Germany. Although she did not serve in the military, Helena Dymond George was a member of the Dow Post Veterans of Foreign Wars (VFW) Women's Auxiliary.[68]

While African Americans generally did well in the city's established institutions, they thrived in those of their own making. The small community established a record of creating and maintaining, with varying degrees of success, organizations tailored to their needs, interests, and sense of civic re-

G-505.68.5

ILLUSTRATIONS 32 (*above*) AND 33 (*opposite*). Black airmen at Dow Air Force Base socialized with local residents. *Collections of the Bangor Museum and Center for History.*

sponsibility. These voluntary organizations included a fraternal organization, a Masonic organization, a social club, two mothers' clubs, and a branch of the NAACP. To a great degree, it was in these organizations that the essence of Black Bangor took place; it is also where the core of its memories resides.

### *The Tarragona Club*

By the early years of the twentieth century — before the community's rising population had even crested — African Americans had created institutions of their own. Blacks in Bangor established the Tarragona Club some time before or during 1905. On 31 May 1905, the Club held its first annual ball at the Jewish Essenic Hall. Perhaps unable to purchase their own building, Blacks relied on and benefited from what appear to have been positive relations with the local Jewish community. At the ball, guests danced the two-step, the quadrille, the waltz, the schottische, the Portland fancy, and assorted variations of the ballroom standards. Those in charge of the ball and of the larger

club comprised a small circle of the community's most well-known men. Charles A. Talbot served on the executive committee and as floor manager. Edgar Buck was both vice-president and assistant floor manager. Charles Smallwood was an aide and the club's secretary. William Stewart, also an aid, served as treasurer. Charles R. Talbot served as president, Charles Burt was an aide, and Sterling Dymond was both an aide and a member of the executive committee.[69]

Led by a small group of well-known men, the Tarragona Club was probably formed because another local men's club, the Tarratine Club, did not allow Blacks to join—or at least Blacks did not feel welcome. Founded in

1884 and incorporated in 1900, the Tarratine was a social club designed for "the promotion of friendly intercourse and social purposes as the club may ordain." The club limited resident membership to 110 men living within ten miles of the site; non-resident members could be elected at any time. Resident members paid an annual membership fee of fifty dollars; non-resident members paid half of that rate. Members had access from nine o'clock in the morning to as late as midnight. The club closed at ten o'clock in the evening on Sundays, the day on which game playing was prohibited.[70]

*The Mothers' Clubs*

The late 1800s and early 1900s were groundbreaking years of women's club activity in the United States. Women across the country maintained or established voluntary organizations to address such issues as temperance, suffrage, motherhood, and race relations. In fact, the state of Maine claims the distinction of having formed the United States' first state federation of women's clubs in 1889; Mrs. Eunice N. Frye of Portland is considered the mother of the Maine state federation. For two days in early October of 1897, the state federation of women's clubs met in the city of Bangor, which at that time was home to four of the state's eighty-seven clubs. One of the more prominent Bangor clubs was the Athene Club, started in 1894, and dedicated to the promotion of educational and literary interests of club members and the larger community. As an indication of its distinction, the Athene Club had as its first president Mrs. Hannibal Hamlin, wife of the former vice-president under Abraham Lincoln.[71]

Based on interviews with surviving children of Mothers' Club members, however, the original Mothers' Club—also known as the Senior Mothers' Club—appears to have been established in Bangor by the late 1910s (illustration 34). Mabel Derricks, Louise Mahoney, Helen Wise, Addie Peters, Carrie Dymond, Janie Dymond, Florence Dymond, Elizabeth Warner, and Edith Johnson all have been identified as members of the Senior Mothers' Club; additionally, Abby Paterson was named as well.[72] A mix of women born in the United States, Canada, and the Caribbean, Senior Mothers' Club members were all women highly visible in the Black community. Some women like Janie Dymond were wives and mothers who did not work outside the home, while others did. Senior Mothers' Club members lived in various wards across the city, and do not appear to have been concentrated particularly in the Parker Street neighborhood.

The Black Women's Club Movement also predated the founding of the

ILLUSTRATION 34. The Mothers' Club, c. 1910s (from left to right): Elizabeth Warner, Abby Paterson, Helen Wise, Carrie Dymond, Janie Dymond, Mabel Derricks, Florence Dymond, Abby Peters, Edith Johnson. *Courtesy Dr. H. Althea Warner Mandel Collection.*

Senior Mothers' Club. While Black women's organizations had existed at the local and state levels prior to the 1890s, one of the pivotal hallmarks of the time was Bostonian Josephine St. Pierre Ruffin's founding of the New Era Club and its monthly newspaper, the *Woman's Era*. The first issue of the *Woman's Era* was published in March of 1894, and in its editorial greeting expressed the purpose of its creation:

> The need of such a journal has long been felt as a medium of intercourse and sympathy between the women of all races and conditions; especially true is this of the educated and refined, among the colored women, members of which class may be found in every state from Maine to Florida, but in nearly all of these places an important factor, and one that receives little or no recognition, and the one more than all others which prevents her from making the most of herself and taking her legitimate place among the advanced women, is the limitation of her surroundings and the circumscribed sphere in which she must move.[73]

The *Woman's Era* newspaper served as the official publication of the National Federation of Afro-American Women (NFAAW), founded in 1895 by a merger of various regional, and often competing, women's clubs, including Ruffin's Woman's Era Club.

In 1896, the National Federation of Afro-American Women and the National League of Colored Women merged to form the National Association of Colored Women (NACW). Mary Church Terrell, of Washington, D.C., served as its first president.[74] By the time Bangor's Senior Mothers' Club was founded, the National Association for the Advancement of Colored Women was more than a decade old. However, the degree to which NACW activities or those of other Black women's clubs may have influenced the founding of the Mothers' Club is unclear. Josephine St. Pierre Ruffin's reference to Maine in the inaugural issue of the *Woman's Era* journal seems anecdotal at best, and there appear to have been no specific references to the activities of Black women in Maine at large or in Bangor. Similarly, there were no distribution agents in Maine for the monthly women's publication. A few Black women in Portland were visible in the Black women's club movement through their work in the Northeastern Federation of Women's Clubs (NFWC). At the ninth annual NFWC meeting in Boston in July 1905, Portland's Julia O. Henson delivered the welcome; Mrs. Corbin Smith of Portland responded. Over the next decade, more Black women in Portland would serve in NFWC leadership positions. Emmeline Green, Sadie Sibley, and Sarah Hill were all elected as NFWC co-vice presidents between 1905 and 1914.[75]

By the early 1940s, the Junior Mothers' Club had been formed in Bangor; they seemed to work in tandem with the Senior Mothers' Club. Fewer members of the Junior Club have been identified than those of the Senior Club, but some Junior Club members were the daughters of Senior Club members. Janie Simmons Dymond's daughter, Helena Dymond George, for example, was a member of the Junior Mothers' Club. Nora Dymond is reported to have been part of the Junior Mothers' Club, although her mother may not have been a member of the original women's organization.[76]

Despite the lack of documentation about the Mothers' Clubs, the very mention of the groups excites memories that are difficult to contain. Sterling Dymond, Jr., recalls:

And the women, they formed what they called a mothers' club. They all got together once a month and had meetings and had sewing circle and things like that, you know, and then they would put on extra big dinners and what not. They even had a hall in the downtown, where they used to hold dances and things like that, you know.[77]

Other accounts report that at the women's monthly gatherings, they helped support each other by coming together to make household necessities including curtains, rugs, and quilts. Lloyd George, whose grandmother, Janie Simmons Dymond, and mother, Helena Dymond George, attended meetings, remembers the group of women working in unison, each woman with her own piece of fabric to work with or task to complete. As a young boy, he hated to see his mother leave for her meetings, but he knew there was no doubt—she was going.[78]

> Holidays were important times for the Mothers' Club members as well: [They] [a]lways had a New Year's Eve dance. Easter dance, and things like that. At Christmas time they had what they called a Christmas tree, for all the kids, and everyone all over the territory came to it. They had the tree, and we were singing hymns that you probably wouldn't see no more. . . . Then in the summertime, they had two or three picnics they would all go to.[79]

Racial uplift, motherhood, hygiene, antilynching, and Black pride were all emphases of the NACW. And although the Mothers' and Junior Mothers' Clubs of Black Bangor do not appear to have left written records, it is possible to link them to the larger ideas of Black women's roles as wives, mothers, and citizens. Edith Delaney Johnson, a longtime member of the original club, had the tripartite conviction that living a happy life involved "doing your duty as a wife and mother, keeping busy and happy, and doing for others and sharing with them." While more extensive than the NACW's motto of "Lifting As We Climb," Edith Johnson's position could have been a provisional motto for the Mothers' and Junior Mothers' Clubs.[80]

Black women in Bangor were also part of a larger local culture that prized motherhood, home life, literacy, and morality. In 1910 the Home Culture Club, the Shakespeare Club, and the Women's Christian Temperance Union were some of the women's organizations in the city. A few decades later, in 1940, there was a preponderance of women's clubs and associations, including the Bangor Woman's Club, which met two Tuesdays per month between October and May, and the Bangor Junior Woman's Club, which met the first Wednesday of each month at the YWCA.[81]

### Odd Fellows and Masons

Black Bangor began its fraternal and Masonic traditions as early as 1912, when the Grand United Order of Odd Fellows (G.U.O.O.F) was meeting the second and fourth Mondays of the month at 12 Harlow Street. W. H. Palmer and Cecil Johnson were the two leading officers, while Herbert Halfkenney served as secretary and J. Robert Mahoney served as treasurer. The Order had two distinct purposes. First, it was to provide personal and financial relief for members in case of illness or disability. Second, it was to help defray members' funeral expenses and ensure members' remains were "followed to the last resting place, and the dust [was] smoothed on [their] grave by the hand of sorrowing friendship."[82]

The Odd Fellows continued to meet during the 1910s and through the early to mid-1920s. In 1914, Ford Clark, William Stewart, J. Robert Mahoney, and Charles R. Talbot were officers; by 1919, Wallace Leek, Goodridge Leek, and Milton Geary joined Mahoney as ranking officers. By the early 1910s, the Odd Fellows of Lodge No. 8750 met twice monthly at the Masonic Hall at 22 Water Street. By 1923, Hubert Scott had become a ranking member of the Odd Fellows. Black Bangor's women organized branch number 5220 of the Household of Ruth, the women's auxiliary of the G.U.O.O.F. The Household of Ruth, which in 1919 included Fahy Heughan Geary, Daisy Clark, Louise Mahoney, and Grace Sekater, also met at 22 Water Street, but on alternating Wednesdays. Like the Odd Fellows, the Household of Ruth continued well into the 1920s; Alta Scott, Gertrude Buck, and Maggie Burtt were also members of the auxiliary.[83]

The Pine Tree Lodge Free and Accepted Masons organized sometime around 1919, and like the Mothers' Clubs, they left little public evidence of their activities. In 1923, the lodge operated under the leadership of J. Robert Mahoney, Hubert Scott, and Alonzo Johnson. As a secret fraternal organization, the inner workings of the Masons are not made public, but the Bangor city directory reports that the Masons met the first Friday of each month at the Masonic Hall at 22 Water Street, and later at the same location, but "at the call of the Worshipful Master." Other members of the Masonic order included Sterling A. Dymond. Later renamed the North Star 22 Lodge, Free and Accepted Masons, it maintains a relationship with the Prince Hall Lodge in Massachusetts.[84]

Sterling Dymond, Jr., continues the family tradition of being a Mason, and the lodge continues to meet to this day. The Masons have filled some of the void left by the disintegration of the Mothers' and Junior Mothers' Clubs. They continue to host Christmas tree parties and sponsor an annual scholarship competition for the Black community's prospective college and university students.[85]

ILLUSTRATION 35. The Bangor chapter of the NAACP on Harlow Street, c. 1920s. *Collection of Maine Historic Preservation Commission.*

## The NAACP

In addition to the Mothers' Clubs, the Odd Fellows, and the Masons, Bangor had the notable achievement of establishing its own chapter of the National Association for the Advancement of Colored People (NAACP). Founded in 1909, the NAACP would become one of the most important civil rights organizations in the twentieth-century United States. NAACP co-founder Mary White Ovington visited Bangor in mid-1920, at which time she chaired the association's board of directors and frequently traveled the country encouraging the formation of new branches. Ovington's address to a Bangor forum was successful: the next month the Bangor chapter of the NAACP began organizing, and in early 1921 it received its charter. J. Robert Mahoney served as president, W. Alonzo Johnson was vice-president, and Fahy Geary served as treasurer. A recent graduate of Bangor High School, stenographer Queenie Peters served as the NAACP's secretary. With more than fifty charter members, the Bangor NAACP was the organization's second branch in Maine (illustration 35).[86]

TABLE 4.1    Charter Members of the Bangor NAACP, 1920[87]

| Name | Occupation | Name | Occupation |
|------|-----------|------|-----------|
| J. Robert Mahoney | Clerk | Alonzo Johnson | Musician |
| Queenie Peters | Stenographer | Fahy Geary | Housewife |
| Mrs. Murray Nelson | Housewife | C. L. Nobleton | Chef |
| Mary Nobleton | Cook | James Beal | Coachman |
| Violet Holmes | Domestic | Jessie Hudlin | Laborer |
| Enos Hudlin | Truckman | Hiram Simmons | Machinist |
| Pearl Simmons | Housewife | Mrs. M. J. Burtt | Housewife |
| Helen Jackson | Domestic | James Warner | Waiter |
| Clara Burtt | At Home | Wm. E. Walz | Prof. Law Sch. |
| Lena Bernard | Housewife | Stella Hudlin | Domestic |
| Louise I. Mahoney | Hairdresser | Bessie Martini | Housewife |
| Blanche Dymond | Domestic | Fillmore Clarkson | M.D. |
| Abbie Peters | Housewife | Hanna Mason | Domestic |
| Edgar S. Buck | Porter R.R. Station | Edith Mae Johnson | At Home |
| Wm. H. Derricks | Porter R.R. Station | Mabel Derricks | Housewife |
| Annie Hudlin | Domestic | Pearl Holmes | Domestic |
| Goodrich A. Leek | Chauffeur | Mrs. Enos Hudlin | Housewife |
| Gertrude Buck | Housewife | Milton R. Geary | Attorney |
| Mrs. Walter Furbler | Housewife | Wm. H. Campbell | Clerk |
| Harry Bernard | Chauffeur | H. W. Scott | Sexton |
| Marion Peters | Housewife | Albert Martini | Chef |
| William B. Stewart | Moulder | Sophia Burt | Domestic |
| Ida Beal | Housewife | John W. Paterson | Laborer |
| Dora P. Clarke | Housewife | Charles A. Talbot | Truckman |
| R. J. Winslow | Waiter | Edward Ambrose | Chef |
| Grace Sekater | Domestic | Blanche McIntyre | Domestic |
| Shenton Peters | R.R. Car Cleaner | Mary Eastman | n/a |
| Mrs. Sterling Dymond | n/a | George Hudlin | n/a |
| Mrs. Charles Talbot | n/a | Josephine Smallwood | n/a |

Source: Application for Charter of Bangor, Maine, Branch of the National Association for the Advancement of Colored People, October 1920. NAACP Branch Files, Box 1-G84, Folder 1, Manuscript Division, Library of Congress.

Given the general esteem that many African Americans enjoyed, one might ask what local concerns engendered the need for a local NAACP chapter. One of the most visible and insidious threats came from the Ku Klux Klan, which, due to Maine's nativist movement of the 1920s, had a reported membership of fifty thousand by 1928. The NAACP's 1921 mass meeting at Bangor city hall directly referenced concerns about the growth of the Ku Klux Klan, which by that time had reorganized as a national organization in 1915, with headquarters in Stone Mountain, Georgia. In fact, Maine's Ku Klux Klan and NAACP branches were growing simultaneously. A mid-October 1922 issue of the *Bangor Daily News* reported KKK chapters operating in Portland and in adjacent Westbrook, and that while Portland hosted the KKK state headquarters, "In Bangor, the work of organization started earlier than [Portland], and as a result it has progressed further" (illustration 36).[88]

Four months after the *Bangor Daily News* reported the Ku Klux Klan's progress in the area, the local newspaper described the organization's buffered attempt to host a public meeting at City Hall. The story is told that a man claiming to represent the Klan approached Bangor's mayor, Albert R. Day, and asked that City Hall be the site of a public meeting; his request was "positively and emphatically refused."[89] The Klan's request was for a forum virtually identical to that granted to the NAACP two years prior, but it seems that an event subsequent to the NAACP meeting had led the city's administration to scrutinize more carefully what groups it would allow to use its facilities. The *Bangor Daily News* reported, rather vaguely, the reason for the policy change:

> The use of City Hall was granted some time ago for a religious gathering, so called, on a Sunday afternoon, but it developed that the meeting was utilized

ILLUSTRATION 36. Parade of the Ku Klux Klan in neighboring Brewer, c. 1920s. *Collections of the Bangor Museum and Center for History.*

for a vicious and bitter attack upon a certain religious sect. Since that time, the custodian has taken great care not to let any persons or organizations which might make an attack upon any portion of the community, as City Hall belongs to all the people.[90]

The *Bangor Daily News* proclaimed that the February 1921 "mass meeting in City Hall Sunday afternoon under the auspices of the Bangor Maine Branch of the National Association for the Advancement of Colored People was an entire success."[91] This February 21 meeting was not a racially exclusive gathering, and was attended by several notable figures, including Judge B. W. Blanchard, whose court record "proved that the colored citizens here were rather an honor to the community than a detriment."[92]

One of the organization's most significant victories came early in the branch's history when the NAACP succeeded in having D. W. Griffith's film, *The Birth of a Nation*, edited for content. In 1921, a committee of NAACP members lobbied the mayor of Bangor to stop what would be the film's third showing, "on the ground that it contained scenes calculated to inspire race hatred." The mayor, however, had no legal power to act, "except in the case of films that are against public morality." The committee then pursued the manager of the Bijou Theatre, who would not cancel, citing expense and extensive advertising. The manager did concede that "if you will send a committee at the first showing of the film, whatever they wish to cut, I will have omitted." After screening the edited version, the committee seemed content, finding "that the film was considerably cut, since last shown in Bangor, and the most objectionable scene was omitted."[93]

The Bangor NAACP met the second Sunday of each month, at three o'-clock in the afternoon, at 22 Water Street. The *Daily News* periodically reported on its activities.[94] The NAACP was clearly a place where the spiritual and the political met. Not only did the Sunday afternoon meeting schedule place the political concerns within the sphere of the Christian Sabbath day, the meetings themselves intertwined biblical and political concerns. The pastor of Bangor's First Baptist Church, Rev. Wayne L. Robinson, preached a "sermon" at the association's January 1925 meeting. Taking his text from John 8:32, Robinson "ably showed how the gospel of Jesus Christ freed men from political, intellectual and spiritual bondage."[95] Milton Geary explained "the local concept of the work" as

the need of the people to encourage greater understanding one with the other; of the need of an extensive educational program; of getting in touch with all the relations of life whether in rural districts or urban localities; of the supreme goal of greater church interest, civic responsibility and moral rectitude.[96]

At the organization's next monthly meeting, the YWCA's general secretary, Martha E. Hopkins, served as principal speaker; she delivered her address, "The Call of God to a Life of Purity, of Service, of Intelligence, and of Determination." Mrs. Harry Smith and Gertrude Buck also "contributed able addresses during the meeting."[97]

In addition to the mixture of the spiritual and the political, musical performance was a part of each meeting. The February 1921 mass meeting at Bangor City Hall was opened with selections by Villas and Alonzo Johnson. The January 1925 meeting featured a violin solo by Dorothy Davis and "a most acceptable piano solo" by Ada Peters. Soloist Charles Mason delighted the assembly at the February 1925 meeting, where Ada Peters, LaRue Dymond, and Alonzo Johnson each provided selections on the piano.[98]

The Bangor NAACP kept up with the organization's national events, and each meeting featured an update on the NAACP's activities. At the February 1925 meeting, for example, J. Robert Mahoney reported on the banquet that honored NAACP national president, the Honorable Morefield Storey. Secretary Bessie Martini outlined the association's achievements of the past year, work that was characterized in the *Bangor Daily News* as "very extensive and intensive," with "remarkable numeric gains."[99]

Despite the promise demonstrated during the early 1920s, the Bangor NAACP declined during the latter part of the decade. President Mahoney resigned, and advised national Director of Branches Robert Bagnall to forward all communications to either Vice-President Gertrude Buck or Secretary Milton Geary. By 1926, the Bangor chapter had become somewhat dormant. Bagnall appealed to William Stewart to serve as president and lead the organization back into an active status. Appealing, perhaps, to Stewart's sense of duty, Bagnall closed his 1926 letter with one final petition:

> I should appreciate it if you would write me telling me whether the National Office can depend on you to do this service for Bangor, for the race and the Association.[100]

The branch continued to falter even more in 1927, during which time Milton Geary informed the New York office that only fifteen people had interest in membership. Geary appealed to Bagnall to accept the branch's lesser apportionment, rather than the necessary fifty dollars.

This assembly seemed to feel that a $25.00 apportionment would meet the situation in Bangor better than a $50.00, and would perhaps mean keeping the society alive. They feel that they do not desire to surrender the charter, but if more money were required than they were able to raise, the only logical thing would be to discontinue the branch. Kindly advise.[101]

While he sympathized with the Bangor situation, Bagnall maintained that the full fifty dollars were required to keep the branch in good standing. NAACP Branch Files are silent on what happened to the Bangor chapter during the rest of the decade, but it is likely that the organization remained inactive. In 1931, the NAACP Conference of the Branches in New England sent no letters to Maine, and in 1939 the newly formed New England Conference noted both Bangor and Portland on its list of inactive branches. Inactive branches were notified of the national board's power to revoke charters if in the best interest of the association; those branches not responding to the notice or unable to return to active status were to be recommended for charter revocation.[102]

### The Columbia Street Community Center

After World War II, the Black U.S.O. recreation center on Columbia Street was turned over to the community, and was renamed the Columbia Street Community Center. As during the war, African Americans remained heavily invested in its management and success. In 1950, Goodridge Leek served as president, Milton Geary, in his sixties and still practicing law, was corresponding secretary. Mrs. Joseph C. Cooper served as recording secretary and Robert Mitchell served as director. Meetings of the Center's board took place on the second Thursday evening of each month.[103] The Columbia Street Community Center served as the platform for the creation of the Carver Club, a Black, semi-professional basketball team that competed across the state and in eastern Canada. Carver Club players included Bobby Nelson, Harold Nelson, William McCarty, Wilfred Dymond, Galen Leek, Richard Nelson, Reginald Clark, Cyril Scott, and Hubert Scott, Jr.[104]

As a competitive, touring team, the Carver Club afforded young men the opportunity to play basketball outside the parameters of school teams and gave them a chance to enhance further their athletic skills. The Carver Club also served to illuminate the African American presence in Bangor even as it allowed players to broaden their experiences on the state and regional levels. In one particular competition, the Carver Club's athletic prowess and showmanship almost exacted a very high cost on the players. When playing opponents at Woodland, in Aroostook County,

> a riot erupted when the Carver Club, with its Harlem Globetrotters style of play, made a mockery of the local club. The referee somehow got flattened by an errant pass, and the fans leaped from their seats.
>
> "We made a dash to the locker room . . . grabbed our clothes and made a quick exit to our cars. We had to be escorted out of town by state police and sheriff deputies."[105]

The history of Black Bangor's voluntary associations mirrors that of its New England counterparts. Newport, Rhode Island, for example, incorporated its branch of the NAACP in 1919, its earlier attempts to organize in the mid-1910s thwarted by World War I.[106] As in Bangor, many of Newport's founding NAACP members held professional, proprietary, managerial, skilled, and semi-skilled positions in the city. As Myra Young Armstead wrote,

> not only did the general community, black and white, accord such workers special stature; these workers defined *themselves* as a high-ranking political vanguard and assumed the responsibilities for race advocacy that they associated with their class.[107]

Newport appears to have been very much in sync with national developments. With anti-lynching as one of its primary campaigns and with visits by W. E. B. DuBois to bolster its visibility, Newport appears to have been a highly engaged chapter from its earliest years.[108]

New Haven organized its local chapter of the NAACP just two years before Newport. The membership is reported to have grown rapidly, incorporating membership from the local Black and White communities alike, or as Robert Warner described, from among White religious liberals and solid, civic-minded Blacks. One of the hallmarks of the New Haven chapter's earlier days were speeches made by NAACP co-founder and *Crisis* editor, W. E. B. DuBois and William Pickens, the organization's national field secretary.[109]

Fraternal organizations, women's clubs, and various civic groups rounded out the bulk of Black New England voluntary associations, either as distinct African American chapters created in response to the racially exclusive policies of established orders or as self-generated organizations designed to address Blacks' specific needs. Portsmouth, New Hampshire, which did not establish a chapter of the NAACP until the late 1950s, supported various Black

organizations through the first half of the twentieth century. Our Boys'
Comfort Club was established in 1919 as a social respite for African American men serving at Portsmouth's navy yard. The club later became known as
the Lincoln American Community Club. The next year, the Colored Pythians
organized a lodge in the city under the name of S. W. Starks Lodge No. 28.
The Colored Pythians' platform was "personal kindness and service to all."
The absence of an early branch of the NAACP in Portsmouth seems to have
been overcome as visiting lodge members related their experiences with and
the larger developments within the NAACP to the city's Colored Pythians.
Membership averaged more than one hundred persons, making the lodge an
important fraternal and civic organization in Black Portsmouth. Other organizations included the Colored Citizens League, founded in 1922, and the
Octagon Club, a Black Masonic order, established in the 1940s.[110]

New Haven, Connecticut, also saw a high rate of Black voluntary activity,
with Black chapters of the Masons, Elks, and Odd Fellows in the late 1800s
and early 1900s. Women's activity in New Haven was no less impressive than
men's. In 1900, Black women formed the New Haven Women's Twentieth
Century Club, and made one of their first campaigns securing and renovat-
ing the Hannah Gray House, a home for the aged. Almost thirty years later,
the Women's Civic League was established, with the founding of a super-
vised residence for employed and unemployed Black women as its goal. In
1936, the League's organizer, Sara Lee Fleming, was able to acquire a local
building to support the organization's mission, and named it the Phyllis
Wheatley Home.[111]

Blacks in Bangor and those in New England cities such as Newport,
Rhode Island, New Haven, Connecticut, and Portmsouth, New Hamsphire,
had much in common. Whether or not all had established early branches of
the NAACP, they all established various voluntary associations to meet their
objectives of fellowship, civic responsibility, social justice, and benevolence.
Where they did not find or were denied access to institutions to meet their
needs, they turned inward—toward themselves—and established what
they needed. Men and women alike were engaged actively in trying to improve the increasingly complex urban conditions in which they lived and into
which their children and grandchildren would be born.

◦⨾◦

Either through lack of formal documentation or because of the confidential
nature of their activities, much of Black Bangor's institutional history is vague.

Nonetheless, the presence of various groups and institutions including the Mothers' Club, the Junior Mothers' Club, the Odd Fellows, the Masons, the Tarragona Club, the NAACP, and the Carver Club all have enough documentation to verify their presence and to offer at least an outline of their early memberships and activities. The histories of these groups place Black Bangor in the company of other New England communities, and makes the African American community in this northern state seem less of an aberration. The five decades from 1900 to 1950 formed a period of incredible institutional development and maturation. Black Bangor went from being a hybrid community of Blacks born across the hemisphere to a multigenerational community capable of creating institutions that served their needs for fraternity, sorority, social justice, leisure, and entertainment. The burdens of institutional formation and maintenance were not distributed evenly. A core group of men like Milton Geary, Alonzo Johnson, J. Robert Mahoney, Charles R. Talbot, and Sterling Dymond, and of women like Louise Mahoney, Mabel Derricks, and Fahy Geary appear again and again in the leadership positions of Black Bangor's own institutions. Nonetheless, it is through the power and impact of their collective activities, whether highly formalized or generally ad hoc, that African Americans in Bangor truly made themselves a community — a community virtually unmatched in the state and one that created a history still celebrated by surviving community members.

# EPILOGUE

## African Americans in Bangor since 1950

After the golden age that was Black Bangor ended by 1950, the rhythms of daily life continued. In 1951, Sterling A. Dymond and Janie Simmons Dymond celebrated their golden anniversary with an afternoon and evening open house in their Fourth Street home. In 1952, Elizabeth Jackson Warner left Bangor to reside in Baltimore, Maryland, next door to her daughter, Beryl Warner Williams. Elizabeth Warner probably never saw Bangor again, for she died in Baltimore the next year. Charles and Panzy Talbot celebrated their fiftieth anniversary in 1958.[1]

In March of 1955, Cora Yvonne Dymond, daughter of Earl and Nora Dymond, married Wayne Galen Norman in an exquisite ceremony at the Columbia Street Baptist Church. Their marriage received considerable attention in the local newspaper with an article that detailed the ceremony, the reception, and the couple's post-wedding plans. A picture of Cora Dymond was included in the article, which describes the bride as follows:

> Given in marriage by her father, the bride was attractive in a full-length gown of ivory satin, fashioned with a fitted bodice, and a V neckline and long pointed sleeves. Her finger-tip veil of nylon tulle was caught to a cap of ivory satin trimmed with seed pearls. She carried a white Bible with camellias.[2]

The 1950s through the 1990s saw the passing of many of the migrants and their children who had built Black Bangor. Sterling A. Dymond died in 1954, and his wife, Janie, died in 1959. Mabel Derricks died in the fall of 1953, and Pearl Leek died in the summer of 1957. Abbie Peters and Helen Wise both died in the early to mid-1950s, and Shenton Peters, Charles Raynsford Talbot, Panzy Dymond Talbot, and Stella Gosman McCarty all died in the 1960s. The 1970s, 1980s, and 1990s were marked by the loss of such noted figures as Emma O'Ree Peters, Linda Brooks Davis, Goodridge Leek, Austin Gordon, Helena Dymond George, and Arvella McIntyre Talbot.[3]

At the passing of Black Bangor's gateway and first-generation populations, their surviving offspring often were living out of state. When Abbie Peters died in 1954, three of her four children lived out of state. When Janie Dymond died in 1959, six of her nine children were living outside of Maine. And when Nora Dymond died in 1973, her daughter Cora Dymond Norman was living in her husband's home state of Ohio.[4]

Sterling Dymond, Jr., Dorothy Simmons, Earl Johnson, Lloyd George, and others still live in Bangor. They still attend services at the city's various churches. Their children matriculated at Bangor's elementary and high schools. The Masons still carry on the traditions of Black Bangor, most notably with seasonal celebrations and scholarship awards. The Odd Fellows no longer meet, and both the Mothers' Club and Junior Mothers' Club have long faded into memory, disbanded by the eventual death of founding members and the outmigration of subsequent generations of young women. The NAACP chapter, which went into decline in the late 1920 or early 1930s, has reorganized as the Greater Bangor Area NAACP. Portland's NAACP branch reorganized various times between the 1930s and the 1950s. Only after its 1964 reorganization did the branch achieve the long-term consistency needed to celebrate its fortieth anniversary in 2004.[5] Bangor also is responsible for another African American milestone. It seems fitting that Maine's first African American legislator should be Bangor born. Gerald E. Talbot, son of Edgerton Talbot and grandson of Charles R. Talbot, was elected to the Maine legislature in 1972. He served three consecutive terms, and although he represented Portland, his accomplishment was a source of pride for Bangor. Sadly, Talbot's father, Edgerton, died before he could see his son take office.[6]

The city of Bangor has changed physically. Bangor High School no longer sits on Harlow Street, but on Outer Broadway. The Bangor Mall opened on Stillwater Avenue in the late 1970s, diverting much of the trade away from the city's downtown core. Businesses such as Freese's department store closed the next decade. Various landmarks, including the Bijou Theatre, Union Station, and the Penobscot Exchange Hotel, were demolished in the name of urban renewal. And, in January 2004, one of the most important stages for Black Bangor's institutional maturation and self-direction was lost when fire completely destroyed the Masonic Hall that stood for decades on the corner of Water and Main.[7]

The changes surrounding Dow Air Force Base have had some of the most profound effects on Black Bangor. After World War II, Bangor's geographic location lost its strategic importance when it was no longer necessary to support the war effort in Europe. African American enlisted men and officers were stationed elsewhere, causing a significant reduction in Black Bangor's population. In 1950, fewer than half of the number of Blacks lived in Bangor than in 1940. When Dow Air Force Base closed in the late 1960s, it dispersed remaining Black service men and women, and closed an important avenue of local employment.[8]

According to the United States Census, 320 African Americans resided in Bangor in 2000, making them 1.0 percent of the city's population. This marked a slight increase over the 1990 population of 305, which, in a city of more than 33,000, comprised 0.9 percent of the population. Blacks also made significant gains in both occupation and income. With African Americans no longer relegated to domestic or general service positions, their jobs more accurately reflected a diversity of ability and training. The top five categories of Black employment were, in descending order: administrative/clerical; precision production, craft, and repair; technical support; sales; and executive and managerial. Together, these categories accounted for two-thirds of African Americans in the city's workforce. Though still few in number, Black professionals accounted for more than 8 percent of the African American workforce. The 2000 Census reports that while the city's total population declined to 31,473, there was a slight increase in the number of Blacks.[9]

The Black populations of 1990 and 2000 are substantially larger than they were at Black Bangor's height in 1930. What they do not do, however, is replicate the cohesiveness, the institutional development, or the very energy that was Black Bangor between 1800 and 1950. As long as the memories persist and the photographs remain, however, we will be able to talk about Black Bangor and about what this small community proved was possible for Blacks in Maine.

# Notes

For space consideration, the author has used the following format when citing from the U.S. Bureau of the Census: "Twelfth (1900) Census of the United States (ms)" (for "manuscript"). Readers will find complete citation information in the primary sources section of the bibliography under "U.S. Bureau of the Census."

## Introduction

1. *Maine Register and State Year-Book and Legislative Manual, 1949–50* (Portland: Fred L. Tower, 1949), 610.

2. Richard W. Judd, "Maine's Lumber Industry," 270; "The Lumber Industry in an Age of Change," 414; Richard R. Westcott, "Tourism in Maine," 434–38; all in *Maine: The Pine Tree State from Prehistory to the Present,* ed. Richard W. Judd, Edwin A. Churchill, and Joel W. Eastman (Orono: University of Maine Press, 1995); Abigail Ewing Zelz and Marilyn Zoidis, *Woodsmen and Whigs: Historic Images of Bangor, Maine* (Virginia Beach: Donning Company Publishers, 1991), 183; Marc Berlin et al., *The Story of Bangor: A Brief History of Maine's Queen City* (Bangor: Bookmarc's Publishing, 1999), 67–73.

3. Berlin et al., *Story of Bangor,* 51–53.

4. Elizabeth Donnan, *Documents Illustrative of the History of the Slave Trade to America,* vol. 3 (New York: Octagon Books, 1969), 28; Lorenzo Johnston Greene, *The Negro in Colonial New England, 1620–1776* (New York: Columbia University Press, 1942), 29, 36. See also Miriam Stover Thomas, *Flotsam and Jetsam* (Maine: by the author, 1973), 26; Randolph Stakeman, "Slavery in Colonial Maine," *Maine Historical Society Quarterly* 27, no. 2 (Fall 1987): 64; *Appleton's Cyclopaedia of American Biography,* vol. 4, s.v. "Pepperell, Sir William."

5. Stakeman, "Slavery in Colonial Maine," 64.

6. William D. Piersen, *Black Yankees: The Development of an Afro-American Subculture in Eighteenth-Century New England* (Amherst: University of Massachusetts Press, 1988), 3.

7. Piersen, *Black Yankees,* xi.

8. Greene, *Negro in Colonial New England,* 29, 36; Donnan, *Documents,* vol. 3, 28; Thomas, *Flotsam and Jetsam,* 26; Stakeman, "Slavery in Colonial Maine," 64; *Appleton's*

*Cyclopaedia of American Biography*, vol. 4, s.v. "Pepperell, Sir William"; Maine Historical Society Collection 73, Box 1 of 15; Elizabeth K. Hobbs Collection, M567–2342; Norman Seaver Frost, *Frost Genealogy in Five Families* (West Newton, Mass.: Frost Family Association of America, 1926). Frost's father, also named Charles, died in July of 1696, and in his will he awarded his son "his negro man servant called Tony" after his wife's death. The same will awarded Nicholas Frost, Charles' brother, a "negro boy called Prince . . . to be delivered to Nicholas when he comes of age." See Frost, *Frost Genealogy*, 229, 230.

    9.  Stakeman, "Slavery in Colonial Maine," 63, 78.

    10.  Edward O. Shriver, *Go Free: The Antislavery Impulse in Maine, 1833–1855* (Orono: University of Maine Press, 1970), 10; *Anchor of the Soul: A Documentary about Blacks in Maine*, prod. and dir. Shoshana Hoose and Karine Odlin, 60 min. 1994, videocassette; William Craft and Ellen Craft, *Running a Thousand Miles for Freedom* (London: William Tweedie, 1860).

    11.  See Hoose and Odlin, *Anchor of the Soul*; Herbert Adams, "SS *Portland*," *Portland Monthly Magazine* (Winterguide, n.d.), 12, 14, 18, 21. African American History Files, Maine Historical Society. In August 2002, the National Oceanic and Atmospheric Administration (NOAA) announced to the public that it had located the wreck of the SS *Portland* off the Massachusetts coast, somewhere in the Stellwagen Bank National Marine Sanctuary. NOAA did not disclose the exact location of the wreckage when releasing news of the discovery to the public. See http://cnn.com/2002/US/08/29/historic.shipwreck (accessed 1 June 2004).

    12.  Randolph Stakeman, "The Black Population of Maine, 1764–1900," *New England Journal of Black Studies* 8 (1989): 19, 23, 33. One of the definitive studies of Black Loyalist movement to the Canadian colonies remains James W. St. G. Walker's *The Black Loyalists: The Search for a Promised Land in Nova Scotia and Sierra Leone, 1783–1870* (New York: Africana Publishing Co., 1976). See also Graham Russell Hodge's inventory of Blacks who left for Canada through New York City after the American Revolution, *The Black Loyalist Directory: African Americans in Exile after the American Revolution* (New York: Garland Publishing, 1996). New Brunswick did not have the subsequent exodus of Black Loyalists and Maroons of late-eighteenth-century Nova Scotia. In 1796, Blacks, disillusioned by their poor treatment and their allotments of inferior lands, left for Sierra Leone, West Africa, under the direction of Thomas Clarkson. See Mavis C. Campbell, *Nova Scotia and the Fighting Maroons: A Documentary History* (Williamsburg: College of William and Mary, 1990) and, more recently, John N. Grant, *The Maroons in Nova Scotia* (Halifax: Formac, 2002). Extensive microfilm materials on the Maroon experience and Thomas Clarkson are housed at the Public Archives of Nova Scotia at Dalhousie University in Halifax.

    13.  See Judd et al., *Maine*, 443, 469, 512. The cities of Portland, Bangor, Auburn, Bath, and Augusta had the largest Black populations in the state in 1920. Portland led with 300 African Americans, followed by Bangor with 208. The numbers were

considerably lower for Auburn, Bath, and Augusta, which recorded 52, 42, and 34 Blacks, respectively, in that year. Fourteenth Census of the United States, 1920 (Population). All five cities hosted KKK or WKKK chapters in the 1920s. See also Hoose and Odlin, *Anchor of the Soul*; John Syrett, "Principle and Expediency: The Ku Klux Klan and Ralph Owen Brewster in 1924," *Maine History* 39 (Winter 2000–2001): 215–39.

14. Papers, Gerald E. Talbot Collection, African American Collection of Maine, Jean Byers Sampson Center for Diversity in Maine, University of Southern Maine Libraries; Selena Ricks, "Cause for Celebration," *Portland Press Herald*, 26 September 2004, 1A. For more on civil rights activity in Maine, see Charles Lumpkins, "Civil Rights Activism in Maine, 1945–1971," *Maine History* 36 (Winter-Spring 1997):70–85.

15. Shoshana Hoose, "Crossroads," *Maine Sunday Telegram*, 24 February 1991, 2F; Elwood Watson, "William Burney and John Jenkins: A Tale of Maine's Two African-American Mayors," *Maine History* 40 (Summer 2001): 113–25; Kelley Bouchard, "Meet the Mayor," *Portland Press Herald*, 29 November 2004, B1, B5.

16. Donald B. Dodd, *Historical Statistics of the States of the United States: Two Centuries of the Census, 1790–1990* (Westport: Greenwood Press, 1993), 40; U.S. Bureau of the Census, 2000 Summary File 1, Matrices P7, P9 (U.S. Census Factfinder.) The Census Bureau advises that the total number of Blacks or African Americans alone and in combination with another race may be inflated, as some people may have reported themselves twice.

### Chapter 1. One Family at a Time: Building Black Bangor

1. Obituary of William A. Johnson, *Bangor Daily News*, 21 January 1913; Twelfth (1900) Census of the United States (manuscript; hereafter "ms"). According to the *Bangor Daily News*, Edith M. Delaney was born in the Virgin Islands in January of 1873, and came to Bangor when she was twelve years old. Johnson and Delaney would have married in the late 1880s or early 1890s, as their first child, W. Alonzo, was born in Bangor in 1891. See Thirteenth Census of the United States, 1910 (ms); Randolph Stakeman, "African American Households in Bangor, 1900–1920" (unpublished manuscript), 1910, 4. For an extensive profile of Edith Delaney Johnson, see Marie Sullivan, "Recipe for Happy Old Age—Be Good Wife and Mother and Do for Others, Says Bangor Nonagenarian," *Bangor Daily News*, 24 January 1963, 22.

2. Nominal census of New Brunswick, 1891, 1901; Thirteenth (1910), Fourteenth (1920), and Fifteenth (1930) Censuses of the United States (ms); Stakeman, "Households," 1910, 4, 6; 1920, 1. According to 1901 census data, Gertrude Leek, whose name is spelled "Leak" in the manuscript census, should have been twenty-four years old in 1910, not twenty-two. Sister Margaret's surname is spelled "Leck" in the 1910 manuscript census of Bangor. William and Evalena added at least two more children to

their family after the 1901 census. Daughter Alma was born in Kingsclear in May of 1901, and son Alton was born in Kingsclear in February of 1903. See Provincial Archives of New Brunswick Online. RS141 Vital Statistics, no. 3223, ref. A5/1901, microfilm F18059 and no. 4281, reference A5/1903, microfilm F19001. Although the cover page of Alton Leek's online birth certificate says that he was born in Fredericton, the actual document says that he was born in Kingsclear.

3.  Twelfth (1900), Thirteenth (1910), and Fifteenth (1930) Censuses of the United States (ms); Stakeman, "Households," 1900, 2; 1910, 3; "Chas. A. Talbot — Well Known Resident Drops Dead at His Home," *Bangor Daily News*, 6 January 1934, 10. The significance of the year 1910 is based on the proportion of African Americans in Bangor at the decennial census. The arrival of African American service personnel at Bangor's Dow Air Force base during World War II inflated Black Bangor's population, but this was a temporary, even artificial migration, as Blacks were stationed there by the U.S. military. Many Black servicemen left after the war.

4.  Carole Marks' study of United States census figures for the years 1870 to 1930 indicates that Black outmigration from the South to the North was building substantially by the end of the nineteenth century. From 1890 to 1900, there was a net outmigration of 168,000. For the next decade, the figure was 170,000, and for the next it had risen dramatically to 454,000. However, the Black outmigration took place between 1920 and 1930, with 749,000 Blacks leaving the U.S. South. Carole Marks, *Farewell — We're Good and Gone: The Great Black Migration* (Bloomington: Indiana University Press, 1989), 2.

5.  U.S. Bureau of the Census, 1870–1950 Censuses of the United States, Population. U.S. Bureau of the Census, *Negro Population in the United States 1790–1915* (New York: Arno Press and the *New York Times*, 1968), 98; *Maine Register, State Yearbook, and Legislative Manual, 1920–21* (Portland: Portland Directory Company, 1920), 848.

6.  Eleventh (1890) Census of the United States, Population, Part 1; Fifteenth (1930) Census of the United States, Population, vol. 3, part 1; Sixteenth (1940) Census of the United States Population, vol. 2.

7.  Twelfth (1900), Thirteenth (1910), Fourteenth (1920), and Fifteenth (1930) Censuses of the United States (ms); Stakeman, "Households," 1900, 1910, and 1920. These figures are approximate and are based on the number of Blacks located in the manuscript census. For the 1900 census, I was able to locate 172 out of the 176 Blacks that the U.S. census reported for the city. For the 1910 census, I was able to locate 200 of 205 Blacks. For the 1920 census, I located 193 out of 208, and for the 1930 census, I located 218 out of 228 reported Blacks in the city. Discrepancies may be caused by poor-quality microfilm, illegible handwriting in the manuscript census, or simple observer error. However, while these numbers may not be set in stone, they are very useful in comparing the Black subpopulations — those born in state, out of state, in

Canada, in the Caribbean, or in other parts of the world. The percentages have been rounded up and may not all equal 100 percent.

8. Conversely, those African Americans of Maine birth living in other states numbered 573 or 43.4 percent in 1900; this rose to 783 or 49.4 percent by 1910. Figures are based on data from the 1900 and 1910 United States censuses. See U.S. Bureau of the Census, *Negro Population*, 71. The percentages have been rounded up and equal 100 percent.

9. Twelfth (1900) Census of the United States (ms); Stakeman, "Households," 1900.

10. Twelfth (1900) Census of the United States (ms); Stakeman, "Households," 1900, 3. The entries for Daniel Mason, John Mason, and Mary Pratt raise some questions about their relationships and about the accuracy of the census data. Daniel Mason's wife is recorded as having been White. John Mason's father is listed has having been born in Spain, his mother in Ireland. Daniel Mason's father is listed as having been born in Peru, his mother in Ireland. Mary Pratt's father is recorded as having been born in Spain and her mother in Ireland. It would appear that Mary Pratt and John Mason could have been siblings, but they are both listed as having been born in 1859—and five months apart.

11. Based on data from the Twelfth (1900) Census of the United States. See U.S. Bureau of the Census, *Negro Population*, 71. The percentages have been rounded up.

12. Based on figures from the Twelfth (1900), Thirteenth (1910), Fourteenth (1920), and Fifteenth (1930) Censuses of the United States (ms); and Stakeman, "Households," 1900, 1910, and 1920.

13. Based on figures from the Twelfth (1900), Thirteenth (1910), Fourteenth (1920), and Fifteenth (1930) Censuses of the United States (ms); and Stakeman, "Households," 1900, 1910, and 1920.

14. See John Hope Franklin and Alfred A. Moss, *From Slavery to Freedom: A History of African Americans*, 8th ed. (Boston: McGraw-Hill Higher Education, 2000), especially chapters 12, 13, and 16; Marks, *Farewell*, 1–2.

15. Joe William Trotter, Jr., "Black Migration in Historical Perspective," in *The Great Migration in Historical Perspective: New Dimensions of Race, Class, and Gender* (Bloomington: Indiana University Press, 1991), 6.

16. See, for example, Marks, *Farewell*; Trotter, *The Great Migration*; Nell Irvin Painter, *Black Exodusters: Black Migration to Kansas After Reconstruction* (New York: Knopf, 1976).

17. Abigail Ewing Zelz and Marilyn Zoidis, *Woodsmen and Whigs: Historic Images of Bangor, Maine* (Virginia Beach: Donning Company, 1991), 31, 67.

18. *Miles of Smiles, Years of Struggle*, prod. Paul Wagner and Jack Santino, California Newsreel, 1983, videocassette; see also Jack Santino, *Miles of Smiles, Years of Struggle: Stories of Black Pullman Porters* (Urbana: University of Illinois Press, 1989); Marc

Berlin et al., *The Story of Bangor; A Brief History of Maine's Queen City* (Bangor: Book-marc's Publishing, 1999), 50; Stakeman, "Households," 1920, 1; Fourteenth (1920) Census of the United States (ms); Shoshana Hoose and Karine Odlin, *Anchor of the Soul: A Documentary about Blacks in Maine*, 1994; Marks, *Farewell*, 3.

19. "New Haven's Labor Problem—Southern Negro Laborers Being Used by the New Haven System," *New York Age*, 20 July 1916, 1.

20. Thirteenth (1910) and Fourteenth (1920) Censuses of the United States (ms).

21. James Oliver Horton and Lois E. Horton, *Black Bostonians: Family Life and Community Struggle in the Antebellum North*, revised ed. (New York: Holmes and Meier, 1999), 6. Based on review of the manuscripts of the Twelfth (1900), Thirteenth (1910), Fourteenth (1920), and Fifteenth (1930) censuses. The general absence of Blacks born in Vermont and New Hampshire from Bangor is supported by census figures. In 1910, for example, only 2 percent of African Americans born in New Hampshire were living in Maine. For that same year, the number of African Americans born in Vermont and living in Maine was less than 1.3 percent and included in the figure for "all other" states. See U.S. Bureau of the Census, *Negro Population*, 80.

22. U.S. Bureau of the Census, *Negro Population*, 43, 44; Twelfth (1900), Thirteenth (1910), Fourteenth (1920), and Fifteenth (1930) Censuses of the United States (ms); U.S. Bureau of the Census, Fourteenth (1920), Fifteenth (1930), Sixteenth (1940), Seventeenth (1950) Censuses of the Population (Washington, D.C.: GPO, 1922, 1932, 1943, 1952).

23. Twelfth (1900) Census of the United States (ms); Stakeman, "Households," 1900, 2. At the time of the 1910 census, William and Lenora Stewart had had four children, but only three survived. Thirteenth (1910) and Fourteenth (1920) Censuses of the United States (ms); Stakeman, "Households," 1910, 4; 1920, 3.

24. Fifteenth (1930) Census of the United States (ms).

25. Ibid.

26. The 1900 manuscript census identifies James Warner's wife as Annie Warner, thirty-one. The census reports that Annie Warner was born in Maine, as were her two sons, Louis A. Warner, seven, and Edward Ambrose, twelve. Ambrose was James Warner's stepson. The 1920 census finds James H. Warner of Connecticut (misidentified as Warren in the actual census) married to Connecticut native Elizabeth Jackson and having two daughters, Beryl, six, and H. Althea, twelve. Annie Warner died in Bangor in 1911 at the age of forty-five years. James Warner soon married Elizabeth Jackson. Twelfth (1900), Fourteenth (1920), and Fifteenth (1930) Censuses of the United States (ms); Stakeman, "Households," 1900, 3; 1920, 2; Obituary of James H. Warner, *Bangor Daily News*, 6 January 1943, 5; Record of Death, Annie A. Warner, 27 June 1911, in Maine Vital Statistics, 1908–1922, microfilm roll #29, Maine State Archives.

27. Fourteenth (1920) Census of the United States (ms); Obituary of Mrs. Elizabeth Warner, *Bangor Daily News*, 23 September 1953, 12.

28. Fourteenth (1920) Census of the United States (ms); Stakeman, "Households," 1920, 1.

29. Thirteenth (1910) Census of the United States (ms); Stakeman, "Households," 1910, 5. The 1930 census records that nineteen-year-old Bedford (or Beckford) Peters was born in Rhode Island. However, the 1910 and 1920 censuses report that he was born in Maine. Peters' parents, Abner and Emma Peters, were both from Canada, and all his other siblings were born in Maine. The Peters were a long-time Bangor family and it appears that the 1930 manuscript is in error. See Thirteenth (1910), Fourteenth (1920), and Fifteenth (1930) Censuses of the United States (ms).

30. Twelfth (1900) Census of the United States (ms); Stakeman, "Households," 1900, 1–3.

31. Virginia London, "Has Practiced Law 50 Years — Milton R. Geary, Minister-Lawyer, Feels Life Guided Directly By God," *Bangor Daily News*, 2–3 March 1963, 12.

32. "Rev. Geary, Noted Maine Negro, Dies," *Bangor Daily News*, 24 June 1964, 1–2; Fourteenth (1920) Census of the United States (ms); Stakeman, "Households," 1920, 4. Virginia had the largest enslaved population in the United States for all censuses from 1790 through 1860. In 1840, Virginia had almost 449,000 enslaved Blacks and almost 50,000 free Blacks. This was the third-largest free Black population in 1840; Maryland had the largest free Black population with more than 62,000 free Blacks and New York followed with more than 50,000. See U.S. Bureau of the Census, *Negro Population*, chapter 5, table 6, p. 57. William Geary does not appear in the 1930 manuscript census for Bangor. Given his advanced age in 1920, he probably had died.

33. London, "Has Practiced Law 50 Years," 12.

34. Fourteenth (1920) Census of the United States (ms); Stakeman, "Households," 1920, 1. There were four border states at the beginning of the Civil War — Maryland, Delaware, Kentucky, and Missouri. President Abraham Lincoln had to walk a political tightrope during the war; he enacted legislation, such as the 1863 Emancipation Proclamation, to end the war, but to retain the allegiance of border states. West Virginia became the fifth border state when it separated from Virginia in 1863. See Franklin and Moss, *From Slavery to Freedom*, Chapter 11, "Civil War."

35. Fourteenth (1920) and Fifteenth (1930) Censuses of the United States (ms); Stakeman, "Households," 1920, 4; obituary of William A. Johnson, *Bangor Daily News*, 21 January 1913.

36. Twelfth (1900) Census of the United States (ms).

37. Twelfth (1900), Thirteenth (1910), Fourteenth (1920), and Fifteenth (1930) Censuses of the United States (ms); Stakeman, "Households," 1900, 3; 1910, 2, 6; Obituary of Mrs. John R. Mahoney, *Bangor Daily News*, 19 February 1934, 11.

38. Twelfth (1900), Thirteenth (1910), and Fifteenth (1930) Censuses of the United States (ms).

39. Twelfth (1900), Fourteenth (1920), and Fifteenth (1930) Censuses of the United States (ms); Stakeman, "Households," 1900, 2; 1920, 1.

40. Twelfth (1900) and Thirteenth (1910) Censuses of the United States (ms); Stakeman, "Households," 1900, 4; 1910, 5. The Joseph surname does not appear among Bangor's Black population during this study.

41. U.S. Bureau of the Census, *Negro Population*, 83. "Other native" is defined by the Bureau of the Census as "persons born in the United States, state of birth not reported; persons born in outlying possessions, or at sea under United States flag; and American citizens born abroad."

42. These figures are based on the number of Blacks located in the manuscript census for each decade.

43. These figures are based on the nativity of Bangor's Blacks located in each manuscript census. In 1900, I was able to locate 172 of the 176 Blacks in the city. For 1910 it was 200 of 205; for 1920 it was 193 out of 208, and for 1930 it was 218 of 228.

44. William Spray writes that a Black man reportedly died at Port Royal in 1606, and that in 1608 a Black—presumably male—was servant to the governor at Port Royal. In the late 1600s, the French apparently captured and carried a Black man from New England into New Brunswick. The same man apparently was freed in 1696 when a force from Massachusetts conducted a counter raid on the St. John River French settlement. W. A. Spray, *The Blacks in New Brunswick* (Fredericton, New Brunswick: Brunswick Press, 1972), 13, 14.

45. Ibid., 16, 17.

46. Robin W. Winks, *The Blacks in Canada: A History*, 2nd ed. (Montreal: McGill-Queen's University Press, 1997), 110–11. Blacks enslaved in the British West Indies also were emancipated under this legislation, but most labored under the apprenticeship system for an additional four years. For more on the abolition of slavery in the British West Indies, see William A. Green, *British Slave Emancipation: The Sugar Colonies and the Great Experiment 1830–1865* (Oxford: Clarendon Press, 1991); Jan Rogozinski, *A Brief History of the Caribbean: From the Arawak and the Carib to the Present* (New York: Meridian Books, 1992); Alvin O. Thompson, ed., *In the Shadow of the Plantation: Caribbean History and Legacy* (Kingston, Jamaica: Ian Randle Publishers, 2002).

47. See William Craft and Ellen Craft, *Running a Thousand Miles for Freedom* (London: William Tweedie, 1860); Winks, *Blacks in Canada*, 142–77; Jane Rhodes, *Mary Ann Shadd Cary: The Black Press and Protest in the Nineteenth Century* (Bloomington: Indiana University Press, 1998), 25–50; Adrienne Shadd, "The Lord seemed to say 'Go': Women and the Underground Railroad Movement," in *"We're Rooted Here and They Can't Pull Us Up": Essays in African Canadian Women's History*, ed. Peggy Bristow (Toronto: University of Toronto Press, 1994), 41–68.

48. Winks also wrote that Loyalist-line Blacks referred to fugitive-line Blacks as "niggers." Winks, *Blacks in Canada*, 465. As Winks' study originally was published in the early 1970s, he referred to Blacks using the term of the day—Negro.

49. Randolph Stakeman, "The Black Population of Maine, 1764–1900," *New England Journal of Black Studies* 8 (1989): 19.

50. Ibid.

51. Randall Kenan, *Walking on Water: Black American Lives at the Turn of the Twenty-First Century* (New York: Alfred A. Knopf, 1999), 91–92.

52. Twelfth (1900) Census of the United States (ms); Stakeman, "Households," 1900, 3.

53. Twelfth (1900) Census of the United States (ms); Stakeman, "Households," 1900, 1, 3.

54. Twelfth (1900) Census of the United States (ms); Stakeman, "Households," 1900, 2. It appears that Fannie Saunders Talbot married very young. She had given birth to two children by the time of the June 1900 census, but Charles Raynsford (also Rainsford) was her only surviving child.

55. Twelfth (1900) Census of the United States (ms); Stakeman, "Households," 1900, 2. According to the census, Bessie had had six children by that June, but only Sadie and Barbara survived.

56. Twelfth (1900) Census of the United States (ms); Stakeman, "Households," 1900, 1.

57. Twelfth (1900) Census of the United States (ms); Stakeman, "Households," 1900, 2.

58. Twelfth (1900) Census of the United States (ms); Stakeman, "Households," 1900, 1.

59. Twelfth (1900) Census of the United States (ms); Stakeman, "Households," 1900, 1. The Hardlings had another boarder from Canada who immigrated in 1898 and who worked as a river driver. His first name was Alfred, but his last name is indecipherable in the manuscript census.

60. Zelz and Zoidis, *Woodsmen and Whigs*, 31; Richard W. Judd, "The Lumber Industry in an Age of Change," in *Maine: The Pine Tree State from Prehistory to the Present*, ed. Richard W. Judd, Edwin A. Churchill, and Joel W. Eastman (Orono: University of Maine Press, 1995), 414.

61. Thirteenth (1910) Census of the United States (ms); Stakeman, "Households," 1910, 1–2. Rosalie's nephew was also living with the Clarks in 1910. He was a nineteen-year-old Canadian native who immigrated to the United States in 1904, the same year as Rosalie Clark. In 1910, the Clarks also lived next door to fellow Canadian natives Abner and Emma O'Ree Peters, and their four Maine-born children, Wesley, ten; Villas, seven; Elden, three; Winnifred, one. Abner Peters was Rosalie's brother. Villas Peters eventually would go on to marry Cecil Johnson, the son of William A. Johnson and Edith Mae Delaney Johnson. See obituary of Mrs. Abner Peters, *Bangor Daily News*, 25 December 1972, 1; obituary of Abner B. Peters, *Bangor Daily News*, 8 July 1938, 21.

62. Fourteenth (1920) Census of the United States (ms); Stakeman, "Households," 1920, 1.

63. Fourteenth (1920) Census of the United States (ms); Stakeman, "Households," 1920, 1.

64. Fourteenth (1920) Census of the United States (ms); Stakeman, "Households," 1920, 4, 5. The 1920 census does not indicate when Violet Holmes immigrated to the United States.

65. Fifteenth (1930) Census of the United States (ms).

66. Lena Bernard, sixty-three, was divorced from her husband Henry by 1930, at which time she was head of the household. Also living with her were two grandnephews, Theodore Dymond, four, and Clyde Dymond, Jr., three. Fifteenth (1930) Census of the United States (ms).

67. Twelfth (1900) Census of the United States (ms); Stakeman, "Households," 1900, 1 3.

68. Fifteenth (1930) Census of the United States (ms).

69. Twelfth (1900), Thirteenth (1910), Fourteenth (1920), and Fifteenth (1930) Censuses of the United States (ms). The figures are based on the number of Blacks located in the manuscript census.

70. Twelfth (1900) and Thirteenth (1910) Censuses of the United States (ms); Stakeman, "Households," 1900, 3; 1910, 2. The 1900 census records Charles Burt's birth date as "c. 1872." The census does not clarify where in the West Indies Burt was born, but according to the 1910 census, he still held alien status some twenty years after immigrating to the United States. Beatrice Burt was born in Maine, although she may not have been born in Bangor itself.

71. Twelfth (1900) and Thirteenth (1910) Censuses of the United States (ms); Stakeman, "Households," 1900, 1, 3; 1910, 2, 4.

72. Fourteenth (1920) and Fifteenth (1930) Censuses of the United States (ms); Stakeman, "Households," 1920, 3; Ed Matheson, "Bangor's Black Community," (Bangor-Brewer) *Register*, 15 June 1988.

73. Thirteenth (1910), Fourteenth (1920), and Fifteenth (1930) Censuses of the United States (ms); Stakeman, "Households," 1910, 4; 1920, 3.

74. Thirteenth (1910), Fourteenth (1920), and Fifteenth (1930) Censuses of the United States (ms); Stakeman, "Households," 1910, 4; 1920, 3.

75. The United States purchased the Danish West Indian islands in 1917 for $25 million. Eric Williams, *From Columbus to Castro: The History of the Caribbean 1492–1969* (New York: Vintage Books, 1984), 426.

76. Sullivan, "Recipe For Happy Old Age," 22; Earl Johnson of Bangor, interview with author, October 1999.

77. Twelfth (1900) and Thirteenth (1910) Censuses of the United States (ms); Stakeman, "Households," 1900, 1; 1910, 1.

78. U.S. Bureau of the Census, *Negro Population*, 62, 63.

79. Ibid., 61. New England also led the country in terms of the proportion of foreign-born Whites as part of the total White population.

80. Advertisement for the West Indian Product and Improvement Company, *New York Age*, 4 July 1907, 6.

Chapter 2. Earning a Living: Laboring Men and Women

1. Eighth (1860), Ninth (1870), and Tenth (1880) Censuses of the United States (ms); "Death of Dr. T. G. Brown," *Bangor Daily Whig and Courier*, 29 October 1887; and Advertisement of Dr. Brown, *Bangor Daily Whig and Courier*, June 1860, Bangor Museum and Center for History. Deborah Thompson, *Bangor, Maine, 1769–1914: An Architectural History* (Orono: University of Maine Press, 1988), 120. Thomas Brown married Belinda Douglas of Prospect, Maine; their granddaughter was Bangor resident and Union Station matron Linda Davis and their great-granddaughter was Dorothy Davis Wilson. The 1997 obituary of Dorothy Davis Wilson identifies her as "the great-granddaughter of Dr. Thomas G. Brown, one of the first physicians in Bangor." See Obituary of Dorothy (Davis) Wilson, *Bangor Daily News*, 16 February 1997; Mount Hope Cemetery Searchable Internment Database, Bangor.

2. Twelfth (1900) and Thirteenth (1910) Censuses of the United States (ms); Randolph Stakeman, "African American Households in Bangor, 1900–1920" (unpublished manuscript), 1900, 4; 1910, 6. "The Death of Fred D. Matheas—Had Served Faithfully for 36 Years in the Bangor Fire Department; Was Highly Esteemed," *Bangor Daily News*, 8 June 1912, 2. The manuscript census of Bangor and the city's directory consistently identify Matheas as a teamster or furniture mover. Only his obituary refers to his more than three decades as a fireman. Had his obituary not been found, this important aspect of his life may well have gone undetected, since it is not part of the local lore among African Americans in Bangor.

3. Carrie Dymond's (also Diamond, Dyamond) family life is difficult to reconstruct. The 1900 manuscript census identifies her husband as Randolph, as does the 1901 city directory, but the 1910 manuscript census identifies him as Gad. The 1900 manuscript census reports that Randolph Dymond was a coachman, and the 1901 city directory records his occupation as a teamster. Information about Carrie Dymond's children is equally confusing. The 1900 manuscript census records only two children for her, sons Elmer Ralph and Edgar, but the next decennial census identifies a fifteen-year-old daughter, Hester. Hester was older than both of the Dymond's sons, but does not appear on the 1900 census. This suggests that Hester Dymond was omitted from the 1900 census or that she was adopted by the Dymonds sometime between 1900 and 1910. Adoption is often recorded in the manuscript census, so the 1900 census may simply be in error. Twelfth (1900), Thirteenth (1910), Fourteenth (1920), and Fifteenth (1930) Censuses of the United States (ms); Stakeman, "Households," 1900, 1; 1910, 2; 1920, 1; 1901 Bangor city directory, 99.

4. Thirteenth (1910) and Fourteenth (1920) Censuses of the United States (ms); Stakeman, "Households," 1910, 4; 1920, 2. At the time of the 1920 census, Josephine Smallwood did share her house with her thirty-two-year-old nephew, Edward Ambrose, and his twenty-three-year-old wife, Rita. Edward Ambrose was the son of Annie

Warner and the stepson of James Warner, leading one to conclude that Smallwood and Annie Warner were sisters. Both Smallwood and Warner were born in Maine, and each listed their mother and father's birthplace as Kentucky.

5. The U.S. Bureau of the Census classifies occupation by category. In 1930, for example, the Bureau had ten different occupational categories for male workers: agriculture, forestry and fishing, mineral extraction, manufacturing and mechanical, transportation and communication, trade, public service not elsewhere classified, professional service, domestic and personal service, and clerical service. In their study of *Black Bostonians*, Horton and Horton reduced this complex classification system to a simple labor hierarchy with three categories: professional, skilled and entrepreneurial, and unskilled and semi-skilled. Myra Young Armstead uses a more complex hierarchy with eight labor categories in her study of Blacks in Newport, Rhode Island, and Saratoga Springs, New York. Armstead's categories are: professional, proprietary, managerial sales/clerical, skilled/semi-skilled, unskilled/service, agricultural, maritime, and military. See Fifteenth (1930) Census of the United States (ms); James Oliver Horton and Lois E. Horton, *Black Bostonians: Family Life and Community Struggle in the Antebellum North* (New York: Holmes and Meier, 1999), 139–40; Myra B. Young Armstead, *"Lord, Please Don't Take Me in August": African Americans in Newport and Saratoga Springs, 1870–1930* (Urbana: University of Illinois Press, 1999), 64. Because the United States workplace became more complex after the Civil War and because Armstead's classification clearly distinguishes proprietors as a separate class of workers, Armstead's hierarchy will be the basis for locating and analyzing Black Bangor's laborers, both male and female.

6. Howard Zinn, *A People's History of the United States 1492–Present*, rev. ed. (New York: HarperPerennial, 1995), 247.

7. Jacqueline Jones, *American Work* (New York: W. W. Norton, 1998), 341, 343.

8. Zinn, *People's History*, 247; "Introduction," in, Martha T. Briggs and Cynthia H. Peters, *Guide to the Pullman Company Archives* (Chicago: The Newberry Library, 1995), v–vii. www.newberry.org/nl/collections/PullmanGuilde.pdf (accessed 27 October 2004).

9. "Death of Dr. T. G. Brown"; *Vital Records of Prospect, Maine*, 176. The article in the *Whig and Courier* reports that Brown's retail shop was "near where D. Bugbee & Co. now keep." David Bugbee and Company was a book-binding company located at 5 Strickland Block. See *Maine State Year-Book and Legislative Manual, 1880–1881* (Portland: Hoyt, Fogg and Donham, 1880), 456.

10. Advertisement of Dr. Brown, *Bangor Daily Whig and Courier*, June 1860.

11. Virginia London, "Has Practiced Law 50 Years—Milton R. Geary, Minister-Lawyer, Feels Life Guided Directly By God," *Bangor Daily News*, 2–3 March 1963, 12.

12. "High Honor for Bangor Lawyer—Milton R. Geary Appointed the Maine Member of National Memorial Asso.," *Bangor Daily News*, 6 June 1925, *Bangor Daily News and Commercial* Scrapbook, v. 80, p. 64, Bangor Room, Bangor Public Library.

13. John Syrett, "Principle and Expediency: The Ku Klux Klan and Ralph Owen Brewster in 1924," *Maine History* 39 (Winter 2000–2001): 215–39. Maine women established chapters of the Women of the Ku Klux Klan (WKKK). Seals for the WKKK of Bath and of Augusta—the state capital, the seat of government, and the governor's headquarters—are held at the African American Collection of Maine, Jean Byers Sampson Center for Diversity, University of Southern Maine Libraries.

14. "High Honor for Bangor Lawyer," 64.

15. Ibid.

16. "Was Ordained as a Minister—Milton R. Geary Admitted to Baptist Conference Pulpit at West Hampden," *Bangor Daily News*, 14 October 1927, *Bangor Daily News and Commercial* Scrapbook, v. 91, p. 6, Bangor Room, Bangor Public Library.

17. "Rev. Geary, Noted Maine Negro, Dies," *Bangor Daily News*, 24 June 1964, 1–2.

18. Penobscot County Records of Probate, File 6568 (W. Johnson), 15620 (C. Talbot), 15619 (F. Talbot), and 26961 (P. Leek).

19. London, "Has Practiced Law 50 Years," 12.

20. *Maine Register, State Year-Book and Legislative Manual* (Portland: Portland Directory Company, 1920), p. 872–73; 1950, p. 620; 1950 Bangor city directory, 575; Penobscot County Probate Records, File for Milton R. Geary and Fahy Heughan Geary.

21. Thirteenth (1910) and Fifteenth (1930) Censuses of the United States (ms); Stakeman, "Households," 1910, 1.

22. "See Johnson First," *Bangor Daily News*, 7 June 1924, 13; "W. A. Johnson Passes Away on Saturday—Esteemed Citizen Prominent in Bangor Music 25 Years," *Bangor Daily Commercial*, 10 April 1937; "Mothers of France Photo Play Supreme at the Nickel Theatre," *Bangor Daily News*, n.d. For samples of Bangor Symphony Orchestra programmes, see Bangor Symphony Orchestra Programmes, microfilm, Bangor Room, Bangor Public Library. During the Bangor Symphony Orchestra's twenty-first season (1916–1917), Johnson played the viola under the direction of conductor Horace Mann Pullen, the same man who taught Johnson to play violin and viola. At this time, Adelbert Wells Sprague played cello. By the orchestra's twenty-sixth season (1921–1922), Johnson continued to play the viola under direction of Sprague, now the conductor.

23. Twelfth (1900) and Thirteenth (1910) Censuses of the United States (ms); Stakeman, "Households," 1900, 2; 1910, 3; Obituary of Dorothy (Davis) Wilson, *Bangor Daily News*, 19 February 1997, B5; "Mrs. Linda Davis Retires after 33 Years with MCRR," *Bangor Daily News*, 20 December 1940, 7; Obituary of Mrs. Charles L. Davis, *Bangor Daily News*, 16 December 1971, 22. Born in Bangor in 1872, Linda Brooks' parents moved her to Massachusetts where she attended the New England Conservatory and apparently lived after her marriage to Charles Davis. The 1900 census still finds Brooks a single woman as she taught music in Bangor. Her daughter, Dorothy, was born in Bangor in late 1905, allowing Linda Brooks Davis a short window of time to have lived in Massachusetts as a married woman.

24. "Mrs. Linda Davis Retires After 33 Years With MCRR," 7.

25. Ibid.

26. Ibid.; Obituary of Mrs. Charles L. Davis, *Bangor Daily News*, 16 December 1971, 22. According to the *Bangor Daily News* article on her retirement, Davis had only planned to winter in Washington, D.C., and to return to Bangor for the summer. It also reported that she had moved in and out of Bangor several times in her life.

27. Fifteenth (1930) Census of the United States (ms); 1930 Bangor city directory, 14–15, 309. Callie Mills Peters' entry in the 1930 city directory confirms her Washington Street residence, but does not identify her occupation. Peters is not listed among the faculty and administrators at Bangor High, the city's only public high school, nor among the city's other urban and suburban schools. Nonetheless, the photograph of the Pond Street School's teachers and students, dated circa 1925 to 1935, includes what appears to be an African American school teacher, quite possibly Callie Mills Peters.

28. Fifteenth (1930) Census of the United States, Population, vol. 1, part 1, 2; Population, vol. 4 (Occupations, by States).

29. University of Maine Alumni Association, *The University of Maine Alumni Directory 2000* (White Plains: Bernard C. Harris Publishing Co., Inc., 2000), 405, 991; 1940 Bangor city directory, 229. In Orangeburg, Beryl Warner probably interned at South Carolina State University. In the video documentary *Anchor of the Soul,* interviewees such as Harold Richardson recounted how they were told that they could not teach in Maine.

30. See Stephanie J. Shaw, *What a Woman Ought to Be and to Do: Black Professional Women Workers During the Jim Crow Era* (Chicago: University of Chicago Press, 1996). For a history of HBCUs, see Henry N. Drewry and Humphrey Doermann, *Stand and Prosper: Private Black Colleges and their Students* (Princeton: Princeton University Press, 2001).

31. 1901, 1914 Bangor city directories; "See Johnson First."

32. Marie Sullivan, "Recipe For Happy Old Age—Be Good Wife and Mother and Do for Others, Says Bangor Nonagenarian," *Bangor Daily News,* 24 January 1963, 22.

33. "See Johnson First."

34. Ibid.

35. "W. A. Johnson Passes Away."

36. Earl Johnson also shared in the family's musical talent. He was a trombonist and would have been a senior in the Bangor High School Band when it won the New England championship in 1928. "Earle's Radio Service Modern Repair Shop," *Bangor Daily Commercial,* 11 March 1939, *Bangor Daily News and Commercial* Scrapbook, v. 124, p. 54–55, Bangor Room, Bangor Public Library.

37. 1923–1924 Bangor city directory, 89; Twelfth (1900) Census of the United States (ms); Stakeman, "Households," 1900, 3.

38. Armstead, *"Lord, Please Don't Take Me in August,"* 94.

39. Twelfth (1900), Thirteenth (1910), Fourteenth (1920), and Fifteenth (1930) Censuses of the United States (ms); Divorce record of Lena Bernard and Henry C. Bernard, Maine Divorce Records, vol. 17, p. 72, microfilm roll #4, Maine State Archives; Stakeman, "Households," 1900, 3; 1910, 4; 1920, 1; 1901 Bangor city directory, 58.

40. Twelfth (1900), Thirteenth (1910), Fourteenth (1920), and Fifteenth (1930) Census of the United States (ms): Stakeman, "Households," 1900, 3; 1910, 4; 1920, 1; 1921–1922 Bangor city directory, 397.

41. Fifteenth (1930) Census of the United States (ms); Obituary of James A. Cromwell, *Bangor Daily News*, 17 July 1974, 27. James Cromwell's wife was Esther Grace Cromwell; see Obituary of Esther Grace Cromwell, *Bangor Daily News*, 21 September 1948, 6.

42. Armstead, *"Lord, Please Don't Take Me In August,"* 64, 65.

43. Twelfth (1900) Census of the United States (ms); Stakeman, "Households," 1900.

44. City of Bangor Record of Mortgage, v. 28: 1; v. 38: 454; v. 43: 185; v. 42: 423; v. 55: 345; Randall Kenan, *Walking on Water: Black American Lives at the Turn of the Twenty-First Century* (New York: Alfred A. Knopf, 1999), 90.

45. City of Bangor Record of Mortgage, v. 25, p. 298–9; v. 35, p. 112, 403.

46. Twelfth (1900) and Thirteenth (1910) Censuses of the United States (ms); Stakeman, "Households," 1900, 4; 1910, 1, 6. "Death of Fred Matheas," *Bangor Daily News*, 8 June 1912, 2.

47. Thirteenth (1910) and Fourteenth (1920) Censuses of the United States (ms); Stakeman, "Households," 1910, 2; 1920, 3. City of Bangor Record of Mortgages v. 41: 98; v. 55: 175.

48. Fifteenth (1930) Census of the United States (ms); Obituary of James H. Warner, *Bangor Daily News*, 6 January 1943, 5.

49. Twelfth (1900) and Thirteenth (1910) Censuses of the United States (ms); Stakeman, "Households," 1900, 3; 1910, 5. The 1900 manuscript census records that Mason's father was born in Spain and that his mother was born in Ireland. Nonetheless, Mason consistently was counted among Bangor's African American population.

50. Twelfth (1900), Thirteenth (1910), and Fourteenth (1920) Censuses of the United States, (ms); Stakeman, "Households," 1900, 2; 1910, 3, 1920, 3; Mount Hope Cemetery Internment Records.

51. Susan Williams McElroy, "Black + Woman = Work: Gender Dimensions of the African American Economic Experience," in *The African American Urban Experience: Perspectives from the Colonial Period to the Present*, ed. Joe W. Trotter, Earl Lewis, and Tera W. Hunter (New York: Palgrave MacMillan, 2004), 144; Fifteenth (1930) Census of the United States (ms); 1930 Bangor city directory, 168, 333, 407.

52. 1880–1881 *Maine Register*, 455; 1900–1901 *Maine Register*, 653; Twelfth (1900) Census of the United States (ms); Stakeman, "Households," 1900, 1, 3, 4.

53. Fifteenth (1930) Census of the United States (ms); *Maine Register*: 1910–1911, 707; 1920–1921, 856–7; 1930–1931, 1010–11; 1940–1941, 516–17; 1950–1951, 612.

54. Fourteenth (1920) and Fifteenth (1930) Censuses of the United States (ms); 1930 Bangor city directory, 260, 434; Obituary of Mrs. John R. Mahoney, *Bangor Daily News*, 19 February 1934, 11. It is unclear if or what Louise Mahoney may have named her shop, for the city directory does not provide a distinct business name for her salon. Louise Mahoney's shop was one floor above the Elite Beauty Shoppe, 16 Post Office Square, room 206. Although Louise Mahoney died in February of 1934, her name still appeared in the 1935 city directory as living with her husband on Division Street. See Bangor city directory, 1935, 142.

55. Fourteenth (1920) and Fifteenth (1930) Censuses of the United States (ms); Jacqueline Jones, *Labor of Love, Labor of Sorrow: Black Women, Work, and the Family from Slavery to the Present* (New York: Basic Books, Inc., 1985), 214–15. For advertisements of Madam C. J. Walker's hair products, see the advertising pages of the African American newspaper, the *New York Age*, ca. 1913. See, for example, 13 July 1913. For the most recent biography of Madam C. J. Walker, see A'Lelia Bundles, *On Her Own Ground: The Life and Times of Madam C. J. Walker* (New York: Scribner, 2001). Bundles is Walker's great-great-granddaughter.

56. Twelfth (1900) and Fourteenth (1920) Censuses of the United States (ms); Stakeman, "Households," 1900, 1; 1920, 1.

57. Thirteenth (1910), Fourteenth (1920), and Fifteenth (1930) Censuses of the United States(ms); Stakeman, "Households," 1910, 2; 1920, 4, 5; 1920–1921 *Maine Register*, 883.

58. Fifteenth (1930) Census of the United States (ms); Richard C. Youngken, *African Americans in Newport: An Introduction to the Heritage of African Americans in Newport, Rhode Island, 1700–1945* (Newport: Rhode Island Historical Preservation and Heritage Commission and Rhode Island Black Heritage Society, 1998), 52; Robert Austin Warner, *New Haven Negroes: A Social History* (New Haven: Yale University Press, 1940), 237–38. Franco-American women comprised one of the largest groups of mill workers in Maine. See, for example, Carol Toner, "'Hard Work to Make Ends Meet': Voices of Maine's Working-Class Women in the Late Nineteenth Century," *Maine History* 42, no. 1 (August 2004): 23–45.

59. Shoshana Hoose, "Proud Roots," *Maine Sunday Telegram*, 17 February 1991, 2F.

60. Kenan, *Walking on Water*, 90. Significant lore has been built around the figure of Panzy Talbot, and she looms large in the memories of Bangor's remaining Black residents.

61. Fourteenth (1920) Census of the United States (ms); Stakeman, "Households," 1920, 2; 1920–1921 Bangor city directory, 344; Ed Matheson, "Retrospective: Bangor's Black Community," (Brewer-Bangor) *Register*, 8 June 1988, 9.

62. Twelfth (1900) Census of the United States (ms); Stakeman, "Households," 1900, 3.

63. Thirteenth (1910) and Fifteenth (1930) Censuses of the United States (ms); Stakeman, "Households," 1910, 3; Bangor city directories: 1930, 360; 1940, 217; 1950, 255.

64. Shoshana Hoose, "Crossroads," *Maine Sunday Telegram*, 24 February 1991, 2F.

65. Fourteenth (1920) and Fifteenth (1930) Censuses of the United States (ms); Stakeman, "Households," 1920, 1; 1930 Bangor city directory, 41, 343.

66. Thirteenth (1910), Fourteenth (1920), and Fifteenth (1930) Censuses of the United States (ms); Stakeman, "Households," 1920, 1, 4; Bangor city directories: 1912, 297, 372; 1921–1922, 337, 411; 1930, 246, 337, 401, 444.

67. During the latter part of the nineteenth century, the choice to work as live-in or live-out help became highly political. Black women exercised the right to control their own labor, to set a respectable wage for their labor, and to safeguard their roles as wives and mothers as much as they could. They also were successful in defeating legislation that sought to regulate their position as domestic workers and to profit from the new regulatory infrastructure. See Tera W. Hunter, "Domination and Resistance: The Politics of Wage Household Labor in New South Atlanta," in *We Specialize in the Wholly Impossible: A Reader in Black Women's History*, ed. Darlene Clark Hine, Wilma King, and Linda Reed (New York: Carlson Publishing, Inc., 1995), 343–57; and Hunter, *To 'Joy My Freedom: Southern Black Women's Lives and Labors after the Civil War* (Cambridge: Harvard University Press, 1997).

68. Fourteenth (1920) and Fifteenth (1930) Censuses of the United States (ms); Stakeman, "Households," 1920, 5; 1920 and 1930 Bangor city directories.

69. Fifteenth (1930) Census of the United States (ms); 1930 Bangor city directory, 167, 222, 424, 467, 505. Worthen and Company occupied room 615 of the building.

70. Twelfth (1900) Census of the United States (ms); Stakeman, "Households," 1900, 1; 1901 Bangor city directory.

71. Twelfth (1900) Census of the United States (ms); Stakeman, "Households," 1900, 3.

72. The 1900 census does not indicate how long Carrie Hardling had been living in the United States. Twelfth (1900) Census of the United States (ms); Stakeman, "Households," 1900, 1, 2, 4.

73. Thirteenth (1910) Census of the United States (ms); Stakeman, "Households," 1910, 2, 3, 5, 6, 7.

74. Fifteenth (1930) Census of the United States (ms).

75. Tera W. Hunter, "'The Brotherly Love for which this City is Proverbial Should Extend to All': The Everyday Lives of Working-Class Women in Philadelphia and Atlanta in the 1890s," in *The African American Urban Experience*, ed. Joe W. Trotter, Earl Lewis, and Tera W. Hunter (New York: Palgrave Macmillan, 2004), 83.

76. Hunter, *To 'Joy My Freedom*, 56–57; Hunter, "Everyday Lives of Working-Class Women," 83.

77. Mary Mills was the widow of George Mills. Fifteenth (1930) Census of the United States (ms); 1930 Bangor city directory, 281, 522.

78. Thirteenth (1910) Census of the United States (ms); Stakeman, "Households," 1910.

79. See Stephanie J. Shaw's discussion of the effects of divorce on Southern Black women in *What A Woman Ought to Be and to Do*, 127–30.

80. Twelfth (1900) Census of the United States (ms); interview by author with Lloyd George of Bangor, October 1999.

81. London, "Has Practiced Law 50 Years," 12; Fifteenth (1930) Census of the United States (ms).

82. Thirteenth (1910), Fourteenth (1920), and Fifteenth (1930) Censuses of the United States (ms); Stakeman, "Households," 1910, 2, 4, 5; 1920, 1, 4.

83. Larry Tye, *Rising from the Rails: Pullman Porters and the Making of the Black Middle Class* (New York: Henry Holt and Company, 2004), 88, 93–96.

84. Ibid., 88, 165; Gerald L. Gill, "Introduction to Part V: Protest and Progress, 1900–1945," in *Making a Living: The Work Experience of African Americans in New England*, ed. Robert L. Hall with Michael M. Harvey (Boston: New England Foundation for the Humanities, 1995), 504.

85. Benjamin E. Mays, "Working for the Pullman Company," in *Making a Living*, 524–27; Tye, *Rising from the Rails*, 79.

86. Fourteenth (1920) and Fifteenth (1930) Censuses of the United States (ms); Stakeman, "Households," 1920, 1; Tye, *Rising from the Rails*, 88.

87. Twelfth (1900) and Fourteenth (1920) Censuses of the United States (ms); Stakeman, "Households," 1900, 1; 1920, 1–4.

88. Kenan, *Walking on Water*, 79.

89. Interview with Helena Dymond George, 16 November 1992, Bangor Historical Society.

90. Twelfth (1900), Thirteenth (1910), Fourteenth (1920), and Fifteenth (1930) Censuses of the United States (ms); Stakeman, "Households, 1900, 1, 2, 4; 1910, 1–6.

91. Thirteenth (1910) Census of the United States (ms); Stakeman, "Households," 1910, 1, 2, 3.

92. Thirteenth (1910) Census of the United States (ms); Stakeman, "Households," 1910, 4, 5.

93. Twelfth (1900), Thirteenth (1910), Fourteenth (1920), and Fifteenth (1930) Censuses of the United States (ms); Stakeman, "Households," 1900, 1, 2; 1910, 4; 1920, 1, 4.

94. Briton Cooper Busch, "Cape Verdeans in the American Whaling and Sealing Industry, 1850–1900," in *Making a Living*, 422–39; Gill, "Introduction," 502.

95. See Sara Mendelson and Patricia Crawford, "The Makeshift Economy of Poor Women," in *Women in Early Modern England, 1550–1720* (Oxford: Clarendon Press, 1998), 256–300.


## Chapter 3. Daily Life: Rhythms of the Community

1. Fifteenth (1930) Census of the United States (ms); 1930 Bangor city directory, 418, 476; Sanborn Fire Insurance Maps, 1914–1949, Reel 3427 (Bangor), 20.

2. Fifteenth (1930) Census of the United States (ms); 1930 Bangor city directory, 476; Sanborn Fire Insurance Map, 66.

3. *Stewart's Atlas of the State of Maine*, 12th ed. (South Paris, Maine: J. H. Stewart and Co., 1902); Fifteenth (1930) Census of the United States (ms); Bangor city directories: 1930, 418, 476; 1940, 304; Sanborn Fire Insurance Map, 20.

4. Fifteenth (1930) Census of the United States (ms);1930 Bangor city directory, 451; Sanborn Fire Insurance Map, 1. The 1930 directory also lists Abe Segal at 98 Oak Street.

5. Fifteenth (1930) Census of the United States (ms); 1930 Bangor city directory, 423, 424.

6. Fifteenth (1930) Census of the United States (ms); 1930 Bangor city directory, 443, 444; Sanborn Fire Insurance Map, 4.

7. Fifteenth (1930) Census of the United States (ms); 1930 Bangor city directory, 457; Sanborn Fire Insurance Map, 70. The Bangor city directory reports that truckman Robert McMahon also resided at 10 Patten Street.

8. Fifteenth (1930) Census of the United States (ms); 1930 Bangor city directory, 457; Sanborn Fire Insurance Map, 70.

9. Fifteenth (1930) Census of the United States (ms); 1930 Bangor city directory, 413; Sanborn Fire Insurance Map, 71.

10. Fifteenth (1930) Census of the United States (ms); 1930 Bangor city directory, 460; Sanborn Fire Insurance Map, 6. According to the 1930 city directory, the Wickers' neighbor, at 6 Pleasant Street, was Frank Toole.

11. *Stewart's Atlas of Maine*; 1940 Bangor city directory, 304. James H. Mundy, *Hard Times, Hard Men: Maine and the Irish, 1830–1860* (Scarborough, Maine: Harp Publications, 1990), 30.

12. Fourteenth (1920) and Fifteenth (1930) Censuses of the United States (ms); Randolph Stakeman, "African American Households in Bangor, 1905–1920" (unpublished manuscript), 1920, 1; Sanborn Fire Insurance Map, 61; 1930 Bangor city directory, 436.

13. Fifteenth (1930) Census of the United States (ms); 1930 Bangor city directory, 436; Sanborn Fire Insurance Map, 61.

14. Fifteenth (1930) Census of the United States (ms); 1930 Bangor city directory, 457; Sanborn Fire Insurance Map, 66.

15. Fifteenth (1930) Census of the United States (ms); 1930 Bangor city directory, 456; Sanborn Fire Insurance Map, 66.

16. Fifteenth (1930) Census of the United States (ms); 1930 Bangor city directory, 472; Sanborn Fire Insurance Map, 66. The Leeks' neighbor at 150 Third Street was Robert Hughes.

17. Fifteenth (1930) Census of the United States (ms); 1930 Bangor city directory, 423; Sanborn Fire Insurance Map, 66.

18. Fifteenth (1930) Census of the United States (ms); 1930 Bangor city directory, 465.

19. Fifteenth (1930) Census of the United States (ms).

20. Fourteenth (1920) and Fifteenth (1930) Censuses of the United States (ms);

Stakeman, "Households," 1920, 3; 1930 Bangor city directory, 404; Sanborn Fire Insurance Map, 66.

21. Fourteenth (1920) and Fifteenth (1930) Censuses of the United States (ms); Stakeman, "Households," 1920, 3; 1930 Bangor city directory, 404; Sanborn Fire Insurance Map, 66. The Sanborn map notation beside the stable reads "for 22 Carroll."

22. Fifteenth (1930) Census of the United States (ms); 1930 Bangor city directory, 475; Sanborn Fire Insurance Map, 65.

23. Fifteenth (1930) Census of the United States (ms); 1930 Bangor city directory, 431; Sanborn Fire Insurance Map, 60. The 1930 city directory identifies Albert P. O'Ree as head of the household at 498 Hammond Street, while the manuscript census for that year clearly indicates that it was Nettie, his older sister, who owned the house.

24. Fifteenth (1930) Census of the United States (ms); 1930 Bangor city directory, 432; Sanborn Fire Insurance Map, 60.

25. Fifteenth (1930) Census of the United States (ms).

26. Fifteenth (1930) Census of the United States (ms); 1930 Bangor city directory, 422, 447, 397. The 1930 city directory conflicts with the census, and records that Sandy Gordon lived at 21 Allen Street.

27. Fifteenth (1930) Census of the United States (ms); 1930 Bangor city directory, 412, 458, 452; Sanborn Fire Insurance Map, 63.

28. Fifteenth (1930) Census of the United States (ms); 1930 Bangor city directory, 437, 440; Sanborn Fire Insurance Map, 56. In July of 1898, William A. Johnson purchased from Mrs. Eunice Dubay, for "one dollar and other valuable consideration," a one-story frame building located on the corner of Washington and Pine streets. In February of 1899, Johnson sold the same one-story building to Louis Kinstein for $19.50. City of Bangor Record of Mortgage, v. 23, p. 66, 67.

29. Fifteenth (1930) Census of the United States (ms); 1930 Bangor city directory, 434, 435; Sanborn Fire Insurance Map, 9.

30. Fifteenth (1930) Census of the United States (ms); 1930 Bangor city directory, 479; Sanborn Fire Insurance Map, 38.

31. Fifteenth (1930) Census of the United States (ms); 1930 Bangor city directory. 399; Sanborn Fire Insurance Map, 37. The Bangor city directory says that Elizabeth McManus occupied the other half of Marion Peters' double house; her address was 5 Blake Place.

32. Fifteenth (1930) Census of the United States (ms); 1930 Bangor city directory, 456, 458, 455; Sanborn Fire Insurance Map, 28, 29, 34.

33. U.S. Bureau of the Census, *Negroes in the United States, 1920–1932* (Washington, D.C.: GPO, 1935), 253.

34. Ed Matheson, "Retrospective: Bangor's Black Community," (Brewer-Bangor) *Register*, 8 June 1988, 1; 1930 Bangor city directory, 404, 423, 456, 457, 472, 475, 476.

35. Fifteenth (1930) Census of the United States (ms).

36. Matheson, "Bangor's Black Community," 9.

37. Ibid.

38. Fifteenth (1930) Census of the United States (ms); 1901, 1914, 1919, and 1923–1924 Bangor city directories.

39. Myra B. Young Armstead, *"Lord, Please Don't Take Me in August": African Americans in Newport and Saratoga Springs, 1870–1930* (Urbana: University of Illinois Press, 1999), 47–48.

40. Ibid., 49.

41. Ibid., 49–50.

42. Robert Austin Warner, *New Haven Negroes: A Social History* (New Haven: Yale University Press, 1940), 196 and corresponding map.

43. Ibid., 195, 197, 200, 201.

44. Ibid., 200–201.

45. Fourteenth (1920) Census of the United States (ms): Stakeman, "Households," 1920, 1–4.

46. U.S. Bureau of the Census, *Mortality Statistics 1931, Thirty-Second Annual Report* (Washington, D.C.: GPO, 1935), 67; U.S. Bureau of the Census, *Negroes in the United States*, 367.

47. *Bangor Daily News*, 2 January 1895; Twelfth (1900) and Fourteenth (1920) Censuses of the United States (ms); Stakeman, "Households," 1900, 4; 1920, 2. According to the 1900 census, Andrew Burtt was born in November of 1871, and Maggie Burtt was born in March of 1874. Daughter Clara was born in September of 1889 and would not yet have reached her sixth birthday when her sister Lydia died on 1 January 1895. Records of the Mount Hope Cemetery, where Lydia Agnes Burtt was interred, indicate that she had been born in Houlton, Maine. See Mount Hope Cemetery Corporation Internment Index, Bangor Room, Bangor Public Library.

48. Twelfth (1900), Thirteenth (1910), and Fourteenth (1920) Censuses of the United States (ms); Stakeman, "Households, 1900, 2.

49. Twelfth (1900) Census of the United States (ms); Stakeman, "Households," 1900, 2, 3. According to the 1900 manuscript census, Daniel Mason's wife, Jennie, was a thirty-seven-year-old White female, who had been born in Maine.

50. Obituary of Murray V. Scott, *Bangor Daily News*, 14 July 1939, 10.

51. "Veteran B&A Employe[e] Is Asphyxiated," *Bangor Daily News*, 25 February 1946, 1–2.

52. Ibid., 2.

53. Ibid., 1, 2; Probate Records of Estate of Albert E. Martini, File #20732, Office of Probate, Penobscot County, Maine; Probate Records of Estate of Bessie E. Martini, File #20733, Office of Probate, Penobscot County, Maine.

54. Probate Records of Estate of Albert E. Martini, File #20732, and Bessie E. Martini, File #20733, Office of Probate, Penobscot County, Maine. Resolving the estates of Albert and Bessie Martini was not without further controversy. Roland A.

Simmons, a long-time friend and seeming confidante of Albert Martini, submitted an affidavit to the probate court that Panzy Talbot and Albert Martini's stepson, Maurice I. Alberts, had taken "in fraud and deceit" materials from Martini's office at the Bangor and Aroostook Railroad. Simmons alleged that Alberts took materials from the office "with the connivance of Talbot," and requested a detailed inventory of everything taken from the office. Simmons depicted himself as Martini's "next and near friend, and personal confident" and that Martini had some of his property at the time of his death. Simmons requested a contempt order be served against Talbot and Alberts, as co-conspirators; Talbot stood to inherit the balance of the Martini estate, valued at more than one thousand dollars. In July 1946, an order was issued to serve Panzy Talbot with a petition to appear before the probate court on 21 July 1946. The probate judge did not find in Simmons' favor, and the claims against Talbot (and Alberts) were thrown out. Bessie Martini would have inherited the estate and would have been able to make a claim against the Bangor Gas Company had she survived. See Estate of Albert E. Martini, File #20732, Office of Probate, Pensobscot County, Maine.

55. "Veteran B&A Employe[e] is Asphyxiated," 2.

56. Twelfth (1900) Census of the United States (ms); Stakeman, "Households," 1900, 2, 3, 4.

57. See *Bangor Daily News*, 6 November 1961, 2; Obituary of Sterling A. Dymond, *Bangor Daily News*, 5 August 1954, 25.

58. Obituaries of Mrs. Elizabeth Warner, *Bangor Daily News*, 23 September 1953, 12; James H. Warner, *Bangor Daily News*, 6 January 1943, 5; William A. Johnson, *Bangor Daily News*, 21 January 1913, 2.

59. Thirteenth (1910) and Fifteenth (1930) Censuses of the United States (ms); Divorce Index Cards 1892–1964, microfilm roll # 1, 7, 10; Maine Divorce Records, Frank and Emma O'Ree, vol. 2: 27; Elizabeth and George O'Ree, vol. 2: 75; Marion and Stanley Peters, vol. 16: 182; Callie and Ernest Peters, vol. 16: 194; Lena and Henry Bernard, vol. 17: 72; Jesse and Jane Hudlan, vol. 19: 99.

60. Fifteenth (1930) Census of the United States (ms).

61. Randall Kenan, *Walking on Water: Black American Lives at the Turn of the Twenty-First Century* (New York: Alfred A. Knopf, 1999), 81.

62. Ibid.

63. Ibid.

64. Ibid.

65. Fifteenth (1930) Census of the United States (ms). Sterling and Janie Dymond were both naturalized by the early 1900s.

66. Kenan, *Walking on Water*, 81–82.

67. Ibid., 92.

68. Ibid., 93.

69. City of Bangor Record of Mortgage, v. 27, p. 453–4; Johnson's watch had case #1875 and works #64146. City of Bangor Record of Mortgage, v. 23, p. 136; v. 27, p. 278–79.

70. Apparently Gordon was selling the property to Henry C. Parker for six dollars; City of Bangor Record of Mortgage, v. 27, p. 295.

71. The firm comprised Frank Noyes, George Nutter, and A. G. Noyes. William Hale Beckford, *Leading Business Men of Bangor, Rockland and vicinity; embracing Ellsworth, Bucksport, Belfast, Camden, Rockport, Thomaston, Old Town, Orono, Brewer* (Boston: Mercantile Publishing Co., 1888), 71. The furnace was a #167 Crown Kineo brand model. The system was to be paid within six months of purchase; City of Bangor Record of Mortgage, v. 33, p. 233.

72. City of Bangor Record of Mortgage, v. 37, p. 317; v. 38, p. 166; v. 40, p. 223. Parlor stove #14; kitchen cabinet #1429. Hodgkins and Fiske Company advertisement, *Bangor Daily News*, 22 May 1916, 9.

73. City of Bangor Record of Mortgage, v. 35, p. 494; v. 37, p. 129.

74. The terms of payment were two dollars per week; City of Bangor Record of Mortgage, v. 57, p. 157.

75. The cost of Stewart's purchase was $114.70 plus a 10 percent interest charge of $11.47. The payment terms were ten dollars down and eight dollars per month; City of Bangor Record of Mortgage, v. 53, p. 56.

76. Judith S. Goldstein, *Crossing Lines: Histories of Jews and Gentiles in Three Communities* (New York: William Morrow and Co., 1992), 103.

77. City of Bangor Record of Mortgage, v. 57, p. 447–48. Range #973. Purchase terms were ten dollars down, eleven payments of eight dollars, and one payment of seven dollars. A 6 percent interest charge was to be levied on overdue charges; City of Bangor Record of Mortgage, v. 57, p. 310.

78. The Monarch typewriter was #35679; City of Bangor Record of Mortgage, v. 37, p. 447.

79. The typewriter was model 2, serial #63063, with a rubber cover; City of Bangor Record of Mortgage, v. 39, p.20. The purchase of the Remington typewriter included exchange of an old machine. Terms on the new typewriter were twenty-five dollars on delivery and ten dollars on the fifteenth of each month; City of Bangor Record of Mortgage, v. 44, p. 445.

80. Studebaker serial #3101984; motor #EL94496, 6 cylinder; City of Bangor Record of Mortgage, v. 55, p.245. The terms of payment for the cash register were eight dollars down, four monthly payments of $7.50, and a twenty dollar trade-in credit for Buck's current National Register machine; City of Bangor Record of Mortgage, v. 56, p. 499.

81. Register #711 with standard denomination keys. Payment terms of ten dollars cash, five monthly payments of ten dollars, and one monthly payment of fifteen dollars.

82. Craig H. Roell, *The Piano in America, 1890–1940* (Chapel Hill: University of North Carolina Press, 1989), 156.

83. Sterling piano style 65, #58481. Purchase terms were ten dollars down, seven dollars per month, and 6 percent interest; City of Bangor Record of Mortgage, v. 35, p. 413.

84. Player piano style #106694 for twenty-nine months. The terms were ten dollars down and six dollars per month; City of Bangor Record of Mortgage, v. 42, p. 13. The Angelus piano style was #25218. Purchase terms were two hundred dollars credit for old piano trade in, and balance at seven dollars per month for twenty-five months, starting July 1918; City of Bangor Record of Mortgage, v. 42, p. 167. "Ad for the Angelus Orchestral Piano," *The Player Piano Page*, www.pianola.demon.co.us, 12 July 2001, accessed 18 October 2004.

85. "Victor Talking Machine Company History Timeline," *The Victor Victrola Page*, www.victor-victrola.com, 7 July 2004, accessed 18 October 2004; City of Bangor Record of Mortgage, v. 30, p. 238.

86. The terms for the piano purchase were fifty dollars credit on current piano, ten dollars down, and monthly payments of six dollars. The interest charged was six dollars; City of Bangor Record of Mortgage, v. 31, p. 98–99. The terms for the stove were monthly payments of five dollars; City of Bangor Record of Mortgage, v. 63, p. 260.

87. City of Bangor Record of Mortgage, v. 32, p. 107–108.

88. The payment terms for the player piano were twenty-five dollars down and twenty dollars on the first of each month; City of Bangor Record of Mortgage, v. 38, p. 158. The payment terms for the phonograph were fifty dollars down and six dollars on the first of each month; City of Bangor Record of Mortgage, v. 41, p. 365.

89. City of Bangor Record of Mortgage, v. 51, p. 333.

90. Cyril Ehrlich, *The Piano: A History*, rev. ed. (Oxford: Clarendon Press, 1990), 134–35; Roell, *The Piano in America*, 158–59.

91. Roell, *The Piano in America*, 159.

92. 1920–1921 *Maine Register*, 855; Goldstein, *Crossing Lines*, 102.

93. The Chevrolet Landau was serial #12AA33481 and motor #3264017. The terms of payment were seventy-five dollars down and the balance in equal monthly payments; City of Bangor Record of Mortgage, v. 55, p. 449–50. The 1929 Chevrolet Sedan was serial #12AC75838 and motor #1004925. The payment terms were two payments of thirty dollars and thirteen payments of twenty-five dollars; City of Bangor Record of Mortgage, v. 64, p. 457. The 1930 Sedan was serial #12AD29423 and motor #1650914; City of Bangor Record of Mortgage, v. 64, p. 289.

94. Condition of payment on the truck was twenty-five dollars per month; City of Bangor Record of Mortgage, v. 44, p. 184.

95. The terms for the seven-passenger touring car were twenty-five dollars a month until paid and 6 percent interest; City of Bangor Record of Mortgage, v. 46, p. 329. The 1927 Dodge sedan was serial #902758 and motor #D977374; City of Bangor Record of Mortgage, v. 63, p. 518–9. The 1930 vehicle was serial #DA-103499 and engine #H-123417; City of Bangor Record of Mortgage, v. 64, p. 424.

96. City of Bangor Record of Mortgage, v. 53, p. 470. Motor #13837561; Wallace Leek agreed to make weekly payments of five dollars; City of Bangor Record of

Mortgage, v. 64, p. 451. Touring car serial #1018475, engine #31521. Alton Leek also had a weekly payment of five dollars on his automobile; City of Bangor Record of Mortgage, v. 62, p. 283. Essex Coach serial #219064, motor # 287398. The automobile cost $380.00, plus $41.80 in financing. The payment terms were $152.00 down, one payment of $22.52, and eleven payments of $22.48 per month; City of Bangor Record of Mortgage, v. 56, p. 430–31.

97.  April 1927: Serial and motor numbers 14 –757– 042. The purchase price was $450, freight and tax were $46, the Warford Transmission surcharge was $120, and a finance charge of $48 was levied. The terms of the purchase were $236 down and the balance in six equal monthly payments; City of Bangor Record of Mortgage, v. 55, p. 439. April 1928: Purchase terms were $195 down and twelve monthly payments of $30.50; City of Bangor Record of Mortgage, v. 58, p. 156.

98.  Ford Sedan and Accessories #6283042. The car cost $737.25, insurance was $4.00, and an interest rate of 6 percent was applied. The terms of the automobile purchase were one hundred dollars down, one hundred on 21 July 1923, and forty dollars or more per month; City of Bangor Record of Mortgage, v. 47, p. 401.

99.  Shoshana Hoose, "Proud Roots," *Maine Sunday Telegram,* 17 February 1991, F1; Kenan, *Walking on Water,* 90.

100.  Probate records of Bessie E. Martini, file #20733, Office of Probate, Penobscot County, Bangor, Maine.

101.  Donald Bogle, *Toms, Coons, Mulattoes, Mammies and Bucks,* 3d ed. (New York: Continuum, 1994), 6, 9.

102.  Ibid., 8.

103.  Ibid., 10 –13; *Ethnic Notions,* prod. and dir. Marlon Riggs, 58 min., California Newsreel, 1987, videocassette.

104.  "All Coons Look Alike," advertisement for M. Lynch and Company, Bangor city directory, 1901, 5.

105.  Sanfords Ginger advertisement, *Bangor Daily News,* 1 September 1916, 4.

106.  Beckford, *Leading Business Men of Bangor,* 52, 57. The Gerald E. Talbot Collection, part of the African American Collection of Maine, includes more than fifty original professional photographs of African Americans taken in Bangor between the mid-1880s and the 1920s. Photographers Weston (23 Hammond Street), Lansil (28 Main Street), Heath (6 State Street), Gerrity (11 State Street), and Chalmers (22 State Street) are all represented in that collection, but the overwhelming majority of photographs were taken at Frank Weston's studio. This is, of course, only a sample of the photographs taken of Blacks over this period, but it seems that Weston was very popular with at least a sector of the Black community. See 1900 –1901 *Maine Register,* 668, for a complete list of photographers in turn-of-the-century Bangor.

107.  Cheryl A. Wall, *Women of the Harlem Renaissance* (Bloomington: Indiana University Press, 1995), 2; quoted in Deborah Willis and Carla Williams, *The Black Female Body: A Photographic History* (Philadelphia: Temple University Press, 2002), 145.

108. Willis and Williams, *The Black Female Body*, 145, 147.

109. See Deborah Willis, *Picturing Us: African American Identity in Photography* (New York: The New Press, 1994), 7.

110. Claudia Brush Kidwell with Nancy Rexford, foreword to *Dressed for the Photographer: Ordinary Americans and Fashion, 1840–1900*, by Joan Severa (Kent, Ohio: Kent State University Press, 1995), xii–xiii.

111. The Davis doll is part of the Brooks Collection at the Bangor Museum and Center for History.

112. bell hooks, "In Our Glory: Photography and Black Life," in *Picturing Us*, 47.

113. Ibid., 47–48.

Chapter 4. Feeling Their Twoness: Black Bangor's Institutional Maturation

1. Randall Kenan, *Walking on Water: Black American Lives at the Turn of the Twenty-First Century* (New York: Alfred A. Knopf, 1999), 82.

2. "U.S.O. Is Carrying on a Successful Program—Columbia Street Home Is Popular with Soldiers," *Bangor Daily News*, 11 January 1943, 3.

3. W. E. B. DuBois, *The Souls of Black Folk* (1903; reprint, New York: Signet Classic, 1995), 45.

4. Kenan, *Walking on Water*, 80.

5. Myra B. Young Armstead, *"Lord, Please Don't Take Me in August": African Americans in Newport and Saratoga Springs, 1870–1930* (Urbana: University of Illinois Press, 1999), 48, 115–16.

6. Robert Austin Warner, *New Haven Negroes: A Social History* (New Haven: Yale University Press, 1940), 211–17.

7. Mark J. Sammons and Valerie Cunningham, *Portsmouth Black Heritage Trail Resource Book*, 2d ed. (Portsmouth: Portsmouth Black Heritage Trail, 1998), 185–86, 206–207. Mark J. Sammons and Valerie Cunningham, *Black Portsmouth: Three Centuries of African-American Heritage* (Hanover, N.H.: University Press of New England, 2004), 145–52. The African Methodist Episcopal Church closed in the 1950s and was leveled in the 1960s in the name of urban renewal.

8. Kenan, *Walking on Water*, 85.

9. The 1921–1922 Bangor city directory and Deborah Thompson's inventory report different dates for the rebuilding of St. John's Episcopal Church. According to the city directory, St. John's was rebuilt in 1913, but Thompson reports that it reopened to worship in 1914 and formally reopened in 1918. 1921–1922 Bangor city directory, 423; Thompson, *Bangor, Maine, 1769–1914: An Architectural History* (Orono, Maine: University of Maine Press, 1988), 180–81, 464–65.

10. Obituaries of Mrs. Charles R. Talbot, *Bangor Daily News*, 19 January 1962, 20; Arvella L. (McIntyre) Talbot, *Bangor Daily News*, 12 September 1995, B5; Mrs. Hubert

Scott, *Bangor Daily News*, 25 August 1942, 13; Herbert D. McCarty, *Bangor Daily News*, 17 June 1935, 5; Goodridge A. Leek, *Bangor Daily News*, 20 December 1978, 33; Mrs. Goodridge A. Leek, *Bangor Daily News*, 5 July 1957, 18; Helena G. (Dymond) George, *Bangor Daily News*, 12 August 1998, B7; Mrs. Jane M. Dymond, *Bangor Daily News*, 20 March 1959, 19; Mrs. Linda Davis, *Bangor Daily News*, 7 December 1971, 28; Mrs. Margaret J. Burtt, *Bangor Daily News*, 22 January 1938, 27; Dorothy Ethel (McIntyre) Dymond, *Bangor Daily News*, n.d.

11. 1921–1922 Bangor city directory, 423; Thompson, *Bangor, Maine*, 335–37; Marie Sullivan, "Recipe for Happy Old Age — Be Good Wife and Mother and Do for Others, Says Bangor Nonagenarian," *Bangor Daily News*, 24 January 1963, 22.

12. 1921–1922 Bangor city directory, 422; Thompson, *Bangor, Maine*, 462.

13. Thompson, *Bangor, Maine*, 463.

14. 1921–1922 Bangor city directory, 422; Thompson, *Bangor, Maine*, 349–50.

15. Obituaries of Shenton A. Peters, *Bangor Daily News*, 13 December 1963, 20; Mrs. John J. Peters, *Bangor Daily News*, 8 November 1954; Viva F. Dymond, *Bangor Daily News*, 1 March 1988, 4; Mrs. Florence Dymond, *Bangor Daily News*, 2 January 1940; Blanche O. Dymond, *Bangor Daily News*, 20 November 1970, 24; Mrs. Mabel Derricks, *Bangor Daily News*, 14 September 1953, 18.

16. Thompson, *Bangor, Maine*, 177.

17. Ibid., 333.

18. Obituary of Mrs. Claude Hoyt, *Bangor Daily News*, 1 August 1938, 12.

19. "The History of Williams Temple Church of God in Christ," Pamphlet of Williams Temple Church of God in Christ, Portland, Maine. n.d. For more on Williams Temple, see www.williamstemple.org.

20. 1890 Bangor city directory, 338–39.

21. Thompson, *Bangor, Maine*, 199–200.

22. Abigail Ewing Zelz and Marilyn Zoidis, *Woodsmen and Whigs: Historic Images of Bangor, Maine* (Virginia Beach: Donning Company Publishers, 1991), 183; Thompson, *Bangor, Maine*, 200

23. Thompson, *Bangor, Maine*, 484.

24. Bangor High School Catalogue, Fall Term 1894, 9, 12, 13. Bangor Room, Bangor Public Library.

25. The languages offered were English, French, German, Greek, and Latin. Mathematics covered algebra, geometry, and trigonometry. History was that of Greece, Rome, France, and England; it also included mythology and civics. Science instruction was in physical geography, botany, physics, chemistry, and astronomy. Bangor High School Catalogue 1904–1905, 21. Bangor Room, Bangor Public Library.

26. Bangor High School Catalogue, 1904–1905, 22, 23.

27. Ibid., 23, 24.

28. Ibid., 24.

29. Booker T. Washington, *Up From Slavery*, ed. W. Fitzhugh Brundage (Boston: Bedford/St. Martin's, 2003), 141–51; DuBois, *Souls of Black Folk*, 79–95.

30. Bangor High School Catalogue, 1916–1917, 7, 8, 9.

31. Ibid., 10, 12, 13.

32. Ibid., 11.

33. Bangor High School Handbook, 1953–1954, 5; Bangor High School Handbook, 1936–1937, 16. Bangor Room, Bangor Public Library.

34. Bangor High School Catalogue 1953–1954. Bangor Room, Bangor Public Library.

35. Ibid.

36. Bangor High School *Oracle*, June 1923.

37. Ibid.

38. Bangor High School *Oracle*, June 1926.

39. Ibid.; Fifteenth (1930) Census of the United States (ms).

40. Bangor High School *Oracle*, June 1926.

41. Bangor High School *Oracle*, June 1927.

42. Ibid.

43. Bangor High School *Oracle*, June 1928.

44. Ibid.

45. Bangor High School *Oracle*, June 1931, 1932, 1933, 1934, 1937, 1938, 1939.

46. Bangor High School *Oracle*, June 1942, 1946.

47. John Bapst High School, *The Bapstonian*, 1946, 22. Bangor Public Library.

48. Bangor High School *Oracle*, June 1950.

49. Ibid.

50. Ibid.

51. Bangor High School *Oracle*, June 1953.

52. Kenan, *Walking on Water*, 82.

53. Ibid.

54. "Campus History." University of Maine Website, www.umaine.edu. n.d. (accessed 20 October 2004).

55. It is somewhat unclear whether Matheas actually graduated in 1907 or 1908. According to the alumni file, Matheas graduated in 1907, but a review of University of Maine commencement programs reveals that the degree was conferred in June 1908. See Fred W. Matheas, Class of '07, University of Maine Alumni Files and University of Maine 37th Annual Commencement Programme, Wednesday, 10 June 1908, Special Collections, Fogler Library, University of Maine. Matheas was buried in Philadelphia's Eden Cemetery. For information on his life in Philadelphia, see obituary of Fred W. Matheas, Philadelphia *Bulletin*, 20 January 1970. A copy of this obituary can be found in the Special Collections' alumni file on Matheas.

56. Milton Roscoe Geary, Class of 1913, University of Maine Alumni File, Special Collections, Fogler Library, University of Maine; "Reverend Geary, Noted

Maine Negro Dies," *Bangor Daily News*, 24 June 1964; "W. A. Johnson Passes Away on Saturday," *Bangor Daily Commercial*, 10 April 1937.

57. University of Maine Alumni Association, *The University of Maine Alumni Directory, 2000* (White Plains: Bernard C. Harris Publishing Co., Inc., 2000), 991.

58. University of Maine *Prism*, 1941, 66, 227; University of Maine Alumni Association, *The University of Maine Alumni Directory, 2000*, 560. According to the *Prism*, Warner transferred to the University of Maine from Bennett College.

59. Kenan, *Walking on Water*, 91–95.

60. Ibid., 93–94.

61. Ibid., 82.

62. Fifteenth (1930) Census of the United States (ms); *Roster of Maine in the Military Service of the United States and Allies in the World War 1917–1919* (Augusta, Maine: Maine State Legislature, 1929), vol. 1, 1141, 495; vol. 2, 97; Obituary of Charles R. Talbot, *Bangor Daily News*, 18 July 1969, 22.

63. Kenan, *Walking on Water*, 80.

64. Ibid.

65. Sammons and Cunningham, *Portsmouth Black Heritage Trail Resource Book*, 225–28.

66. "Geary Named Director of U.S.O. Unit," *Bangor Daily News*, 18 July 1944, 13; "U.S.O. Is Carrying on a Successful Program," 3.

67. "U.S.O. Is Carrying on a Successful Program," 3.

68. Obituaries of Sterling A. Dymond, Sr., *Bangor Daily News*, 5 August 1954, 25; Mrs. Jane M. Dymond, 20 March 1959, 19; George R. Leek, 5 January 1945, 3; David J. Sickles, 16 February 1967, 23; Mrs. Mabel Derricks, 14 September 1953, 18; Helena G. (Dymond) George, 12 August 1998, B7.

69. "First Annual Ball of the Tarragona Club, Essenic Hall, Wednesday Evening, 31 May 1905" (Bangor: Bangor Co-operative Printing Co.), Gerald E. Talbot Collection, African American Collection of Maine, Jean Byers Sampson Center for Diversity in Maine, University of Southern Maine Libraries.

70. "Tarratine Club, Bangor, Maine, 1900," Special Collections, Fogler Library, University of Maine, 367.T177.

71. Mrs. J. C. Croly, *The History of the Woman's Club Movement in America*, (New York: Henry G. Allen and Co., 1897), 523, 525, 535–37, 556. Hannibal Hamlin had a highly significant political life in Maine before and after he became Lincoln's vice-president. He became a congressman in 1843, served eight years as a Maine senator, and became governor of the state in 1856. After serving under President Abraham Lincoln from 1861 to 1865, Hamlin served an additional eleven years in the Senate. Born in Paris Hill, Maine, Hannibal Hamlin retired to Bangor in 1882 after his political career. In Bangor, Hamlin helped found the exclusive Tarratine Club, the private club at which several members of the Black community eventually would find employment. After Hamlin's death in July 1891, citizens commis-

sioned a bronze statue in his likeness. The monument, which stands eight feet tall, was installed on the Kenduskeag Mall in 1927. Zelz and Zoidis, *Woodsmen and Whigs*, 114.

72. Interview by the author with Herbert Heughan, October 1999, Hampden, Maine; H. Althea Warner Mandel to Maureen Elgersman Lee, September 1999.

73. The *Woman's Era* 1, no. 1 (24 March 1894): 8.

74. Dorothy Salem, "National Association of Colored Women," in *Black Women in America: An Historical Encyclopedia*, vol. 2, ed. Darlene Clark Hine, Elsa Barkley Brown, and Rosalyn Terborg-Penn (Brooklyn: Carlson Publishing, 1993), 845.

75. "Women's Clubs at Boston," *New York Age*, 17 August 1905, 3; "New England Women Meeting this Week," *New York Age*, 23 July 1914, 1; "Women's Federation of Northeast Meet," *New York Age*, 15 July 1915, 5.

76. Interview by the author with Lloyd George, October 1999; Obituary of Nora Dymond, *Bangor Daily News*, 27–28 January 1973, 24.

77. Kenan, *Walking on Water*, 80.

78. Interview with Lloyd George, October 1999.

79. Kenan, *Walking on Water*, 80.

80. Sullivan, "Be Good Wife and Mother and Do for Others," 22.

81. Bangor city directories: 1910–1911, 393, 394; 1940, 307, 308.

82. 1912 Bangor city directory, 388; Charles H. Brooks, *The Official History and Manual of the Grand United Order of Odd Fellows in America* (Freeport, New York: Books for Libraries Press, 1971), 226.

83. The directory identifies G.U.O.O.F. treasurer, and later secretary, Mahoney as James R. Mahoney, rather than John R. or J. Robert Mahoney. Bangor city directories: 1912, 388; 1914, 388; 1919, 386; 1921–1922, 424; 1923–1924, 47; obituaries of Mrs. Margaret J. Burtt, *Bangor Daily News*, 22 January 1938, 27; Mrs. Hubert Scott, 25 August 1942, 13.

84. 1919 Bangor city directory; 1923–1924 Bangor city directory, 478; Elwood Watson, interview with Lloyd George and Sterling Dymond, Jr., 17 October 1994, Maine Folklife Center, Accession no. 2355, University of Maine. According to the interview, the lodge continued strong until approximately 1945; it went into "recess," restarted in the mid-1960s, and has continued ever since.

85. Elwood Watson, interview with Lloyd George and Sterling Dymond, Jr., 17 October 1994.

86. Carolyn Wedin, *Inheritors of the Spirit: Mary White Ovington and the Founding of the NAACP* (New York: John Wiley and Sons, Inc., 1998), 169; Mary White Ovington, *Black and White Sat Down Together: The Reminiscences of an NAACP Founder*, ed. Ralph E. Luker (New York: The Feminist Press, 1996), xiii, xv, 89, 94; Application for Charter of Bangor, Maine, Branch of the National Association for the Advancement of Colored People, October 1920; NAACP Secretary to Queenie Peters, 12 January 1921; J. Robert Mahoney to James W. Johnson, 14 October 1920, NAACP

Branch Files, Box G-84, Folder 1, Manuscript Division, Library of Congress. The NAACP Portland Branch received its charter in mid-1920. See Application for Charter of Portland, Maine Branch of the National Association for the Advancement of Colored People, March 1920; NAACP Field Secretary to Edgar B. Howard, 24 July 1920; NAACP Branch Files, Box G-84, Folder 3, Manuscript Division, Library of Congress.

87. In November 1920, President J. Robert Mahoney requested that Mrs. Charles Talbot and Josephine Smallwood be added to the list of charter members. See J. Robert Mahoney to James W. Johnson, 6 November 1920, NAACP Branch Files, Box G-84, Folder 1, Manuscript Division, Library of Congress.

88. "Ku Klux Klan Makes Progress in Bangor," *Bangor Daily News*, 18 October 1922, *Bangor Daily News* Scrapbook, vol. 68, p. 16. "Eloquent Plea for Colored Race—Work of National Association Set Forth by Able Speaker," *Bangor Daily News*, 21 February 1921, *Bangor Daily News* Scrapbook, vol. 61, p. 48, Bangor Room, Bangor Public Library; Maine PBS, "Home: The Story of Maine—A Timeline of Maine History," www.mainepbs.org/hometsom/timelines, 4 March 2003.

89. "No K.K.K. in City Hall," *Bangor Daily News*, 28 February 1923, *Bangor Daily News* Scrapbook, vol. 69, p. 152.

90. Ibid.

91. "Eloquent Plea for Colored Race."

92. Ibid.

93. Queenie Peters to NAACP National Office, 22 July 1921, NAACP Branch Files, Box G-84, Folder 1, Manuscript Division, Library of Congress.

94. "Colored People Held a Meeting—Organization to Aid Progress of Negroes Plan for Future Activities," *Bangor Daily News*, 12 January 1925; "Colored People's Association Has Interesting Session," *Bangor Daily News*, 9 February 1925, *Bangor Daily News* Scrapbook, vol. 77, p. 176; vol. 78, p. 80.

95. "Colored People Held a Meeting."

96. Ibid.

97. "Colored People's Association Has Interesting Session."

98. "Eloquent Plea For Colored Race"; "Colored People Held a Meeting"; "Colored People's Association Has Interesting Session."

99. "Colored People's Association Has Interesting Session."

100. Robert W. Bagnall to Mr. W. B. A. Stewart, 3 November 1926, NAACP Branch Files, Box G-84, Folder 1, Manuscript Division, Library of Congress.

101. Milton R. Geary to Robert W. Bagnall, 28 February 1927, NAACP Branch Files, Box G-84, Folder 1, Manuscript Division, Library of Congress.

102. Form Letters to New England Chapters Re: 1931 New England Conference; E. Frederic Morrow to Joseph G. LeCount, 25 August 1939, NAACP Branch Files, Box I-G114, Manuscript Division, Library of Congress.

103. 1950 Bangor city directory, 411.

104. Ed Matheson, "Retrospective: Bangor's Black Community" (Brewer-Bangor) *Register,* 8 June 1988, 9; Matheson, "The Parker Street Kids: A Look Back at Bangor's Black Athletes" (Brewer-Bangor) *Register,* 8 June 1988.

105. Matheson, "Parker Street Kids," n.p.

106. Armstead, *"Lord, Please Don't Take Me in August,"* 106, 129.

107. Ibid., 106–107.

108. Ibid., 128, 129.

109. Warner, *New Haven Negroes,* 287–88.

110. Sammons and Cunningham, *Portsmouth Black Heritage Trail Resource Book,* 209–214; Sammons and Cunningham, *Black Portsmouth: Three Centuries of African-American Heritage* (Hanover, N.H.: University Press of New England, 2004), 141–59.

111. Warner, *New Haven Negroes,* 284, 285.

## Epilogue: African Americans in Bangor since 1950

1. "Married Fifty Years Ago," *Bangor Daily News,* 6 November 1951, 2; Jeanine Fenwick, "Well-Loved Bangor Woman Is Leaving," *Bangor Daily News,* 12 November 1952, 12; Obituary of Mrs. Elizabeth Warner, *Bangor Daily News,* 23 September 1953, 12; "Mr. and Mrs. Raynsford Talbot Celebrate Golden Anniversary," *Bangor Daily News,* 10 June 1958, 11.

2. "Columbia Street Church Scene of Attractive Wedding Saturday," *Bangor Daily News,* 14 March 1955.

3. See the following obituaries, all in the *Bangor Daily News:* Sterling A. Dymond, Sr., 5 August 1954, 25; Mrs. Janie M. Dymond, 20 March 1959, 19; Mrs. Mabel Derricks, 14 September 1953, 18; Mrs. Goodridge Leek, 5 July 1957, 18; Mrs. John J. Peters, 8 November 1954; Mrs. Helen Wise, 30 October 1951; Mrs. Cleveland McCarty, 18 January 1968; Charles R. Talbot, 18 July 1969, 22; Shenton A. Peters, 13 December 1963, 20; Mrs. Charles R. Talbot, 19 January 1962, 20; Mrs. Abner Peters, 25 December 1972, 19; Mrs. Linda Davis, 7 December 1971, 28; Goodridge A. Leek, 20 December 1978, 33; Austin L. Gordon, 19 May 1986, 8; Helena G. (Dymond) George, 12 August 1998, B7; Arvella L. (McIntyre) Talbot, 12 September 1995, B5.

4. Obituaries of Mrs. John J. Peters, *Bangor Daily News,* 8 November 1954; Janie Dymond, 20 March 1959, 19; Nora Dymond, 27–28 January 1973, 24.

5. Selena Ricks, "Cause for celebration," *Portland Press Herald,* 26 September 2004.

6. Shoshana Hoose, "Proud Roots," *Maine Sunday Telegram,* 17 February 1991; and "Crossroads," *Maine Sunday Telegram,* 24 February 1991, 2F.

7. Abigail Ewing Zelz and Marilyn Zoidis, *Woodsmen and Whigs: Historic Images of Bangor, Maine* (Virginia Beach: Donning Company, 1991), 183–84; Marc Berlin et al., *The Story of Bangor: A Brief History of Maine's Queen City* (Bangor: Bookmarc's Publishing, 1999), 72–73; Ryan R. Robbins, "Masonic Hall a total loss—Fire still burn-

ing nearly 24 hours later—Hundreds watch demolition," 16 January 2004; "Bangor says goodbye to piece of history," 17 January 2004; "Masons hope to salvage some relics from rubble," 25 January 2004; *The Journal,* http://bangorinfo.com/Journal/january2004journal.html (accessed 20 October 2004).

8. Berlin et al., *Story of Bangor,* 72–73.

9. U.S. Bureau of the Census, *1990 Census of the Population,* vol. 1, part 21 (Washington, D.C.: GPO, 1992), 16, 55, 42. The 2000 Census allowed respondents to identify themselves as members of more than one racial group. In Bangor, 320 persons identified themselves as Black or African American alone; 447 identified themselves as Black or African American and another race. Those who identified themselves biracially may have been included already in the former group, and, therefore, may have been counted twice. For that reason, I am using the figure of 320 Blacks in Bangor in 2000. U.S. Bureau of the Census, *2000 Census of Population and Housing PHC-3–21* (Washington, D.C.: GPO, 2003), 8; U.S. Bureau of the Census, Table DP-1, Profile of General Demographic Characteristics—Bangor, 2000. http://censtats.census.gov/dtata/ME/1602302795.pdf (accessed 27 October 2004).

# Selected Bibliography

Primary Sources

Bangor City Directory. Bangor Room, Bangor Public Library; Maine State Library; Maine Historical Society.

*Bangor Daily News.* Bangor Room, Bangor Public Library; Maine State Library.

*Bangor Daily News and Commercial.* Bangor Room, Bangor Public Library.

*Bangor Daily Whig and Courier.* Bangor Room, Bangor Public Library.

Bangor High School *Oracle.* Bangor Public Library.

Bangor High School Catalogue. Bangor Room, Bangor Public Library.

Bangor Probate Records. Office of Probate, Penobscot County, Maine.

Bangor Symphony Orchestra Programmes (microfilm). Bangor Room, Bangor Public Library.

City of Bangor Record of Mortgages. Special Collections, Fogler Library, University of Maine.

Interview with Helena Dymond George. 16 November 1992. Bangor Historical Society.

Interview with Sterling Dymond, Jr. 16 November 1992. Bangor Historical Society.

*Maine Register, State Yearbook, and Legislative Manual 1920–21.* Portland: Portland Directory Company, 1920.

*Maine Register and State Year-Book and Legislative Manual, 1949–50.* Portland: Fred L. Tower, 1949.

*Maine State Year-Book and Legislative Manual, 1880–1881.* Portland: Hoyt Fogg and Donham, 1880.

Maine Vital Statistics, 1908–1922, Maine State Archives.

Maine Divorce Index Cards, 1892–1964. Maine State Archives.

Maine Divorce Records, vol. 18, 20. Maine State Archives.

*Maine Sunday Telegram.* Portland Public Library.

Mount Hope Cemetery Corporation Internment Index. Bangor Room, Bangor Public Library.

Nominal Census of New Brunswick, 1881, 1891, 1901. Fogler Library, University of Maine.

NAACP Branch Files. Manuscript Division, Library of Congress.

*New York Age*

*Portland Press Herald*. Portland Public Library.

*Roster of Maine in the Military Service of the United States and Allies in the World War 1917 – 1919*. Augusta, Maine: Maine State Legislature, 1929.

Sanborn Map Company. Sanborn Fire Insurance Maps. Teaneck, N.J.: Chadwych-Healey, 1983. Microfilm, University of Southern Maine Libraries.

U.S. Bureau of the Census. Eighth (1860) Census of the United States (ms), micro-film reels 445 – 447. Maine State Archives.

———. Ninth (1870) Census of the United States (ms), microfilm reels 553 – 554. Maine State Archives.

———. Tenth (1880) Census of the United States (ms), microfilm reels 485 – 486. Maine State Archives.

———. Twelfth (1900) Census of the United States (ms), microfilm reels 597 – 598. Maine State Archives.

———. Thirteenth (1910) Census of the United States (ms), microfilm reels 544 – 545. Maine State Archives.

———. Fourteenth (1920) Census of the United States (ms), microfilm reels 645 – 646. Maine State Archives.

———. Fifteenth (1930) Census of the United States (ms), microfilm reels 836 – 837. Maine State Archives.

———. *Mortality Statistics 1931, Thirty-Second Annual Report*, Washington, D.C.: GPO, 1935.

———. *Negro Population in the United States, 1790 – 1915*. New York: Arno Press and the New York Times, 1968.

———. *Negroes in the United States, 1920 – 1932*. Washington, D.C.: GPO, 1935.

———. *Ninth (1870) to Seventeenth (1950) Censuses of the United States*. Population. Washington, D.C.: GPO, 1873 – 1952.

———. *1990 Census of the Population*. Vol. 1, part 2. Washington, D.C.: GPO, 1992.

———. *2000 Census of the Population and Housing PHC-3 – 21*. Washington, D.C.: GPO, 2003.

University of Maine Alumni Records. Special Collections, Fogler Library, University of Maine.

University of Maine *Prism*. Special Collections, Fogler Library, University of Maine.

Watson, Elwood. Interview with Lloyd George and Sterling Dymond, Jr., 17 October 1994. Maine Folklife Center, University of Maine.

*Woman's Era*. Microfilm, Boston Public Library.

Secondary Sources

Albans, Constantine, Alan R. Miller, James H. Mundy, Jerome J. Nadelhaft, Charles G. Roundy, Earle G. Shettleworth Jr., and David C. Smith, eds. *Bygone Bangor*. Bangor: Bangor Publishing Co., 1976.

Alexis, Marcus. "Patterns of Black Consumption, 1935–1960." *Journal of Black Studies* 1, no. 1 (1970): 55–74.

*Anchor of the Soul: A Documentary about Blacks in Maine.* Produced and directed by Shoshana Hoose and Karine Odlin. 60min. 1994. Videocassette.

*Appleton's Cyclopaedia of American Biography*, vol. 4. New York: D. Appleton, 1889.

Armstead, Myra B. Young. *"Lord, Please Don't Take Me in August": African Americans in Newport and Saratoga Springs, 1870–1930.* Urbana: University of Illinois Press, 1999.

Beckford, William Hale. *Leading Business Men of Bangor, Rockland and Vicinity; embracing Ellsworth, Bucksport, Belfast, Camden, Rockport, Thomaston, Old Town, Orono, Brewer.* Boston: Mercantile Publishing Co., 1888.

Beedy, Helen Coffin. *Mothers of Maine.* Portland: Thurston Print, 1895.

Berlin, Marc, Ardeana Hamlin, Richard Shaw, and Gig Weeks. *The Story of Bangor: A Brief History of Maine's Queen City.* Bangor: Bookmarc's Publishing, 1999.

Blee, Kathleen M. *Women of the Klan: Racism and Gender in the 1920s.* Berkeley: University of California Press, 1991.

Bogle, Donald. *Toms, Coons, Mulattoes, Mammies and Bucks.* 3d ed. New York: Continuum, 1994.

Bolster, W. Jeffrey. *Black Jacks: African American Seamen in the Age of Sail.* Cambridge: Harvard University Press, 1997.

Briggs, Martha T., and Cynthia H. Peters. "Introduction" in *Guide to the Pullman Company Archives.* Chicago: The Newberry Library 1995. www.newberry.org/nl/collections/PullmanGuide.pdf, accessed 27 October 2004.

Bristow, Peggy, ed. *"We're Rooted Here and They Can't Pull Us Up": Essays in African Canadian Women's History.* Toronto: University of Toronto Press, 1994.

Brooks, Charles H. *The Official History and Manual of the Grand United Order of Odd Fellows in America.* Freeport, N.Y.: Books for Libraries Press, 1971.

Bundles, A'Lelia. *On Her Own Ground: The Life and Times of Madam C. J. Walker.* New York: Scribner, 2001.

Busch, Briton Cooper. "Cape Verdeans in the American Whaling and Sealing Industry, 1850–1900." In *Making a Living: The Work Experiences of African Americans in New England*, ed. Robert L. Hall and Michael M. Harvey, 422–42. Boston: New England Foundation for the Humanities, 1995.

Campbell, Mavis C. *Nova Scotia and the Fighting Maroons: A Documentary History.* Williamsburg, Mass.: College of William and Mary, 1990.

Castillo, George R. *My Life between the Cross and the Bars.* Shalimar, Fl.: G & M Publications, 1996.

Clark-Lewis, Elizabeth. *Living In, Living Out: African American Domestics in Washington, D.C., 1910–1940.* Washington, D.C.: Smithsonian Institution Press, 1994.

Collins, Patricia Hill. *Black Feminist Thought: Knowledge, Consciousness, and the Politics of Empowerment.* 2d ed. New York: Routledge, 2000.

Connolly, Michael C., ed. *They Change Their Sky: The Irish in Maine.* Orono, Maine: University of Maine Press, 2004.

Cowan, Ruth Schwartz. *More Work for Mother: The Ironies of Household Technology from the Open Hearth to the Microwave.* New York: Basic Books, Inc., 1983.

Craft, William, and Ellen Craft. *Running a Thousand Miles for Freedom.* London: William Tweedie, 1860.

Croly, Mrs. J. C. *The History of the Woman's Club Movement in America.* New York: Henry G. Allen and Co., 1897.

Curtis, Nancy C. *Black Heritage Sites: The North.* New York: The New Press, 1996.

Dodd, Donald B., compiler. *Historical Statistics of the States of the United States: Two Centuries of the Census, 1790–1990.* Westport, Conn.: Greenwood Press, 1993.

Donnan, Elizabeth. *Documents Illustrative of the History of the Slave Trade to America,* vol. 3. New York: Octagon Books, 1969.

Drewry, Henry N., and Humphrey Doermann. *Stand and Prosper: Private Black Colleges and Their Students.* Princeton: Princeton University Press, 2001.

DuBois, W. E. B. *The Souls of Black Folk.* 1903. Reprint, New York: Signet Classic/Penguin Putnam, 1995.

Ehrlich, Cyril. *The Piano: A History.* Rev. ed. New York: Oxford University Press, 1990.

*Ethnic Notions.* Produced and directed by Marlon Riggs. 58 minutes. California Newsreel, 1987. Videocassette.

Foy, Jessica H., and Thomas J. Schlereth, eds. *American Home Life, 1880–1930: A Social History of Spaces and Services.* Knoxville: University of Tennessee Press, 1992.

Franklin, John Hope, and Alfred A. Moss, Jr. *From Slavery to Freedom: A History of African Americans.* 8th ed. Boston: McGraw-Hill Higher Education, 2000.

Frost, Norman Seaver. *Frost Genealogy in Five Families.* West Newton, Mass.: Frost Family Association of America, 1926.

Giddings, Paula. *In Search of Sisterhood: Delta Sigma Theta and the Challenge of the Black Sorority Movement.* New York: William Morrow and Company, 1988.

———. *When and Where I Enter: The Impact of Black Women on Race and Sex in America.* New York: William Morrow and Company, 1984.

Ginger, Ray. *Age of Excess: The United States from 1877 to 1914.* New York: Macmillan, 1965.

Goings, Kenneth W., and Raymond A. Mohl, eds. *The New African American Urban History.* Thousand Oaks, Calif.: Sage Publications, 1996.

Goldstein, Judith S. *Crossing Lines: Histories of Jew and Gentiles in Three Communities.* New York: William Morrow and Co., 1992.

Grant, John N. *The Maroons in Nova Scotia.* Halifax: Formac, 2002.

Green, William A. *British Slave Emancipation: The Sugar Colonies and the Great Experiment 1830–1865.* Oxford: Clarendon Press, 1991.

Greene, Lorenzo Johnston. *The Negro in Colonial New England, 1620–1776.* New York: Columbia University Press, 1942.

Gregory, Alexis. *Families of Fortune: Life in the Gilded Age.* New York: Rizzoli International Publications, 1993.

Grizzle, Stanley G., with John Cooper. *My Name's Not George: The Story of the Brother-*

*hood of Sleeping Car Porters in Canada: Personal Reminiscences of Stanley G. Grizzle.* Toronto: Umbrella Press, 1998.

Groh, George W. *The Black Migration: The Journey to Urban America.* New York: Weybright and Talley, 1972.

Gross, Ernie. *Advances and Innovations in American Daily Life, 1600s–1930s.* Jefferson, N.C.: McFarland and Company, 2002.

Hall, Robert L., with Michael M. Harvey, eds. *Making a Living: The Work Experience of African Americans in New England.* Boston: New England Foundation for the Humanities, 1995.

Harris, William H. *Keeping the Faith: A. Philip Randolph, Milton P. Webster, and the Brotherhood of Sleeping Car Porters, 1925–1937.* Urbana: University of Illinois Press, 1991.

Haskell, John D., Jr., ed. *Maine: A Bibliography of Its History.* Hanover, N.H.: University Press of New England, 1983.

Henri, Florette. *Black Migration: Movement North, 1900–1920.* Garden City, N.Y.: Anchor Press/Doubleday, 1975.

Hine, Darlene Clark, and Kathleen Thompson. *A Shining Thread of Hope: The History of Black Women in America.* New York: Broadway Books, 1998.

Hirsch, Susan Eleanor. *After the Strike: A Century of Labor Struggle at Pullman.* Urbana: University of Illinois Press, 2003.

Hodges, Graham Russell, ed. *The Black Loyalist Directory: African Americans in Exile after the American Revolution.* New York: Garland Publishing, in Association with the New England Historic Genealogical Society, 1996.

hooks, bell. *Black Looks: Race and Representation.* Boston: South End Press, 1992.

———. "In Our Glory: Photography and Black Life." In *Picturing Us: African American Identity in Photography,* ed. Deborah Willis, 43–53. New York: The New Press, 1994.

Horton, James Oliver, and Lois E. Horton. *Black Bostonians: Family Life and Community Struggle in the Antebellum North.* Rev. ed. New York: Holmes and Meier, 1999.

Hunter, Tera W. "'The Brotherly Love for Which This City is Proverbial Should Extend to All': The Everyday Lives of Working-Class Women in Philadelphia and Atlanta in the 1890s." In *The African American Urban Experience,* ed. Joe W. Trotter, Earl Lewis, and Tera W. Hunter. New York: Palgrave Macmillan, 2004.

———. "Domination and Resistance: The Politics of Wage Household Labor in New South Atlanta." In *We Specialize in the Wholly Impossible: A Reader in Black Women's History,* ed. Darlene Clark Hine, Wilma King, and Linda Reed. New York: Carlson Publishing, 1995.

———. *To 'Joy My Freedom: Southern Black Women's Lives and Labors after the Civil War.* Cambridge: Harvard University Press, 1997.

Ierley, Merritt. *Open House: A Guided Tour of the American Home, 1637–Present.* New York: Henry Holt and Company, 1999.

Jackson, Kenneth T. *The Ku Klux Klan in the City, 1915–1930.* New York: Oxford University Press, 1967.

Johnson, Daniel M., and Rex R. Campbell. *Black Migration in America: A Social Demographic History.* Durham, N.C.: Duke University Press, 1981.

Jones, Jacqueline. *American Work.* New York: W. W. Norton and Co., 1998.

———. *Labor of Love, Labor of Sorrow: Black Women, Work, and the Family from Slavery to the Present.* New York: Basic Books, 1985.

Judd, Richard W., Edwin A. Churchill, and Joel W. Eastman, eds. *Maine: The Pine Tree State from Prehistory to the Present.* Orono, Maine: University of Maine Press, 1995.

Kenan, Randall. *Walking on Water: Black American Lives at the Turn of the Twenty-First Century.* New York: Alfred A. Knopf, 1999.

*The Ku-Klux Klan: Hearings before the Committee on Rules, House of Representatives, Sixty-Seventh Congress, First Session.* Washington, D.C.: GPO, 1921. Reprinted as Robert M. Fogelson and Richard E. Rubenstein, eds., *Mass Violence in America: Hearings on the Ku Klux Klan, 1921.* New York: Arno Press and the *New York Times*, 1969.

Kusmer, Kenneth L. "African Americans in the City since World War II: From the Industrial to the Postindustrial Era." In *The New African American Urban History*, ed. Kenneth W. Goings and Raymond A. Mohl, 320–68. Thousand Oaks, Calif.: Sage Publications.

Leavitt, Sarah A. *From Catharine Beecher to Martha Stewart: A Cultural History of Domestic Advice.* Chapel Hill: University of North Carolina Press, 2002.

Lemann, Nicholas. *The Promised Land: The Great Black Migration and How It Changed America.* New York: Alfred A. Knopf, 1991.

Lenz, Peter A. *Colonial New England Slavery (African, African-American, Indian) in Massachusetts, N.H. and Maine.* Noway, Maine: Dawnfire Educational Collective, 1996.

Lifshey, Earl. *The Housewares Story: A History of the American Housewares Industry.* Chicago: National Housewares Manufacturers Association, 1973.

Logan, Shirley Wilson. "'What Are We Worth': Anna Julia Cooper Defines Black Women's Work at the Dawn of the Twentieth Century." In *Sister Circle: Black Women and Work*, ed. Sharon Harley and The Black Women and Work Collective, 146–63. New Brunswick: Rutgers University Press, 2002.

Lumpkins, Charles. "Civil Rights Activism in Maine, 1945–1971." *Maine History* 36 (Winter–Spring 1997): 70–85.

Macrae, David. *The Americans at Home.* New York: E. P. Dutton and Co., 1952.

Marks, Carole. *Farewell—We're Good and Gone: The Great Black Migration.* Bloomington: Indiana University Press, 1989.

Mayo, Edith. *American Material Culture: The Shape of Things Around Us.* Bowling Green: Bowling Green State University Popular Press, 1984.

Mays, Benjamin E. "Working for the Pullman Company." In *Making a Living: The Work Experience of African Americans in New England*, ed. Robert L. Hall with Michael M. Harvey, 524–27. Boston: New England Foundation for the Humanities, 1995.

McAlester, Virginia, and Lee McAlester. *A Field Guide to American Houses.* New York: Alfred A. Knopf, 1984.

McCracken, Grant. *New Approaches to the Symbolic Character of Consumer Good and Activities.* Bloomington: Indiana University Press, 1988.

McElroy, Susan Williams. "Black + Woman = Work: Gender Dimensions of the African American Economic Experience." In *The African American Urban Experience: Perspectives from the Colonial Period to the Present,* ed. Joe W. Trotter, Earl Lewis, and Tera W. Hunter, 141–55. New York: Palgrave MacMillan, 2004.

Melish, Joanne Pope. *Disowning Slavery: Gradual Emancipation and "Race" in New England, 1780–1860.* Ithaca: Cornell University Press, 1998.

Mendelson, Sara, and Patricia Crawford. *Women in Early Modern England, 1550–1720.* Oxford: Clarendon Press, 1998.

*Miles of Smiles, Years of Struggle.* Produced by Paul Wagner and Jack Santino. 58 min. California Newsreel, 1983. Videocassette.

Morton, Desmond. *A Short History of Canada.* 3d ed. Toronto: McClelland and Stewart, 1997.

Mundy, James H. *Hard Times, Hard Men: Maine and the Irish, 1830–1860.* Scarborough, Maine: Harp Publications, 1990.

Mursaskin, William A. *Middle-Class Blacks in a White Society: Prince Hall Freemasonry in America.* Berkeley: University of California Press, 1975.

National Park Service. *Maine Catalog: Historic American Buildings Survey.* Augusta: Maine State Museum, 1974.

Osterweis, Rollin G. *Three Centuries of New Haven, 1638–1938.* New Haven: Yale University Press, 1953.

Ovington, Mary White. *Black and White Sat Down Together: The Reminiscences of an NAACP Founder.* Ed. Ralph E. Luker. New York: The Feminist Press, 1995.

Painter, Nell Irvin. *Black Exodusters: Black Migration to Kansas after Reconstruction.* New York: Knopf, 1976.

Parakilas, James, et al. *Piano Roles: Three Hundred Years of Life with the Piano.* New Haven: Yale University Press, 1999.

Perata, David D. *Those Pullman Blues: An Oral History of the African American Railroad Attendant.* New York: Twayne Publishers/Simon and Schuster Macmillan, 1996.

Piersen, William D. *Black Yankees: The Development of an Afro-American Subculture in Eighteenth-Century New England.* Amherst: University of Massachusetts Press, 1988.

Pleck, Elizabeth H. *Celebrating the Family: Ethnicity, Consumer Culture, and Family Rituals.* Cambridge: Harvard University Press, 2000.

Rhodes, Jane. *Mary Ann Shadd Cary: The Black Press and Protest in the Nineteenth Century.* Bloomington: Indiana University Press, 1998.

Rice, Arnold S. *The Ku Klux Klan in American Politics.* Washington, D.C.: Public Affairs Press, 1962.

Robinson, William H. *Black New England Letters: The Uses of Writings in Black New England.* Boston: Trustees of the Public Library of the City of Boston, 1977.

Roell, Craig H. *The Piano in America, 1890–1940.* Chapel Hill: University of North Carolina Press, 1989.

Rogozinski, Jan. *A Brief History of the Caribbean: From the Arawak and the Carib to the Present.* New York: Meridian Books, 1992.

Ross, Lawrence, Jr. *The Divine Nine: The History of African American Fraternities and Sororities.* New York: Kensington Publishing Corp., 2000.

Roth, Leland M. *A Concise History of American Architecture.* New York: Harper and Row Publishers, 1979.

Salem, Dorothy. "National Association of Colored Women." In *Black Women in America: An Historical Encyclopedia,* ed. Darlene Clark Hine, Elsa Barkley Brown, and Rosalyn Terborg-Penn, 842–51. Brooklyn: Carlson Publishing, 1993.

Sammons, Mark J., and Valerie Cunningham. *Black Portsmouth: Three Centuries of African-American Heritage.* Hanover, N.H.: University Press of New England, 2004.

———. *Portsmouth Black Heritage Trail Resource Book.* 2d ed. Portsmouth: Portsmouth Black Heritage Trail, 1998.

Santino, Jack. *Miles of Smiles, Years of Struggle: Stories of Black Pullman Porters.* Urbana: University of Illinois Press, 1989.

Seale, William. *The Tasteful Interlude: American Interiors through the Camera's Eye, 1860–1917.* New York: Praeger Publishers, 1975.

See, Scott W. *Riots in New Brunswick: Orange Nativism and Social Violence in the 1840s.* Toronto: University of Toronto Press, 1993.

Severa, Joan. *Dressed for the Photographer: Ordinary Americans and Fashion, 1840–1900.* Kent, Ohio: Kent State University Press, 1995.

Shaw, Richard. *Images of America: Bangor,* Vol. 2: *The Twentieth Century.* Dover, New Hampshire: Arcadia Publishing, 1997.

———, compiler. *The Old Photographs Series: Bangor.* Bath and Augusta, Maine: Allan Sutton, 1994.

Shaw, Stephanie J. *What a Woman Ought to Be and to Do: Black Professional Women Workers during the Jim Crow Era.* Chicago: University of Chicago Press, 1996.

Shriver, Edward O. *Go Free: The Antislavery Impulse in Maine, 1833–1855.* Orono, Maine: University of Maine Press, 1970.

Siebert, Wilbur H. "The Underground Railroad in Massachusetts." *New England Quarterly* 9, no. 3 (September 1936): 447–67.

Smith, Henry Atterbury, compiler. *500 Small Houses of the Twenties.* New York: Dover Publications, 1990.

Smith, Jessie Carney. *Black Firsts: 4,000 Ground-Breaking and Pioneering Historical Events.* 2d. rev. ed. Canton, Mich.: Visible Ink Press, 2003.

Spain, Daphne. *How Women Saved the City.* Minneapolis: University of Minnesota Press, 2001.

Spray, W. A. *The Blacks in New Brunswick.* Fredericton, New Brunswick: Brunswick Press, 1972.

Stakeman, Randolph. "African American Households in Bangor, 1900–1920." (Unpublished manuscript), August 1999.

———. "The Black Population of Maine, 1764–1900." *New England Journal of Black Studies* 8 (1989): 17–35.

———. "Slavery in Colonial Maine." *Maine Historical Society Quarterly* 27, no. 2 (Fall 1987): 58–81.

*Stewart's Atlas of the State of Maine,* 12th ed. South Paris, Maine: J. H. Stewart and Co, 1902.

Susman, Warren I. *Culture as History: The Transformation of American Society in the Twentieth Century.* New York: Pantheon Books, 1984.

Sutherland, Daniel E. *The Expansion of Everyday Life, 1860–1876.* New York: Harper and Row, 1989.

Syrett, John. "Principle and Expediency: The Ku Klux Klan and Ralph Owen Brewster in 1924." *Maine History* 39 (Winter 2000–2001): 215–39.

Thernstrom, Stephan. *Poverty and Progress: Social Mobility in a Nineteenth Century City.* Cambridge: Harvard University Press, 1964.

Thernstrom, Stephan, and Richard Sennett, eds. *Nineteenth-Century Cities: Essays in the New Urban History.* New Haven: Yale University Press, 1969.

Thomas, Miriam Stover. *Flotsam and Jetsam.* Maine: by the author, 1973.

Thompson, Alvin O., ed. *In the Shadow of the Plantation; Caribbean History and Legacy.* Kingston, Jamaica: Ian Randle Publishers, 2002.

Thompson, Deborah. *Bangor, Maine, 1769–1914: An Architectural History.* Orono, Maine: University of Maine Press, 1988.

Toner, Carol. "'Hard Work to Make Ends Meet': Voices of Maine's Working-Class Women in the Late Nineteenth Century." *Maine History* 42, no. 1 (August 2004): 23–45.

Trotter, Joe William, Jr. "African Americans in the City: The Industrial Era, 1900–1950." In *The New African American Urban History,* ed. Kenneth W. Goings and Raymond A. Mohl, 299–319. Thousand Oaks, Calif.: Sage Publications, 1996.

———, ed. *The Great Migration in Historical Perspective: New Dimensions of Race, Class, and Gender.* Bloomington: Indiana University Press, 1991.

Tye, Larry. *Rising from the Rails: Pullman Porters and the Making of the Black Middle Class.* New York: Henry Holt and Company, 2004.

University of Maine Alumni Association. *The University of Maine Alumni Directory 2000.* White Plains: Bernard C. Harris Publishing Co., 2000.

Walker, James W. St. G. *The Black Loyalists: The Search for a Promised Land in Nova Scotia and Sierra Leone, 1783–1870.* New York: Africana Publishing Co., 1976.

Wall, Cheryl A. *Women of the Harlem Renaissance.* Bloomington: Indiana University Press, 1995.

Warner, Robert Austin. *New Haven Negroes: A Social History.* New Haven: Yale University Press, 1940.

Washington, Booker T. *Up From Slavery,* ed. W. Fitzhugh Brundage. Boston: Bedford/ St. Martin's Press, 2003.

Watson, Elwood. "William Burney and John Jenkins: A Tale of Maine's Two African-American Mayors." *Maine History* 40 (Summer 2001): 113–25.

Wedin, Carolyn. *Inheritors of the Spirit: Mary White Ovington and the Founding of the NAACP.* New York: John Wiley and Sons, 1998.

White, Deborah Gray. *Too Heavy a Load: Black Women in Defense of Themselves, 1894– 1994.* New York: W.W. Norton and Co., 1999.

Williams, Eric. *From Columbus to Castro: The History of the Caribbean 1492–1969.* New York: Vintage Books, 1984.

Williams, Loretta J. *Black Freemasonry and Middle-Class Realities.* Columbia: University of Missouri Press, 1980.

Williamson, Judith. *Decoding Advertisements: Ideology and Meaning in Advertising.* New York: Marion Boyars, 1987.

Willis, Deborah. *Picturing Us: African American Identity in Photography.* New York: The New Press, 1994.

Willis, Deborah, and Carla Williams. *The Black Female Body: A Photographic History.* Philadelphia: Temple University Press, 2002.

Wilson, Francine Rusan. "'All of the Glory . . . Faded . . . Quickly': Sadie T. M. Alexander and Black Professional Women, 1920–1950." In *Sister Circle: Black Women and Work,* ed. Sharon Harley and The Black Women and Work Collective, 164–83. New Brunswick: Rutgers University Press, 2002.

Wilson, Joseph F. *Tearing Down the Color Bar: A Documentary History and Analysis of the Brotherhood of Sleeping Car Porters.* New York: Columbia University Press, 1989.

Winkler, Gail Caskey, and Roger W. Moss. *Victorian Interior Decoration: American Interiors 1830–1900.* New York: Henry Holt and Company, 1986.

Winks, Robin W. *The Blacks in Canada: A History.* 2d. ed. Montreal: McGill-Queen's University Press, 1997.

Wrinn, Stephen M. *Civil Rights in the Whitest State: Vermont's Perceptions of Civil Rights, 1945–1968.* Lanham, Md.: University Press of America, 1998.

Youngken, Richard C. *African Americans in Newport: An Introduction to the Heritage of African Americans in Newport, Rhode Island, 1700–1945.* Newport: Rhode Island Historical Preservation and Heritage Commission and Rhode Island Black Heritage Society, 1998.

Zelz, Abigail Ewing, and Marilyn Zoidis. *Woodsmen and Whigs: Historic Images of Bangor, Maine.* Virginia Beach: Donning Company Publishers, 1991.

Zinn, Howard. *A People's History of the United States, 1492–Present.* Rev. ed. New York: HarperPerennial, 1995.

# Index

Page numbers in *italics* represent illustrations.